MW01436596

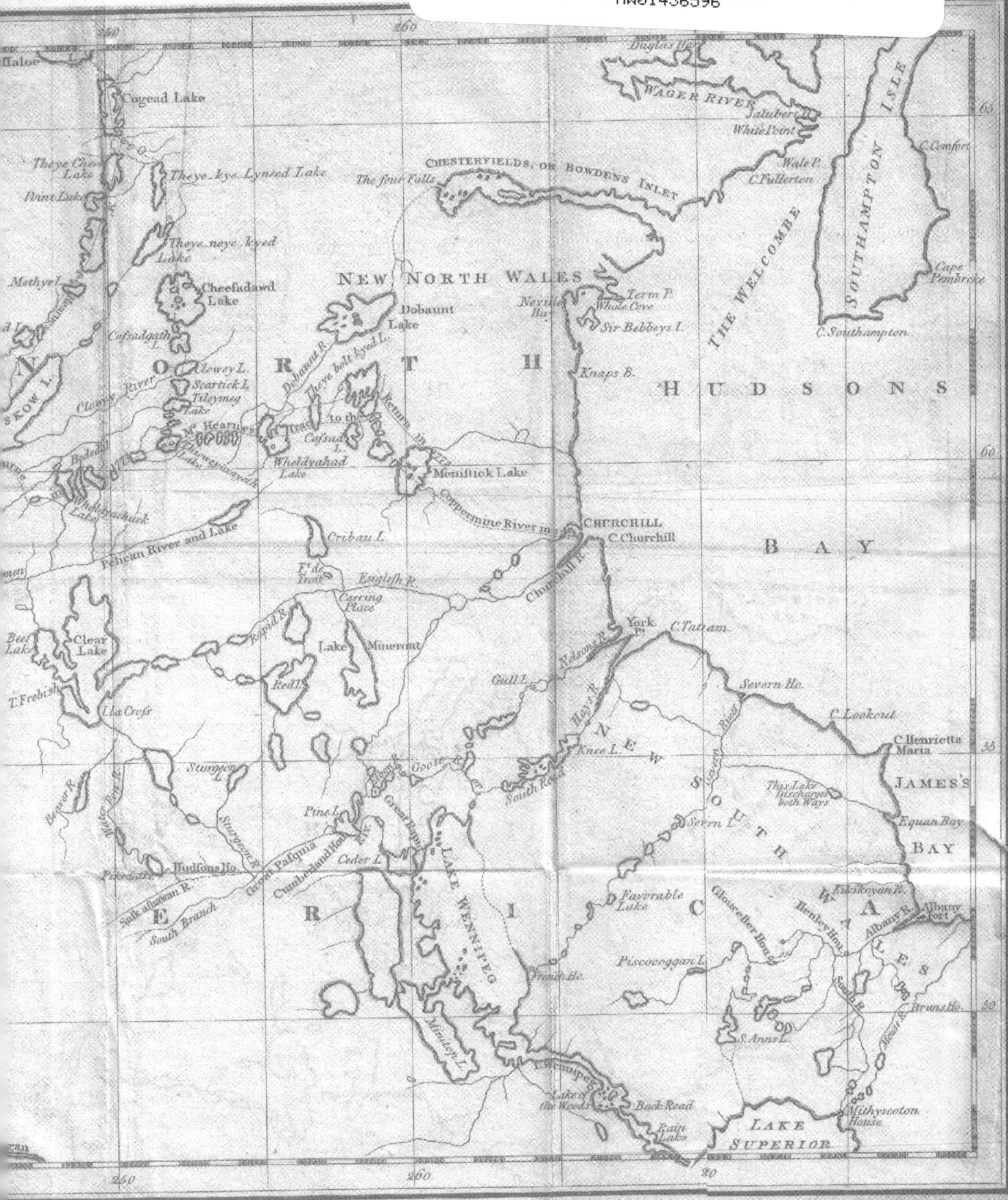

Woodman & Mutlow Sculp. Russel Court

POSSESSING MEARES ISLAND

Also by Barry Gough
The Royal Navy and the Northwest Coast
Gunboat Frontier
First Across the Continent: Sir Alexander Mackenzie
Fortune's a River
Juan de Fuca's Strait
The Elusive Mr. Pond

POSSESSING MEARES ISLAND

A Historian's Journey into the Past of Clayoquot Sound

BARRY GOUGH

Copyright © 2021 Barry Gough
1 2 3 4 5 — 25 24 23 22 21

All rights reserved. No part of this publication may be reproduced, stored in a retrieval system or transmitted, in any form or by any means, without prior permission of the publisher or, in the case of photocopying or other reprographic copying, a licence from Access Copyright, www.accesscopyright.ca, 1-800-893-5777, info@accesscopyright.ca.

Harbour Publishing Co. Ltd.
P.O. Box 219, Madeira Park, BC, V0N 2H0
www.harbourpublishing.com

Edited and indexed by Audrey McClellan
Text design and maps by Terra Firma Digital Arts
Printed on 100% recycled paper certified by the Forest Stewardship Council®
Endsheet: "A Chart of the Interior Part of North America Demonstrating the very good probability of an Inland Navigation from Hudsons Bay to the West Coast", from John Meares' book, *Voyages to the North-West Coast of America* (1790) | From the collection of Gary Little
Page vi : Clayoquot Sound aerial | Wilderness Committee Archive
Printed and bound in Canada

Harbour Publishing acknowledges the support of the Canada Council for the Arts, the Government of Canada, and the Province of British Columbia through the BC Arts Council.

Library and Archives Canada Cataloguing in Publication
Title: Possessing Meares Island : a historian's journey into the past of Clayoquot Sound / Barry Gough.
Names: Gough, Barry M., author.
Description: Includes index.
Identifiers: Canadiana (print) 20210289899 | Canadiana (ebook) 2021028997X | ISBN 9781550179576 (hardcover) | ISBN 9781550179583 (EPUB)
Subjects: LCSH: Meares Island (B.C.)—History. | LCSH: Clayoquot Sound (B.C.)—History. | LCSH: Indigenous peoples—British Columbia—Meares Island—History. | LCSH: Indigenous peoples—Land tenure—British Columbia—Meares Island—History. | LCSH: Environmental protection—British Columbia—Meares Island—History.
Classification: LCC FC3845.M42 G68 2021 | DDC 971.1/2—dc23

We see our territory as a massive feast dish with the mountains as its rim; the dishes that we use in our feasts are, in turn, symbols of the territory and its resources.

Ki-ke-in, Hupacasath artist

The people of the west coast of Vancouver Island used to be called Nootka by Europeans. We know ourselves as Nuu-chah-nulth, which can be translated as "along the mountains" and refers to our traditional territories.

Nuu-Chah-Nulth Tribal Council

CONTENTS

Notes on Names and Terms	ix
Maps and Charts	xiii
Preface	xix
Introduction	1
Acknowledgements	13
PART I The Empire of Fortune	
1 Out of the Mists	17
2 First Encounters	26
3 Sea Otter Hunters	48
4 Buying and Selling Clayoquot	75
5 Fort Defiance and the Destruction of Opitsat	84
6 Tales the *Tonquin* Tells	101
7 The In-between Time	128
PART II War for the Woods	
8 Possessions and Dispossessions	161
9 Maximum Yield in the Balance	179
10 Contested Ground	188
11 History's Possession	199
Notes	208
Index	224

Winter quarters at Fort Defiance, Adventure Cove, Lemmens Inlet, Meares Island. In this sprightly watercolour by George Davidson, illustrator on Captain Gray's voyage in the famed Boston ship *Columbia Rediviva*, the artist portrays himself showing off this very illustration. On the left, the *Columbia* is shown in Adventure Cove. On the stocks below Fort Defiance and the Stars and Stripes is the sloop *Adventure*, being built as a coaster for the sea otter business. The location of Fort Defiance was found after diligent searches by American and local historians. In 1966, Ken Gibson of Tofino established the exact site.
Oregon Historical Society Research Library

Notes on Names and Terms

Magical, and symbolically laden with history, its forests still standing, its mountains and rugged coasts facing across the waters to today's Tofino, British Columbia, Canada, Meares Island lies within the southern part of Vancouver Island's Clayoquot Sound. The Sound itself is a labyrinth of inlets, islands and passages. This is the Nuu-chah-nulth nations' territory of traditional lands and waters.

The names of the leading Nuu-chah-nulth chiefs of the late 1700s and early 1800s appear as Wickaninnish, Maquinna and Sitakanim, though they are variously spelled in documents and published narratives of the time, and I have not sought to change the original spellings given by my documentary sources. Wickaninnish is invariably named in the records as a chief; however, the Nuu-chah-nulth word for his rank, possessions and station is *Ha'wiih*.

For such technical matters as the elevation of Lone Cone and Mount Colnett and the longitude and latitude of Opitsat, I have used modern scientific data, though I am conscious that historical records disclose earlier observation coordinates, and that magnetic variations have changed over time. By and large, in the late eighteenth and nineteenth century, British nautical measurement of longitude was based on distances west of Greenwich, England.

Great Britain did not acquire sovereignty of the area we now call British Columbia through conquest or by doctrine of discovery. Rather, its claimed sovereignty was recognized in 1846 by treaty with the United States (the Oregon Treaty). When the Colony of British Columbia joined Canada by Act of Union in 1871, the direction of "Indian Affairs" passed to the Dominion (later Government) of Canada. Thus, Indian reserves and bands became (and are to this day) regulated by that government, headquartered in Ottawa. The term "band" is used here in the context of the *Indian Act* of Canada. No formal system exists in law for the authorized naming of bands.

The word "Nu-tka-," or more commonly "Nootka," has now been supplanted by the terms "Nuučaańuɫ," "Nuu-chah-nulth" or, occasionally, "the west coast peoples." The language spoken is now referred to as Nuu-chah-nulth. This language is part of the Wakashan language grouping. Representing constituent components is the Nuu-Chah-Nulth Tribal Council (NTC). The term "Nuu-chah-nulth," meaning loosely "all along the mountains and sea," was formally adopted by the NTC in 1980.

I have generally used the common spelling "Clayoquot"; that being said, the reader's forbearance is requested, for all variant spellings appear in quoted passages. To complicate matters, the Indigenous people formerly called Clayoquot changed their name to Tla-o-qui-aht First Nation effective November 21, 1988. The reader's attention is therefore specifically drawn to the following: in this book Clayoquot usually means the location (though sometimes, particularly when referring to events in the eighteenth and nineteenth centuries, can mean the peoples or band); Tla-o-qui-aht means the Clayoquot First Nation. Wherever possible I have followed the Canadian convention of using the single form of a First Nation rather than the plural form (thus, Ahousaht rather than Ahousahts). Note that all sorts of variant spellings of names and places exist in the

Notes on Names and Terms

historical documentation, and I have not standardized these when I am quoting from the source documents.

Meares Island contains two Indian reserves: I.R. 1, Opitsat, and I.R. 2, Cloolthpich, the latter west of Lone Cone. I.R. 1 was dedicated in 1890 as a Clayoquot Indian reserve. I.R. 2 was dedicated in 1890 as a Kelsemaht Indian reserve. Numerous other reserves exist within the Clayoquot Sound area including Marktosis, Sutaquis, Clayoquot, Tofino.[1] The *Indian Act* of Canada specifies that an Indian reserve is a "tract of land, the legal title to which is vested in Her Majesty, that has been set apart by Her Majesty for the use and benefit of a band."

During the sea otter trade of the 1700s and 1800s, which features in Part I of this book, Haida Gwaii was known as the Queen Charlotte Islands to the Europeans (and many Boston traders called them Washington's Isles). I have used this name in that context, but Haida Gwaii when referring to more contemporary events.

The terms used to refer to Native Peoples remain unsettled. Most of the historic documents use "Indian," and this is still the term used in the *Indian Act* and as part of the tri-partite definition of "the Aboriginal Peoples of Canada" given in Article 35 of the Canadian Constitution (*Constitution Act, 1982*), that is, "Indians, Inuit and Métis."[2] The capitalized form "Aboriginal Peoples" is also used in Canadian legal contexts. "Indigenous" is usually an adjective ("indigene" is the noun), meaning "native and belonging to the soil, born of it." I prefer to use "Native," as in my view it best represents those who were here before the modern era (which I date as the era beginning with the arrival of the Norse). However, again, when quoting material from the historical record, I use the term used by the writer. And whenever possible I use the specific name of a group or nation.

Different terms are used abroad. I have lectured on Canadian history in Australia, New Zealand and South Africa, and consequently know that I will get into trouble with local experts in Australia when I use the term "aboriginal" to mean Canadian Indigenous person, and I will certainly get into equal if not more hot water in South Africa if I use the word "native." In Alaska the current usage is

"Alaska Natives," organized in 1971 as Alaska Native Tribes. In the continental United States, "American Indian" passes as standard. American informants tell me that "Indian" is still widely used without difficulty in many locales. (This may be the case in places in Canada.) Odd it is that Columbus called the original inhabitants of some Caribbean Islands "Indians" and left for all of us (at least in Canada) this tortured legacy still in need of working out terms for clarification and accuracy.

Legal cases, whether in short or full form, are shown in italics: thus, *Meares Island*.

"Old-growth forest" means a mature forest ecosystem, one that contains a broad diversity of plant and animal species, and which is relatively uninfluenced by the human race.

Maps and Charts

Possessing Meares Island

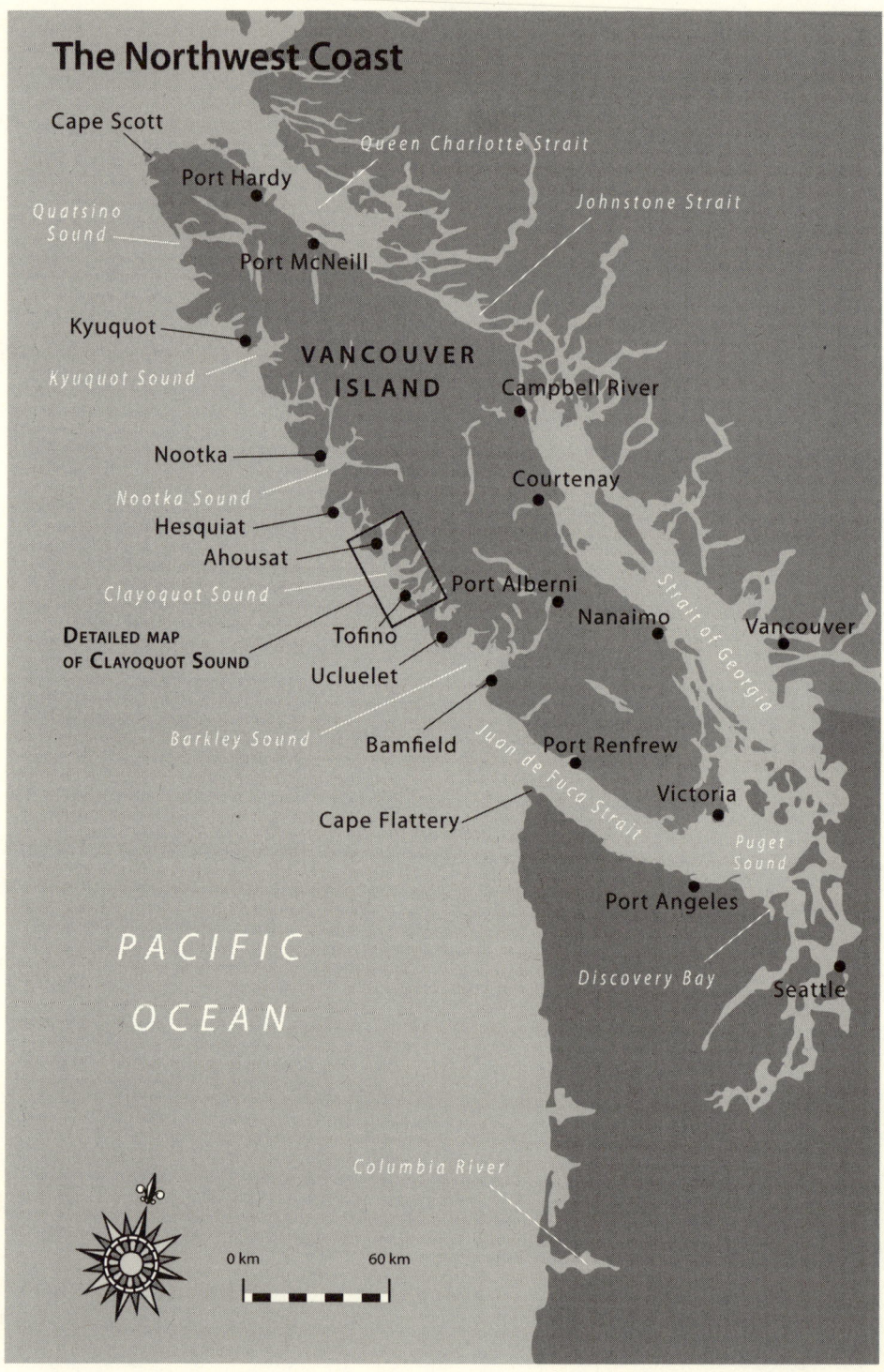

Maps and Charts

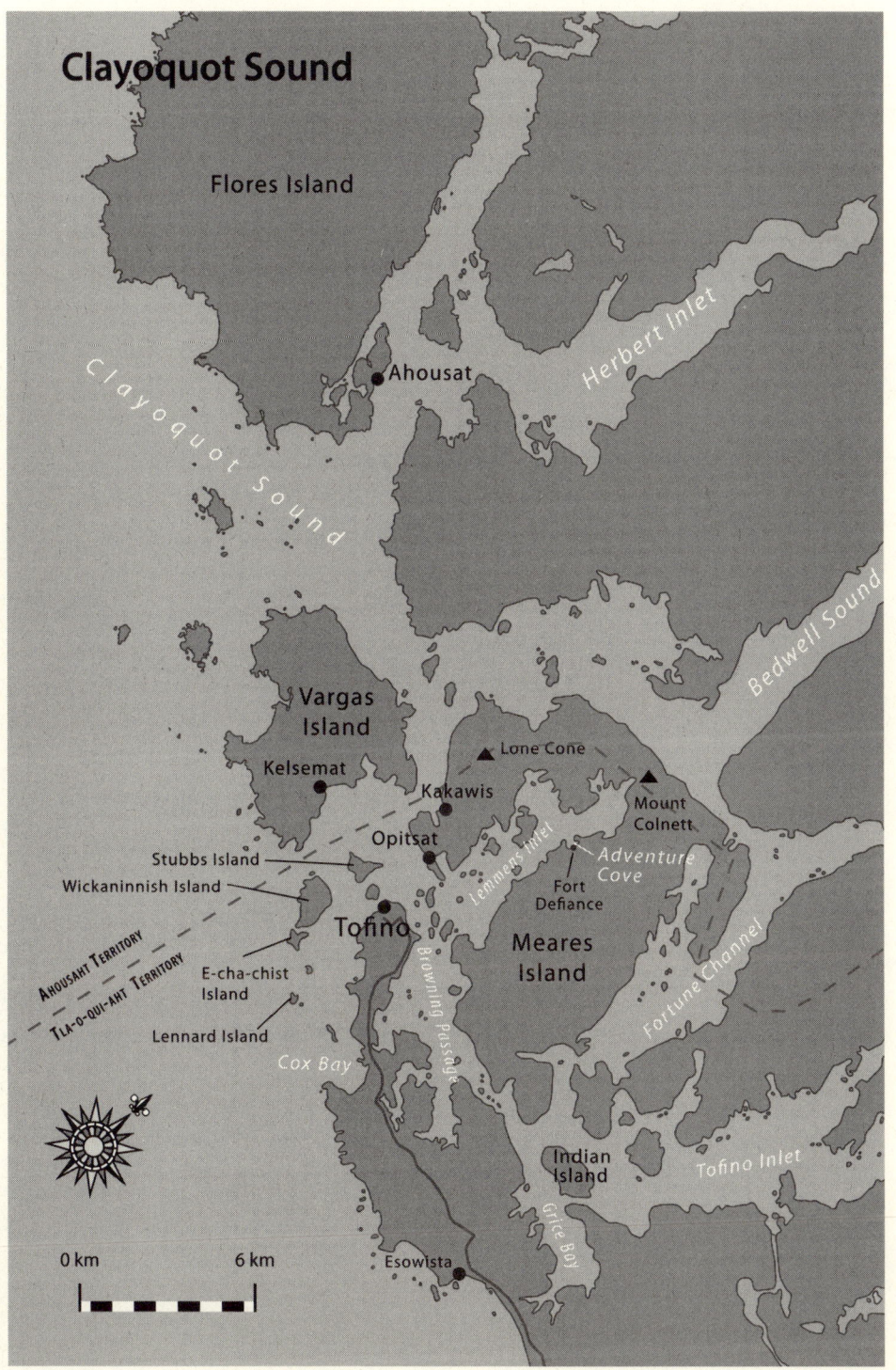

Possessing Meares Island

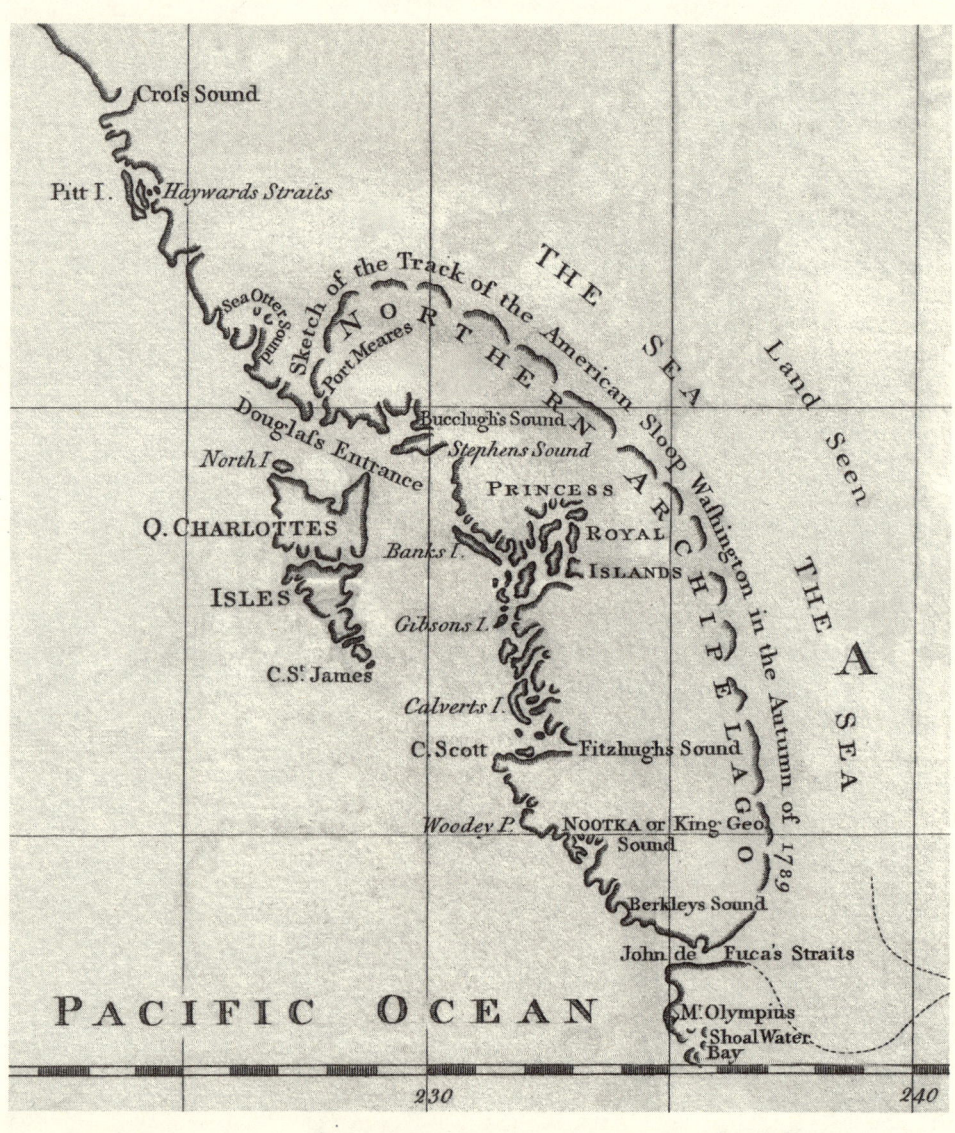

The west coast section of "A Chart of the Interior Part of North America Demonstrating the very good probability of an Inland Navigation from Hudsons Bay to the West Coast" from John Meares' book, *Voyages to the North-West Coast of America*, published in London in November 1790. Note "the sea" surrounding most of present-day British Columbia accessed via Juan de Fuca Strait and extending north of Haida Gwaii.
From the collection of Gary Little

Maps and Charts

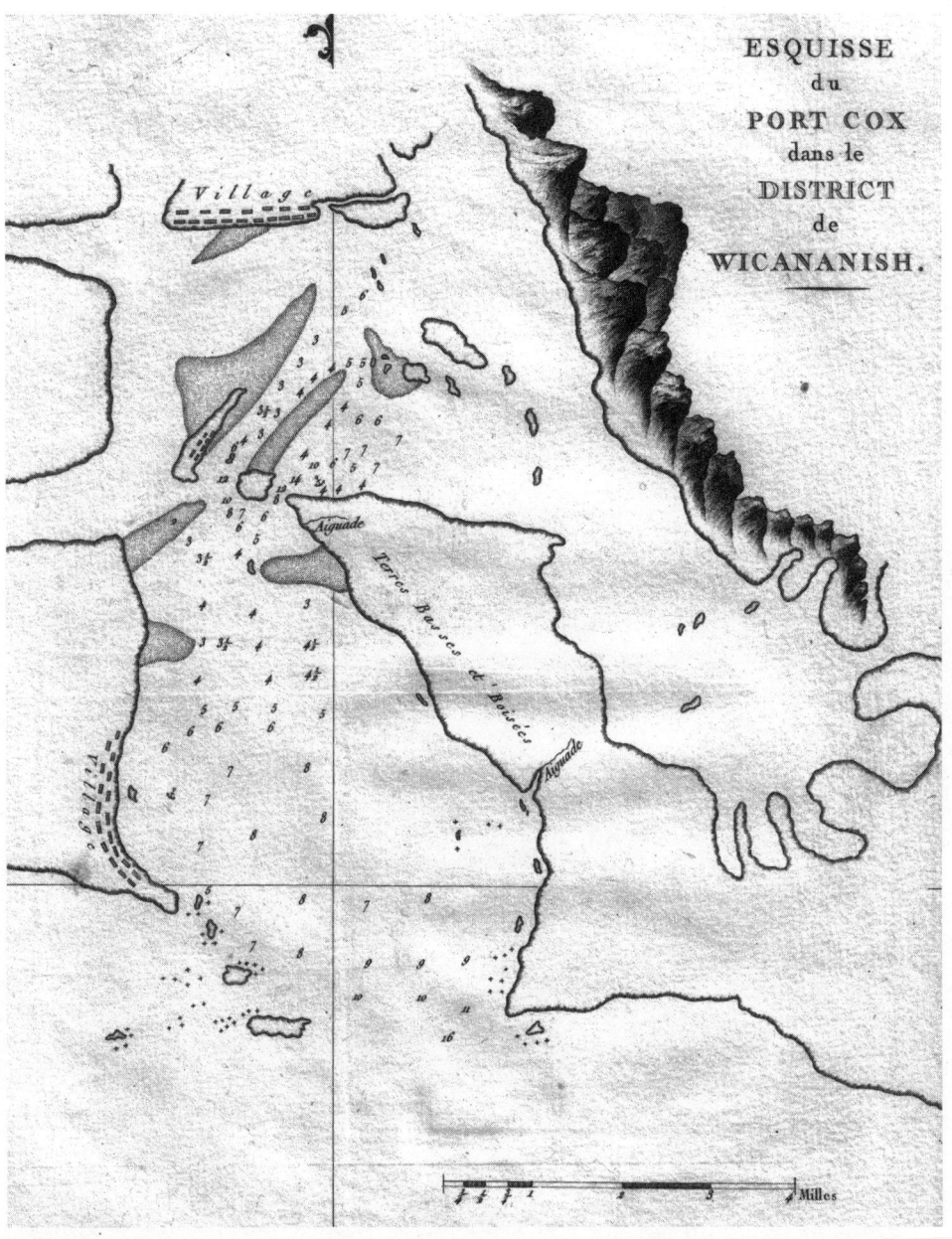

The sketch of Port Cox from the French edition of Meares' *Voyages*. Note that Meares Island, featuring Lone Cone, is shown lying in profile upper right. The top village is Opitsat. Today's Tofino lies at the end of the peninsula. The hazards to navigation are apparent.
From the collection of Gary Little

Preface

One day in early 1986, I received a phone call from a British Columbia lawyer, Jack Woodward. Our discussion was cordial and, after customary pleasantries by way of introduction, yielded from him this combined commendation and question: "We understand you know something about the colonial history of Vancouver Island. You have been recommended by an anthropologist to undertake the legal history of Meares Island. You would leave no stone unturned in reporting on the details of the encounter between outsiders and the Native peoples. We understand that you have special knowledge of the British records. You would have about three years to complete your work. Would you be interested in preparing a dossier on the history of Meares Island in defence of the claim by Ahousaht and Clayoquot tribes?"

Our conversation moved at breakneck speed. I could sense the urgency of the matter. The forest of heavily treed Meares Island, rich with western red cedar and hemlock, seemed in danger of falling to the chainsaw. Mr. Woodward explained that he was acting on behalf of the Nuu-Chah-Nulth Tribal Council (NTC) in a recently filed case known as *Moses Martin et al. v. H.M. the Queen et al.*

Moses Martin, I soon learned, was chief councillor of the Clayoquot Nation, and the et al. were the claimant nations of the NTC—specifically the Clayoquot and Ahousaht, with the Kelsemaht peoples soon to join, all ancestral claimants to Meares Island and constituent members of the NTC. This was a *comprehensive claim* on the part of the NTC—that is, on behalf of its constituent member entities. As to the second et al., this turned out to be the world's biggest logging company, MacMillan Bloedel (later Weyerhaeuser), with head offices on Georgia Street, Vancouver, as well as the Crown in right of the Province of British Columbia, and the Crown in right of the Government of Canada—altogether a formidable and well-heeled opposition.

This was heady stuff, a true David and Goliath scenario. I knew from years of teaching Canadian constitutional history that in the evolution of Native rights, the small tended to find itself pitted against the giant. Court rulings defined the new law, directed the course of justice and shaped the future. Did the long curve of history bend toward justice? Here was a test case.

In short order all the details were explained to me. At issue was Tree Farm Licence 22, held by MacMillan Bloedel; TFL 22 gave the lumber barons, or their contracted partners, the right to log on Meares Island. For several years the island had been the scene of protests, largely ineffective. Then came the crisis. On November 21, 1984, loggers arrived to begin cutting down trees. They were met by a group of Ahousaht and Clayoquot men and women, led by Moses Martin, who greeted the loggers, welcomed them to a Tribal Park, which he described as the Tla-o-qui-aht's garden, and told them they were not to cut the trees. Instead of responding with force, MacMillan Bloedel brought court action against the protesters and the First Nations. In response, the NTC, assisted by the Friends of Clayoquot Sound and backed by the Western Canada Wilderness Committee and the Sierra Club of British Columbia, sought a court injunction to halt the further cutting of the trees of Meares Island. The legal challenge hinged on the matter of Aboriginal title. November 21, 1984, is thus a significant date in Meares Island's modern history, for it began a process that would stop clear-cut logging. One might call it a threshold event.

Preface

In order to present the claimants' case to its best advantage, the NTC had hired the legal firm Rosenberg, Rosenberg and Woodward, and Jack Woodward told me that he and his law partners, the cousins David and Paul Rosenberg, with offices in False Creek, Vancouver, were putting in place a crack team of "subject experts" to prepare documentation for the court when the matter came to trial. He explained who was who on the impressive list of experts, including a pair of anthropologists, an archaeologist, a genealogist, and a tree and soils science expert.[3]

Charmingly, Mr. Woodward went on to say that he had read my book *Gunboat Frontier: British Maritime Authority and Northwest Coast Indians, 1846-1890*, recently published by UBC Press, which he noted had been awarded the Lieutenant Governor's Medal for Historical Writing. He said that my account and analysis of contact and conflict on Vancouver Island's west coast had sparked his personal interest and, getting to the point, it had critical importance to the case. The NTC and its lawyers would have to demonstrate the living presence of history, the continuities of occupation and resource use over time. To do so, they needed someone who could read, understand and analyze historical records. They needed a historian, one who had researched and published in the field.

It was a long phone call. Mr. Woodward advanced the cause in legalistic detail. He said that the preparation of the case and the experts' studies would take considerable time, necessary in the search for data relevant to the case. Authenticity was the requirement. He explained that the Hon. Thomas Berger, former BC New Democratic Party leader, a leading Native rights lawyer in his own right, would be an adviser and would lead the case arguments at the appropriate time. This further piqued my interest, as Berger had chaired the famed federal Mackenzie Valley Pipeline Inquiry and written the brave report *Northern Frontier, Northern Homeland* (1977), which recommended a ten-year moratorium on pipeline development. Certainly, Berger's expected involvement raised the profile of the *Meares Island* case. The larger prospect of entering a new world, that of legal scholarship, presented its own attraction for me. And Woodward assured me I would be answerable to Rosenberg, Rosenberg and Woodward, and not to those bringing the case, allowing me some independence from the clients.

Jack Woodward asked me if I would undertake the project and write up the historical account that eventually would be filed at court. I had never had a lawyer define a research topic for me, nor had I ever charged a nickel for any historical work done. As a historian, I was unaccustomed to being among those acclaimed by anthropologists! But the matter duly offered was of a different order. Something very unusual—something of weighty moment—lay in the offing.

Fortunately, I had completed my most recent project and could turn to a new challenge. I took a deep breath and agreed. And I have never regretted my decision to accept the challenge, though of course I did not know what the final outcome would be. I am not fond of being on the losing side.

A few months later, in my first face-to-face meeting with Woodward and the Rosenbergs, I quickly gathered that these were some of the young lawyers whose passion for Native law made them a new breed in British Columbia and Canadian justice. They would go on to greatness. Jack Woodward was then preparing his classic reference work, *Native Law* (Toronto: Caswell, 1989 and many subsequent editions). He was a "float-plane lawyer," operating from his seaside home on Saltspring Island. A graduate of the UBC School of Law, he was also an instructor of law at the University of Victoria. He liked to say that all lawyers learn the law at their clients' expense, but that was an exaggeration for he had taken a very serious interest in the history of Canadian and British Columbia legal practices and rulings. He knew that the unique nature of the rights and powers of Native peoples in Canada required an understanding of their origins. Mr. Woodward held that these origins are truly indigenous, and as such were unlike Canadian legal practices.

His law partners brought complementary skills to the team. David Rosenberg's later triumph was in a 2014 Supreme Court

Preface

of Canada decision, which in effect awarded the Tsilhqot'ín title and rights to a substantial portion of their ancestral territories.[4] That case rested on the shoulders of many others, not least *Meares Island*, which began as a case of Aboriginal title. Our discussions around the great table in their office reminded me of my own training in the Imperial History Seminar at the Institute of Historical Research, London University, where the wonderful cut and thrust of arguments posed in discussions of contentious points of history ensured that any frauds were exposed and arguments of a spurious nature destroyed.

But to return to the *Meares Island* case. A couple of long summers of research and writing awaited. The prospect appealed to me in another way, for "Indian law" in Canada was moving at a breakneck speed, with new case law expanding Native rights. Several years of teaching university history courses on Indigenous peoples in Canada (First Nations, Métis and Inuit, as specified in the *Constitution Act, 1982*) had given me a vague understanding of the complexities of land claim cases—for example, in Canada, provinces regulate lands, resources and forests while the federal government has other responsibilities under the *Indian Act*, including reserves (which are Crown lands), marine matters and fisheries. But in the *Meares Island* case, who knew what lay ahead?

The lawyers had hired some bright-spark student researchers to unearth documents, compile inventories of documents and get ready for an exchange of documents with the opposition, or the lawyers for the defence. This exchange, I was told, was called "disclosure." And when the bulky files kept arriving for my examination and comment, I realized not only the thoroughness of those working on the legal team but also the immense capacity required to organize, collate and catalogue materials. Here is one reason why treaty claims processes take so very long even to get to discussion, let alone conclusion.

In due course the case came to trial. It reached a conclusion in the form of an injunction against logging on the island. The injunction was for five years and has since been renewed several times, giving the illusion of permanence. Meares Island's trees were saved for the immediate future: at the time, that was the all-important item of business. Perhaps the trees were saved forever. A silence descended over the island: the searching cry of the chainsaw was not heard, nor the heavy thump of falling timber.

Truth to tell, the results of our findings were profound. The documentation breathed authenticity. As the case progressed, in and out of court, and the evidence kept piling up in favour of "our case," the Province of British Columbia made final admission that Aboriginal title, so long denied, so long contested, would be acknowledged. This constituted a dramatic turnaround in provincial public policy, for not long before the cast-in-stone argument ran, basically, that "all the lands of British Columbia belong to all the people." Thus, the Province of BC and the Government of Canada both recognized the principle for which the Aboriginal peoples had so long argued.

The achievement was of momentous proportions, with ongoing legacies. In *Meares Island*, Moses Martin et al. had defended by legal process their native interests against the encroaching power of the Crown in right of British Columbia, its agents and the licensed commercial interest, MacMillan Bloedel Ltd., which held the lease. The rising tide of outsiders' exploitation had been stopped.

Though history could not be reversed, existing Aboriginal rights had recently been entrenched in the *Constitution Act, 1982*, section 35(1). This highly influential piece of Canadian constitutional legislation confirmed the common-law doctrine of Aboriginal rights and, along with its companion, the Canadian Charter of Rights and Freedoms (especially Section 25, which shields Aboriginal rights), was a significant breakthrough in the recognition of Native claims. In short, the constitutional adoptions of 1982 opened new chapters in the history of Aboriginal rights.

Likewise, *Meares Island*, coming at the same time other key cases were being decided by the courts (*Bartleman* [1984] and *Sparrow* [1987], for instance) was a watershed of modern law. Other cases—*Calder* (1973) and *Delgamuukw* (1997)—are of much higher profile, but *Meares Island* had lasting legacies. For one, it opened individual or specific claims of the constituent tribes of the Nuu-Chah-Nulth Tribal Council, the strong multi-band force behind the case. Other British Columbia tribes that were not members of the NTC also benefited from the decision—and from our hard work.

Even at this date, long after the events, I cannot forget the excitement of beginning this research, nor the satisfaction of carrying it to completion. All sorts of new information was uncovered, by myself and by the other subject experts. If we gather all the reports together, we can say that perhaps no specific island's history had been so extensively covered. The records and reports are on file in the BC Law Courts in Vancouver, and many can be found elsewhere in law school libraries and corporate head offices. This epoch was a heady time in the history of BC and Canadian Aboriginal law, the most dramatic and influential in our national history. Confirmation of this can be found in commentaries and elucidations in UBC *Law Reports*, *BC Studies* and elsewhere.

I did not know this at the time of Jack Woodward's phone call, only that we were on the edge of a great legal adventure. Law and constitutional rights drive history like no other force when a showdown is expected in court, and in my case, my disciplinary obligation was to get the facts right. The lawyers also requested my opinions as a historian. They told me not to be shy in making my own estimations of how time and tide had influenced the history of Meares Island. Thus, with my mind in a gigantic whirl of prospects, I began to research widely all that had happened on and near these 8,500 acres of land. I came up with some surprising details of history, coupled with some delightful insights into the historical record and the historian's processes.

Introduction

This book is a historian's perspective—a historical progress, so to speak—concerning Meares Island and nearby waters of Clayoquot Sound. It is not the report I prepared for the Nuu-Chah-Nulth Tribal Council's 1985 court case, but something quite different. I like to think of this book as a vertical inquiry, by which I mean that it is a study of a place and its peoples across layered spans of time, from the beginning of the historical record (when written documents about the area began to appear in the 1770s) right through to our present time. The book bears a personal stamp as a record of my own work in disclosing this past.

Although a book on Meares Island and Wickaninnish's world may seem at first sight like history in miniature, this is far from the case. The history of Meares Island is not the history of Vancouver Island, any more than the history of Vancouver Island is the history of British Columbia, much less western Canada. Perhaps this book could be called an extended essay, a historian's mediation of matters of the past, bringing into literary form historical data across a wide range of interrelated topics from out of the mists of time. Local becomes global.

In many respects this is a book about the land and waters of renowned sea otter chief Wickaninnish. This famed lord of

Clayoquot Sound was powerful and influential. I find him an engaging figure and certainly the most dominant personage in Clayoquot Sound. He must have been a great warrior but, even more, a person of tremendous commercial acumen. In the literature he ranks second to the legendary Maquinna of Yuquot, Nootka Sound, but by the 1830s, as will be shown, their positions had been reversed.

The British trader John Meares, in the late 1780s, was struck by the fact that he encountered a highly structured society. The Clayoquot, Ahousaht and Kelsemaht peoples were autonomous social and political entities, each having lineages, traditions and legends. Members of each group were either lords or commoners, and had slaves, who were chattel. Then as now, hereditary rank and kinship dominated their social system.[5] The rank into which one was born determined the course of life. As units, as peoples, they were subject to no outside authority. Such was the freedom that they enjoyed. Democracy was an alien concept. They lived in the here and now, yet were highly conscious of tradition, ranking, material possessions, property and rights related to the same. Power and position stemmed from inherited property, real and non-material (songs, dances and names are in the latter category). A house would consist of closely related families. Prestigious ceremonies and conspicuous consumption were social and political demonstrations of power and rank. Traditional privileges, including cultural inheritance and lineage, were prized properties—and were accepted by those who did not have them. These people were, in all ways, masters of possession.

Non-material property could be possessed even into the modern age. But the ownership of physical property could not be sustained under the pressure of changes brought from outside. Thus, these people faced a partial social and political revolution as outsiders came to possess their waters, sea resources, mountains and forests.

Understanding this vibrant era of the maritime, or sea otter, trade is essential to an appreciation of the Meares Island legal case. Particulars will be explained at appropriate places later in the book. But here we note that there are several reasons global attention was drawn to the case. Voyage accounts by mariners of British, American

Introduction

and Spanish nationality tend to prove the existence of Aboriginal rights on Meares Island. They reveal that the First Nations of Clayoquot Sound were an organized society as evidenced by their villages; arts and handicrafts, including the production of clothes, musical instruments, canoes and furniture; their religion; and their government (as ruled by one superior chief, Wickaninnish). They had social and political organization, and they could wage war and make peace. The voyage accounts detail the Native occupation of Meares Island at Opitsat. Descendants live there to this day, a marvellous continuity over centuries. And the accounts also reveal that the First Nations of Clayoquot Sound used the forests in almost every aspect of their lives—for buildings, furniture, clothing, canoes and much else. These accounts, scarce as they are, disclose that First Nations of Clayoquot Sound occupied Meares Island to the exclusion of other organized societies, exhibited exclusive use of their land and, not least, occupied Meares Island before British rights of trade and navigation were asserted (with the signing of the Nootka Convention in about 1790). These travel and voyage accounts allow us to reconstruct local conditions, usefully so by virtue of the absence of archival sources of the age. Certainly, the voyages, and the narratives of these voyages, demonstrate that Aboriginal rights on Meares Island were not extinguished. No voluntary surrender of any land to the British occurred. The Indigenous peoples made treaties just as they pleased, to suit their needs and purposes. Aboriginal rights to Meares Island were not extinguished by the "Kendrick deeds" sale of August 11, 1791, for not only did the Nootka Convention terms apply, but also the First Nations could only voluntarily sell their lands, and thus extinguish their Aboriginal rights, to the British crown.

I like to think that this book exhibits the "living presence," so to speak—a great continuity going back to the time of what anthropologists like to call "contact." In fact, this living presence goes back deeper than that: the present comes out of the mists of time, though we have no archival record of this, only archaeological records and the people's oral history. Here, then, is living history known, comprehended and remembered by a living society.

The Northwest Coast Native culture that flourished into the modern era, when travellers, agents, and missionaries arrived to take note of its features for the first time, had been stimulated by the early phases of its people's contact with European mariners and traders. This was a time of vigorous trade and of cultural changes, including the development and elaboration of the potlatch. The Northwest Coast nations were fishing peoples, un-agrarian in their ways of existence. They lived communally on their jungle-fringed beaches, with their backs to the mountains, facing out into the channels, sounds and passages that led to Vancouver Island's outer coast, its coastal routes and the broad Pacific. Sea lions, sea otter, whales, porpoise, seals and river otter were creatures of the sea, and bear and wolf of the land. Shellfish were in profusion.

The saw and the axe had replaced bone and stone tools, and the monarchs of the forest, the great Douglas fir and cedar, the carver's favourite, now lay at the mercy of the industrial age and the rapacious forest industries. But still the posts and supporting timbers held the stories of the village and allied kin. The carvings, writes Bill Reid, "told the people of the completeness of their culture, the continuing lineages of the great families, their closeness to the magic world of myth and legend." Reid goes even farther in his elegiac description *Out of the Silence*: "Perhaps they told more, a story of little people, few in scattered numbers, in a huge dark world of enormous forests and absurdly large trees, and stormy coasts and wild waters beyond, where brief cool summers gave way forever to long black winters, and families round their fires, no matter how long their lineages, needed much assurance of their greatness."[6]

We leave the discussion of these things now, marvelling at their complexity, yet understanding that artistic creation and linguistic uniqueness gave identity, provided unity, accorded pride and rendered reassurance.

I have not attempted a social history of the Nuu-chah-nulth peoples over two centuries. This is a book about property and possession. Here again, travel and voyage accounts allow us to reconstruct

Introduction

local conditions in the absence of archival sources. Charles Edward Barrett-Lennard, George Henry Richards and Father A.J. Brabant left graphic observations of a world in flux and one entering furious changes. Naturally the writers' cultural references, understandings and biases inform the texts they produce about new people, practices, and places. How could it be otherwise?

For me, only yesterday the world was young. For First Nations, this is far from the case. There is little written testimony on the First Nations' side, and I have combed through Native accounts of Nuu-chah-nulth ethnography looking for hard evidence. Time and again I have wished for more Native historical evidence, but it is not there in the documents, which are what I relied on. Nothing more clearly distinguishes the original inhabitants from those who came to live among them in the modern period than the difference in recording history. First Nations did not write down their stories or histories. Furthermore, they had concepts of history that differ radically from professional historical epistemology and practice. I accept this limitation and I ask readers to understand the matter. Given what presents itself in the written record, there is no shortage of documentation upon which to build up a history of Meares Island and the *Meares Island* case.

And another matter: in my research efforts I found so much material on late eighteenth-century history (and so much descriptive material available to the historian about the pre-1871 period) that it towers over the records of Clayoquot Sound history since that time. Surely, the reader will say, it must have been the other way around, with less data for the earlier period. This is not the case: the late eighteenth century holds many insights into the life and trade of Clayoquot Sound, a richness I could not deny and, indeed, wanted to bring to the fore. This explains why I have devoted a good deal more attention to the earlier period, "The Empire of Fortune," than I have to the later period, "War for the Woods."

Gathering the whole together and composing it into an understandable narrative is the greatest task facing the historian. One of my model historians, Arthur Marder, liked to talk about Ariadne's thread and how that golden thread wove almost magically in and out of his themes. Working historians often pull their hair trying to find such a thread. But try they must so as to make sense out of a vast amount of information—hard facts, usually—and to arrange them as they occurred in time: you can't play fast and loose with the order of developments.

By contrast, a chronicler faces the easier task of simply listing events as they happened, with no connections, no cause and effect. But that is not strictly history and is not the historian's craft. Following the thread and arranging the facts is only the beginning, for it is the testing of the evidence, and the looking at it from various viewpoints, that is so essential to a reliable narrative. Time and again in the writing of this book I have faced these challenges and wondered at the possibilities of a sensible final result, one comprehensible to the reader.

And here is where a little magic can come in handy: for instance, some flash may occur to a historian in the middle of the night, and all of a sudden a segment of the past is illuminated and all the problems the author has been pondering and worrying about are solved, at least to the writer's satisfaction. Reviewers and other critics, of course, may have different views, as well they should.

Going back to what I said at the outset, it is the drawing together of things that counts so much—the figuring out of relationships. In addition, you have to beware of the bogus, and leave doctrine and bias aside. At the same time, judgments are required, and one hopes that these, when made, are sober judgments, ones that will stand the test of time. Any book has a complex structure because of shifts of time and place, and it is always grand when personalities and characters make their appearance and brighten the story or illuminate the past by their actions, opinions and pronouncements. This is when history truly comes to life. In cross-cultural matters, and in this case a field of history known as ethnohistory (the study of race relations or interrelations), the historian is often bereft of details about those

Introduction

who form part of the history but who had no written records. Then the great challenge presents itself concerning the other side of the frontier, so to speak. As any historian knows, they must do the best they can with what they have found or are presented with. The writing of British Columbia and Pacific Northwest history (or indeed any other kind of history where people of oral cultures come in contact and conflict with people of literary culture) therefore poses special problems. Of all the challenges the historian faces, this is the most formidable. And so it is with this book.

Insofar as this book may be a contribution to the history of history (or "historiography" as we call it in my trade), I make no claim as to how it fits into the larger corpus except to say that the subject has never been tackled before. Certainly, it does not fit easily into the settler-colonialist category, for there were no permanent settlers on Meares Island until a residential school was established in 1900. "Settler anxiety" holds no water here, though it might have been felt elsewhere, especially in Victoria. Clayoquot Sound was, in its first phase, an open, maritime place of exchange or *makúk* (that is, to buy or to sell—or "let's make a deal"). In its second phase, in the mid-twentieth century, it moved directly into what might be called the industrial age of clear-cut logging. There was no gold rush at Clayoquot Sound, such as occurred in the Fraser River watershed. There was no mass gathering of Indigenous peoples, upsetting the local authorities who called for forced removal, as occurred in Victoria. It is hard to gauge the impact of infectious diseases: smallpox, syphilis, diphtheria and others would have taken their terrible toll. However, the 1862 smallpox epidemic, perhaps the most severe calamity to befall the Indigenous population of British Columbia, certainly would have affected the peoples of Clayoquot Sound, though not to the degree it did the Haida, Tsimshian and people in Fort Rupert and Bella Bella, for Clayoquot Sound lay off the main arterial of coastal travel, the Inside Passage separating Vancouver Island from the mainland. My point—and the striking thing revealed here—is that Clayoquot Sound stood as a world apart, free from many external pressures, and its residents were less influenced than other peoples in other locales.

Possessing Meares Island

Persons familiar with British Columbia history, and that of the Northwest Coast of North America more generally, will appreciate the fact that all too often generalizations are made about our history that do not apply in certain locations and at certain times. I also think historians have been far too careless in the generalizations that they have made. British Columbia is a complicated piece of geography; its Indigenous peoples showed some uniform cultural changes over time, but these peoples, or individual nations, retained their uniqueness in language, places of occupation and responses to outside authority. I have tried diligently to focus on Clayoquot Sound and Meares Island and not to distract the reader with what was occurring in such places as Nootka Sound, Barkley Sound, Victoria, Nanaimo and Fort Rupert. I have fought against the tendency to wander, always the historian's nightmare.

The modern history of Clayoquot Sound, including Tofino with side glances at Meares Island, has been successfully told by Margaret Horsfield in her wonderful contemporary history *Voices from the Sound* (2008). In *Tofino and Clayoquot Sound: A History* (2014), Horsfield and Ian Kennedy brought the account up to date, enriched and broadened. And what a lovely account it is. This, my book, is of a different order—an analysis of how Meares Island came out of the mists of time, how the sea otter was hunted to the brink of extinction, how the last internecine war of 1855 changed that world, how colonial and Canadian law and regulation spread enveloping arms over Clayoquot Sound, subverting or destroying local mores, and how, at the climax of the modern age, the chainsaw and clear-cut logging threatened Meares Island. This led to the fights for the woods, the alliances of convenience and the rise of the Nuu-Chah-Nulth Tribal Council and its constituent First Nations, which sought to either possess Meares Island or keep it out of the clutches of industrial logging. At the end of the day, this historian has come to possess the island even more than he did in 1991, when his report demonstrated decisively to the court the active use of the forests by persons who had always occupied that place, had never been conquered or swept aside, and

Introduction

who—a true and living presence of Native bands—continued to guard and exploit the resources of mountainous Meares Island.

Here is an epic of survival and resistance, the story of continuous occupation and possession, and of the triumph of the guardians going back to Wickaninnish. The weight of this Meares Island story has slowly increased over time, its importance strengthened. Events, in the retelling, take on heroic status. Years hence we will look back on the Meares Island crisis of 1984 and all that followed over the next few decades, and realize this was drawing a line in the sand and saying, "None shall pass."

Now, a word about how this book is ordered. The issues it explores are best raised in the form of questions. How does history come to possess a certain place, and how did Meares Island in particular come to be possessed by the historical record? This is the focus of Part I, "Empire of Fortune." Commercial activities run throughout its chapters. Chapter 1, "Out of the Mists," sets the locale, while Chapter 2, "First Encounters," takes us down a different trail. When we think of Meares Island in recent history we immediately think of trees and how they were saved from the chainsaw. Two centuries before this the waters of Meares Island were filled with, and then stripped of, *Enhydra lutris*, the sea otter. The history contained in this chapter thus belongs to the age of sea otter exploitation. Chapter 3, "Sea Otter Hunters," is a chapter about cargoes. As such, it reverts to a time—the late eighteenth century—when British and American fur traders, and, almost as an afterthought, Spanish explorers on imperial purpose, came in their sailing vessels to Meares Island and its water approaches, inlets and passages. They arrived for various purposes: to trade, to seek shelter, to take on wood and water, to winter, to engage in shipbuilding and repair. This chapter adds to discussions by historians of Indigenous control of the sea otter trade and the ability to engage in price fixing. This was a more wide-open commercial frontier than has been imagined. It also calls into question the safeguarding of marine resources on a basis of sustained yield. Sea otter were hunted to near extinction.

Chapter 4, "Buying and Selling Clayoquot," flows from its predecessor, disclosing phases of the encounters that came one after the other. When traders arrived for their various purposes, they came vigorously and unavoidably into contact and, in some cases now notorious, conflict with the Aboriginal peoples of Meares Island and Clayoquot Sound. There were many unrecorded peaceful encounters but, understandably, these seldom warrant a mention in any historical narrative. Once again, crisis drives history. There were bloody and violent times that we cannot wish away from our past. British, Americans and Spanish were all involved in violent encounters at Clayoquot Sound. I have brought the Native side of the story to the fore as much as space, and particularly documentation, will allow. Historians have engaged in lively discussion about the intensity and meaning of these cross-cultural encounters, and these also are worth noting here.

Chapter 5 deals specifically with the destruction of the village of Opitsat on Meares Island, as ordered by the American fur trade captain Robert Gray. There is much more to this than meets the eye, and I present new evidence plus in-depth discussion of the matter as it came before the courts in 1993. The trade in muskets and ammunition intensified cross-cultural exchanges and made that world all the more dangerous. This is not—indeed, it cannot be—a benign story. We always want finality in our judgments, but sober ones are harder to make.

Chapter 6 tells the story of the ill-starred ship *Tonquin*. Many a historian has tried to bring closure to the issue of the location of this episode; I review the various possibilities and add some new explanatory detail on the Native side.

Chapter 7, "The In-between Time," is the closing segment of Part I. The subjects covered are perhaps the most elusive imaginable. I have not strained for grand overarching themes: there are none to be found. There is no Native testimony, only observations from transient visitors. And yet this was a central time, for new influences were replacing old. The old "empire of fortune" of the sea otter trade had given way to a "dominion of influence." Indigenous peoples

Introduction

had controlled the trade by controlling the supply of pelts. With the establishment of the colonial jurisdiction at Victoria, the Hudson's Bay Company held the commercial and political monopoly, which, though benign on the west coast of Vancouver Island, nonetheless changed the commercial activity there: it kept foreign shipping out. Clayoquot Sound became a backwater, and only the occasional trader or yachtsman called there. The Indigenous population declined, owing to disease and spirituous liquors, some poisonous, as well as individuals travelling to other places for work. Internecine warfare continued but was in its last phase. The old vitality of commercial rivalry and wealth gathering had given way to something more warlike and certainly less commercial.

Part II, "War for the Woods," is the modern history of Meares Island, running from the latter part of the nineteenth century to the present. It answers a related web of questions: What circumstances led to the island's transfer, in historical memory, from Native occupancy and maritime fur-trading realm to Indian Reserves 1 and 2 and, later, Tree Farm Licence 22? Who has rights of possession to the island and its waters? Must possession be on the spot, or can it be from some faraway place or places—or can it even be an imagining of the mind? How did the legal case brought forward by the NTC bring all these issues together? And how did it leave as legacy a quite different and indeed startlingly new perception of Meares Island—as a place saved from forest exploitation by the alliance of Native voices and environmental groups? Chapter 8, "Possessions and Dispossessions," is all about chainsaws, protests and commercial disputes. It focuses on the historical issues of the legal file. Generally speaking, I have left the legal pleadings, arguments and counterarguments to others. These can be traced in court records. My intent here has been to restage the deep-seated grievances brought forth so long ago and yet still persistent.

There is much about real estate in this chapter, mainly regarding the size and contracted limits of Indian reserves. There are appeals to the Crown and its agents for justice and for due recognition of Native rights. Native peoples claiming a hereditary interest in Meares Island called for righteous action on the part of the Crown. Their voices, cutting through legalese and administrative obfuscation, are striking testimony that all they really wanted was fair treatment under the law. Native resentments were disclosed in many of the documents I examined; these same resentments are with us today.

Chapter 9 looks at the forest and the trees, examining how MacBlo came to have the right to log Meares Island, but also tracing the development of industrial logging on the BC coast generally, and its slow but steady march to Clayoquot Sound and Meares Island. Chapter 10 gives a taste of the courtroom drama and the judgment of the Appeal Court justices, and then turns to other cases that built on the *Meares Island* decision, as well as to the Clayoquot Sound protest that drew worldwide attention a decade after the Meares Island protest.

A final chapter offers some observations about the continuing assault on the forest and the downward slide of old-growth timber stands. It is not a happy story, but a tragic conclusion and sad commentary on the rapaciousness of humankind.

Meares Island is now symbolic. The inescapable conclusion we are bound to draw is that it is *crisis* that gives uniqueness to the history of otherwise unknown locales such as, in our case, Meares Island. As so often in history, crisis drives the agenda.

Barry Gough
Victoria, British Columbia, Canada

Acknowledgements

First, my thanks go to the Nuu-Chah-Nulth Tribal Council. The late Earl George was my constant companion on research trips and visits to Ahousat.[7] Hesquiaht Chief Simon Lucas offered valuable wisdom. Many Chiefs and Elders supported my efforts but never made any attempt to check my own voice; there has been enough in the written historical record and public documents to tell a story that runs generally parallel to theirs. At the grand council of the NTC at Ahousat I was asked to present my findings, in this way repaying the kindnesses shown to me. I had come to pay homage and to honour the history of these people. "How should I dress for this?" I asked lawyer Jack Woodward in advance.

"I will wear my best suit," he replied, "My clients like to see that I am treating their case with every respect as a trial lawyer."

I took a cue from this, and I dressed similarly. When later that same day I saw the Native regalia and dress that was worn, I realized I had come properly attired. This is a sidelight on the story of Meares Island as I tell it, but it serves to demonstrate the seriousness and formality with which we tackled the case and its historic significance. We were, in our own ways, making history. The research was as exciting as it was compelling, and all sorts of stories and secrets were revealed as the past was brought to light.

Except where noted, documentation comes from the National Archives of Canada; British Columbia Archives; Department of Northern Affairs, Government of Canada (Vancouver office); the National Archives, Kew (Admiralty and Colonial Office Papers); Hydrographic Records Office, Taunton, Somerset; Massachusetts Historical Society; Oregon Historical Society; and Maritime Museum of British Columbia. I thank the archivists and librarians for their assistance. British Columbia Archives' inspired *Sound Heritage* series, in which William Langlois, Barbara Efrat, Bob Bossin and others made truly outstanding contributions to British Columbia's early history, provided aural evidence and explanatory commentary essential to many of the revelations found in this book. Their work was heroic. The story of Father Brabant derives from his memoir. F.W. Howay, Robin Fisher, James Gibson, Mary Malloy and Valerie Sherer Mathes have made significant contributions to cross-cultural and trade studies, and I am in their debt. I also thank Richard Blagborne for details on the yacht *Templar*; Rick Charles, for advice on John Meares' sailing into Clayoquot Sound, and also for taking me on a charming personal voyage of discovery to Adventure Cove; Malcolm Crockett, for advice; Kim Davies and Gordon Miller, for items various about my text; Greg Dening, for inspiration and insistence that I must keep writing history; John Dewhirst, for advice on so many of the themes of this work; E.W. Giesecke, for knowledge about the *Tonquin*; Ken and Dot Gibson, for advice and friendship over decades; David W. Griffiths, Tonquin Foundation, for information on the possible anchor of Astor's *Tonquin*; Walter Guppy, for his history of the settlement period; Edmund Hayes, for explanations about the expedition he made with Samuel Eliot Morison in

Acknowledgements

search of Adventure Cove, and for many discussions about *Tonquin*; Margaret Horsfield and Ian Kennedy, historians of Tofino and Clayoquot Sound, for help in many ways; Robin Inglis, for material on why Maquinna called John Meares a liar; Hewitt Jackson, Steve Mayo and Gordon Miller for artistic appreciations; John Lutz, for inspired revelations about makúk; Don Mitchell, for archaeological evidence and interpretation; John Motherwell, for land title searches; J. Richard Nokes, for insights into John Meares; Camilla Turner, for discussion of Chinook jargon as trade language; J.S. Whittaker, for advice and information on land law and survey techniques. It is a matter of regret and sadness that numerous persons who aided me in my quest are no longer with us. I owe a debt of grateful thanks to my esteemed editor Audrey McClellan and to the editors and staff of Harbour Publishing. I alone am responsible for errors of omission and commission.

PART I

The Empire of Fortune

1
Out of the Mists

I have in my study an old streamer trunk that nowadays is my treasure trove of Meares Island history. I doubt if there is such a cache of materials on this subject elsewhere, for the various items included are fragments of memory and politics brought together, conveniently, and at considerable cost, under legal instructions to leave no stone unturned in my research.

In that trunk are legal files, statements of claim, legal questions and responses, lists of documents, injunctions, correspondence with lawyers, personal jottings, and notes of all sorts gathered from near and far. These materials contain Spanish references, ghostly traces of the first Europeans to voyage to Vancouver Island's shores. Some American traders' papers are also to be found in the trunk. These are hard-nosed in character, reflective of the traders' mindset. Missionary records make their appearance, symptomatic of a search for the possession of souls. Most of the documentation, as could be expected, is British and colonial. Given the British fetish for keeping records for legal purposes, the short colonial period of Vancouver Island history suffers from no shortage of documentation. Successor governments—British Columbia and Canada—continued the tradition, and the modern practice of photocopying means that literary fragments of Meares Island history are now scattered globally.

It was not always so. Only fifty years ago, Meares Island was *terra*

PART I The Empire of Fortune

incognita to the outside world. Like many other places on this earth, it was possessed and comprehended solely by its inhabitants and near neighbours. Isolation moulded a separate identity of a world apart.

"We still don't know how long people have lived on the West Coast, or where they came from." That is the view of archaeologist John Dewhirst, who estimates that 4,200 years ago is the likely time of occupation of Yuquot specifically. Based on his extensive oral history research, Dewhirst further states that the Nuu-chah-nulth resent the view that they had ultimately come from Asia: "the Nootkans maintain that they have *always* lived on the West Coast."[8] From my perspective as a historian, this startling Native view does not square with assembled anthropological and archaeological evidence, which suggests the first occupants came vast distances from the Asian periphery 10,000 or more years ago, crossing the Beringia land bridge or coasting the shore, and taking preliminary possession in and around the place we now call Meares Island. However, 10,000 years or even 4,200 years is an ancient history, and these occupants have been on Meares Island and the coast of Vancouver Island since time out of mind. By contrast, the modern era seems like the twinkling of an eye—but so much has passed in this short epic era. It is one of dizzying intensity.

Today, and in the relatively recent past, we have come to possess Meares Island variously: as Native homeland, as forest preserve lying dormant, as Native ecological park, and even in memory as battleground in a dogged court fight. Plucked from virtual obscurity in the day-to-day prosaic political affairs of British Columbia, Meares Island attained importance, even notoriety, out of proportion to its geographical size. It was "put on the map," so to speak, by crisis. Outsiders came to know of it in consequence of the crisis. Nowadays we possess it in more symbolic ways: as a survivor of clear-cutting timber practices, as nature preserved in the face of industrial-age onslaughts. We might also wonder how we will possess it in decades and centuries hence.

Where is this island of history and politics? It is best described as being near Tofino, north across intervening waters. Today, if going by the customary land route, you drive by car from the city of Alberni and wend your way along the highway crossing the mountainous spine of Vancouver Island. Near a small building indicating that you are at last in splendid Pacific Rim National Park you halt at the stop sign, and then, turning right when almost in sight of the open Pacific Ocean, you travel on until you come to the village or town of Tofino. This municipality, incorporated 1983, lies mainly at the tip of the low-lying Esowista Peninsula, northwest of undeniably magnificent and well-named Long Beach, now possessed by Canada in Pacific Rim National Park. The coastline forming an immense backdrop to this theatre of nature is steep and sharp. Mountains three or four thousand feet high come down to water's edge. Here and there are low-lying places, some islands, suitable for human occupation.

In geographical terms, you are just about on the forty-ninth parallel and approximately 130 miles due west of the city of Vancouver. In another sense, you are far away from the maddening noise and bluster of the metropolis, on the rim of the world. Tofino and Clayoquot Sound, they say, is life on the edge. "But on the edge of what?" ask Dave Duffus and Nancy Turner of the University of Victoria, who then respond: "It is, of course, the edge of the vast Pacific Ocean and the west coast of Vancouver Island. But it is also the edge of two planes of existence, the edge between the white industrial world and the world of aboriginal tradition."[9] Named for an eighteenth-century Spanish cartographic and navigation specialist, Don Vincente Tofiño, the place acquired military distinction as an air station during the Second World War and now boasts a fine small landing strip. In later years it has become a refuge for the disaffected, a mecca for surfers, a retreat for urbanites, a platform for media seekers, and much else.

Before the days of commercial air travel—indeed, before the road (Highway 4 from Tofino/Ucluelet to Alberni) was "punched through" by logging companies and the BC Highways Department in 1959—the place was accessible only by sea or air, mainly float plane.[10] Remoteness, when you think of it, has been its secret for so long. All the same, new forces were coming to possess it from the late 1700s.

Maritime fur traders seeking sea otter pelts formed the first wave

PART I The Empire of Fortune

of intruders. When the sea otter were hunted to near extinction locally, a dormant era ensued. Later, itinerant traders established makeshift quarters here. But nothing seemed permanent in the days before the coastal steamships began arriving on a schedule. For a time, Roman Catholic priests made conversions here, and on Meares Island they built a residential school.

In the early years of contact, and well into the twentieth century, the Nuu-chah-nulth peoples maintained seasonal camps for fishing and for hunting sea mammals on the open beaches of small islands, on what they refer to as the "outside," the rough and rugged coast of storms. By contrast, their principal villages are built on the "inside," in sheltered locations within sounds and inlets. As a rule, summer occupation was on the outside, winter on the inside. This was the case at Clayoquot. Characteristic of the locale is its protected inner waterways. There exist two entries to the same, one in the southeast, leading to today's Tofino, and the other to the north, nearer to Ahousat and Hesquiat.

From late October to early spring, violent storms lash the coast, creating mountainous surf pounding outer beaches and rocky shores. Spring and summer are relatively calm periods, but even then heavy ground swells are found outside, and fog banks come crawling in from the sea. The interior channels are largely free from storms and winds. The Japanese current sweeping by the west coast keeps the winter temperatures above freezing, while in summer the climate is mild and unlikely to be hot for humans. The annual rainfall is 96 to 100 inches, about twice that of Vancouver and three times that of Victoria. Heavy forest and ground cover plus fallen trees keep habitation to the shore. For Aboriginal people, seasonal migrations were dictated by northwest winds, and drenching rains would require the seeking of shelter and abandonment of the economic pursuits of summer's kinder weather. In all, it may be said that this is a benign climate, though prone to torrential rain and storms—nowadays a tourist attraction.

Father Augustin Brabant, the Belgian-born and -educated Oblate priest, described the area in his reminiscences of 1900: "The coast is rugged and rocky, presenting in its entire extent the appearance of desolation and barrenness. The hills and mountains run down to the beach; the valleys are lakes, and a few patches of low land, to be encountered here and there, are covered with worthless [unmarketable] timber. No clear land is to be seen anywhere, and no hopes can be entertained that the west coast of Vancouver Island will ever be available for agricultural settlements."

Brabant arrived in Victoria in 1869, and in 1874 went to Hesquiat, north Clayoquot Sound, as a missionary. He faced much resistance. But he came to know the area and people well, and he had a strong interest in its history, taking note of Native accounts. At Hesquiat the church building, ready for service in 1875, soon proved inadequate, and a new one, Sacred Heart Church, with stepped buttresses or gables with parapets, gave it a unique look (it decayed to ruin in 1936). Brabant thought the climate differed little from Victoria. About half the time it was fine weather, about half rain. Heavy frost was rare; snow seldom fell in any depth. The local peoples—"Indians," he called them—"seem not to notice the general depression of the seasons, but for one born and raised elsewhere, accustomed to the society of his fellow white men, there are no words to convey how monotonous it is, and how lonesome one would feel were it not for the thought of the sacredness of the object for which he is here."[11]

Anthropologist Philip Drucker writes that a distinctive feature of North Pacific culture is the use of wood, which is one of the area's chief natural resources. Red cedar and redwood, both soft and tractable, long and straight and easily split and opened, are still in common use. So are yellow cedar, alder, Douglas fir, true firs, spruce and hemlock, all with different properties and degrees of difficulty to work. With adzes, chisels, wedges, hammers and mauls, drills, knives and limited sanding materials, much can be completed by hand. Fire is also used. Iron appeared on the coast before contact and may have come via Japanese sea drifters or by other ways—for example, shipwreck. Native development of tools and implements gave all sorts of opportunity for the fashioning of boxes, rattles, masks, ornaments, carved doors and posts, and, not least, large roof beams and planks

PART I The Empire of Fortune

for shelter. According to Drucker, "The exteriors of wooden containers and dishes were usually simple geometric forms, sometimes modified into stylized zoomorphic shapes, but always symmetrical both externally and in relation to the hollowed-out portion."[12] Symmetry and neatness were characteristics of items manufactured out of wood. There were wooden clubs and spears, too, but many were crafted out of sea lion bones, which were stronger and more durable. But this was, and is, a culture dependent on wood, and not least among its requirements were transportation and trade. Canoes, crafted from red cedar, were best made on the Northwest Coast by the Nuu-chah-nulth peoples. They were used locally and were sold or bartered in trade with other nations.

Meares Island was, and in many ways still is, a world apart. From the main wharf of Tofino, on most days you can see the island clearly, for its horizon is dominated by a large cone-shaped mountain, now shown on maps as Lone Cone (743 metres, 2,438 feet). From the time of human occupation the mountain has served as a sentinel. The Ahousaht know Meares Island as *Hilhooglis* (the closest rendering in English phonetics; *Hithuugis, ipa* is the transliterated spelling). Lone Cone Mountain is *wanacks*. The meaning of Hilhooglis, explained to me by Peter S. Webster, an Ahousaht Elder,[13] is "People who go, or steer, by the Mountain"—that is, are guided by it.

It is easy to see why this is so. From offshore, in clear weather, Lone Cone offers an aid to navigation. It is distinct from the other hills or mountains of the immediate vicinity, including the more southeasterly Mount Colnett (802 metres, 2,631 feet), also on Meares Island, which though slightly higher in elevation is not so dramatic in shape. Given the blue-grey hues of the landscape, such variations as these curiosities in terrain can be an essential and lifesaving marker to a mariner approaching from a distance. In inshore waters, through the labyrinthine paths and in some cul-de-sacs, the Ahousaht, and others, steered by the mountain. Webster, born 1908, recounts how he accompanied his grandmother to strip bark from cedar trees for clothing. He remembers trapping black bear with his grandfather and building dugout canoes. And he recalls the shifts of his people to take advantage of nature's bounty: in spring and summer, catching herring and spring salmon near Vargas Island; in the fall, dogfish could be found at Bedwell Sound; later they would move to a sheltered bay on Meares Island, where they would find ling cod, clams, duck and loon. He and his kin survived on what nature could provide.

The principal village of Meares Island, then as now, is Opitsat. Originally a Kelsemaht village, it was conquered by the Clayoquot, who then numbered about 350 warriors and counted eighteen big houses. The Clayoquot declared war on the Kelsemaht to obtain their fishing waters in about 1720. Oral tradition holds that it was a stubborn battle, after which the Kelsemaht were driven away and made their home at Tloo tlpich (Cloolthpich), also on Meares Island, north of the future site of Christie Indian Industrial School. The Clayoquot's earliest place of residence, by their traditions, was Tla a qua, a spot about ten miles east on Tofino Inlet from present-day Tofino, at the north end of Kennedy Lake.[14] At Opitsat the Clayoquot flourished, being closer to salmon and herring. They had a summer village at Clayoquot (Stubbs Island) and another at E-cha-chist, and perhaps others elsewhere. E-cha-chist was their whalers' station, and there they awaited their next quarry.

To the naked eye the land thereabouts seems all greys and greens, and when taken all together it forms one harmonious whole. Toward the seashore, the land is generally of a low character but appears to rise in increments the farther the distance away, often to snow-clad mountains. The higher mountains are frequently and magically wreathed in low-lying clouds. Behind, the flanking mountains form a barrier to the lands beyond and to the straits and inlets even farther to the east. Farther still, the Cordilleran mountains form the formidable spine of North America.

In the inlets immediately within view from our vantage point of Tofino we see small islands and islets as well as big ones, all with twisted deciduous trees that we note have strongly held up against the storms that sweep in here from the open and often wild Pacific. A fog bank lying offshore may obliterate the view; if not, the eye

PART I The Empire of Fortune

looks to the vanishing horizon, all the while perhaps imagining Japan, Russia or China beyond the rim of the sea.

From the viewpoint of the mariner approaching offshore, there is an outer shore, a difficult channel, and an inner sanctuary or port. Tofino lies as if cradled by the protective islands, sandbars and reefs that form the outside, or southeast, entrance. From the rocky entrance, Templar Channel, named for the cutter of the yachtsman Charles Barrett-Lennard, who called here in 1860 as part of his stupendous pioneering circumnavigation of Vancouver Island, leads to the safer anchorage off the point of Tofino, on the north side. This is Port Cox. By dint of experience, seaborne mariners from far away learned how to approach, then steer through and ultimately come to anchor in this place of magnificent safety. Here is how John Hoskins of Boston described the tricky entrance in March 1792:

> This Harbour or rather this district or tribe is called by the natives Clioquot and as has been before observed by Captain Gray Hancock's Harbour [Port Cox]. It is situated about twenty leagues to the east south east of Nootka in the latitude of 49°9′ north and longitude 125°26′ west. The entrance to this harbour is through a roads [Templar Channel] about five miles in length where there is good anchorage. The only obstruction in the passage through the roads is two sand spits the one running off the eastern the other from the western shore. [T]o go clear of these you will run close in to Observatory Island steer from thence north north west until you get the passage into the harbour open on the eastern side of Harbour Island (there is a passage on the other side of the island but not so good). You may then venture to keep away for [from] it keeping Harbour Island shore aboard till you are in the gap then doubling round the eastern point you will find good anchorage in six or seven fathoms water over a sandy bottom about a mile from the shore.[15]

A number of islands lie scattered about the harbour, and in those early days there were many sandbanks or spits that presented hazards to navigation. There were many coves, too, and the anchorage seemed well sheltered from any wind, though tides run very strongly off Tofino. Hoskins took his bearings using various landmarks and the flagstaff at Opitsat.

What is true for Clayoquot Sound is generally true for the west coast of Vancouver Island. The Admiralty *Pilot*, or sailing directions, published in London in 1864, puts the problems of navigation this way:

> [The coast is] fringed by numerous rocks and hidden dangers, especially near the entrances of the sounds, and the exercise of great caution and vigilance will be necessary on the part of the navigator to avoid them . . . On no occasion, therefore, except where otherwise stated . . . should a stranger attempt to enter any of the harbours or anchorages during night or thick weather, but rather keep a good offing until circumstances are favourable; and when about to make the coast, it cannot be too strongly impressed on the mariner to take every opportunity of ascertaining his vessel's position by astronomical observations, as fogs and thick weather come on very suddenly at all time of the year, more especially in summer and autumn months.[16]

Forewarned mariners sailing these waters were always aware of the devious currents and treacherous tides. They knew, as their successors do, that access from the open Pacific can be a tortuous passage from the entrance through to safe moorage. The same is true for a return to open sea: in short, it is a dangerous passage.

Sailors aboard a sea otter trading vessel must have expressed much wonder at the richness offered by the forests, the great trees, particularly cedar, standing in majesty. Bernard Magee, in 1793, wrote in his log this account of the region: "the whole face of the Country is covered with woods having a most beautiful appearance . . . & in some places that were Clair of wood was Covered with beautifully green verdure most pleasing to the Eye & in my opinion as fine a Country as any in the globe."[17] Spanish pilot Juan Pantoja, there in May 1790, thought Clayoquot milder than Nootka and certainly drier. "The surface of the country is likewise full of woods and is rough for travel, although not so dismal and gloomy. Wherever I have gone with the longboat I have seen small pieces of flat land on which there is good pasture for cattle."[18]

These were agreeable views of summertime visitors. In wintertime a different prospect presented itself from offshore. And for this we turn to Captain Cook, the master mariner.

2
First Encounters

In March 1778, when he made landfall on the Oregon coast—referred to as Nova Albion by the British in recognition of seadog Francis Drake's 1579 claim for his sovereign Queen Elizabeth I at Drakes Bay, California—Cook observed that the land appeared high and craggy and mostly covered with snow. There were prodigious flocks of birds. As to the weather, it was squally, with fogs and frequent showers of snow, hail and sleet, making it dangerous to approach an unknown coast where no known shelter existed. This last he would have to find (and he did) at Nootka. There he took on wood and water, and repaired spars and rigging.

Such were the conditions when he passed the Strait of Juan de Fuca's entrance that he thought it unlikely a strait existed there. Generally speaking, therefore, mariners from the outside world avoided this coast in wintertime, leaving the Native inhabitants in quiet isolation. All the same, James Cook put Friendly Cove, or Yuquot ("Where the wind blows"), on charts for all time, and where he had sailed, others would come in his wake. Cook concluded that the local peoples derived much from sea animals, and he found evidence of whaling implements though he did not see whaling carried out. Here was a marine culture dependent on ritual replenishment. Not only was the larder filled, so to speak, but it gave the Nuu-chah-nulth a position of power in trade with non-whaling cultures along the coast.[19]

Cook's arrival at Nootka in stormy late March 1778 is such a demarcation in the history of British Columbia that one is tempted to call the time before his visit "Before Cook," or BC, and the years after AC. In the BC era the coast was an absolutely Aboriginal world; AC, the contact and interaction of societies changed the old order almost beyond recognition—and very quickly as well.

Cook's ships and ship companies were greeted cordially, with masked performances and extensive orations. Not only was there an easy interaction of races, but there was also a mixing of technologies, for the Industrial Revolution sailed into Nootka Sound with Cook's ships and with the trading vessels that followed in their wake. At the time of Cook's arrival, the Indigenous peoples were related in various ways, and ownership of beaches, land and resources were delineated, defined. Forests and banks were tribal possessions, sometimes linked by close relations to hereditary chiefs. The search for power and prestige was driven by possession of the natural world's resources.

Europeans were driven by different expectations. Cook came to the coast in search of a northern passage that would shorten the distance and sailing time from England to Asia. This potential trade route had been a grail, real or imagined, of mariners for a couple of centuries by the 1770s. A passage had been shown on Ortelius's chart of 1570, and this may have encouraged those who advised Francis Drake to search for a "Strait of Anian." He was more intent on piracy than exploration, however, and from Nova Albion's Drakes Bay he sailed via the Pacific and the Moluccas, trading for spices en route to England. Before the end of the sixteenth century, Juan de Fuca, sailing for Spain, contended to have sailed where Drake failed, finding a strait at the forty-seventh parallel of latitude. Spanish reports also indicated a current from the east of Japan that would bring ships across toward the Aleutians, then into the Gulf of Alaska and south.

Twenty-five years before Cook sailed for the North Pacific, Vitus Bering and Aleksei Chirikov, for Russia, had examined the Alaska

PART I The Empire of Fortune

coast from about Mount St. Elias south toward the Queen Charlotte Islands (Haida Gwaii). Because their work was cursory, Cook was ordered to follow the coast northward from 45 to 65 degrees north, searching especially for a passage to Hudson Bay. Cook's River (Cook Inlet) proved a blind alley, and passing through the Aleutian Archipelago he entered the Bering Sea, sailing north then east to appropriately named Icy Cape, the limits of his exploration before fog, high winds, drifting ice and the approaching season of darkness caused him to go south to winter quarters. From this he never returned. However, he left a vast amount of new knowledge in the form of navigational and scientific data, including significant ethnographic details of the Nuu-chah-nulth peoples of Nootka Sound and of other Natives to the north in high latitudes.

We need to expand our understanding of the state of geographical knowledge at this time, to remember how little Europeans knew of the greater northwest (of course, the Indigenous Peoples were familiar with the area all along). In 1776, the year Cook set forth from England in the British warships *Resolution* and *Discovery* in quest of a western entrance to the Northwest Passage, the Pacific flank of North America was largely *terra incognita* to Europeans—and the subject of much speculation. Curious outsiders held various views of what the country consisted. The River of the West was reputedly there—later located and named the Columbia River. In Cook's time, rumours were rife of passages and straits through this mountainous western flank, and the most charming and seductive of these, already alluded to, was advertised in the 1625 publication (by Purchas in London) of Michael Lok's interview in a bar in Venice with an intrepid though shadowy Kefalonian pilot known to the Spanish as Juan de Fuca. Fuca claimed that in 1592 he had taken part in an expedition that discovered a broad strait, between 47 and 48 degrees N latitude—remarkably where the gateway strait eventually proved to be—that led to a great inland sea.[20] Encouragement to find the elusive strait was provided by the allure of a 20,000 pounds sterling reward to the finder of any northern passage "for vessels by sea between the Atlantic and Pacific Ocean—a North West Passage."[21] Cook sailed with high expectations.

First Encounters

As students of Northwest history, we need to be reminded of the Spanish presence that features in this dramatic age. Spain claimed Vancouver Island, the continental mainland and adjacent waters by virtue of the doctrine of discovery, and we will look at this claim later in the book. Spain pursued its interests through marine discoveries and occupation.

In 1769 the port of San Blas in New Spain (now Mexico) was established for the renewal of Spanish control of its northwestern frontier, where missions and presidios had been established. San Blas was a marine depot, a place of supply and a location to build ships and send them to sea to guard shipping. Closer than Acapulco to the China trade, San Blas was to be the beachhead and base of supply for the expanding frontier.

In 1775, naval vessels on exploration and supply sailed northward from San Blas. Bruno de Hezeta in the frigate *Santiago*, accompanied by the schooner *Sonora* under Juan Francisco de la Bodega y Quadra, anchored near Point Grenville, in what is now Washington State, on July 14. Hezeta landed and took possession for the Spanish crown. Local Natives killed a boat's crew from the schooner.[22] In succession came Bodega y Quadra's voyage to the Gulf of Alaska, and later Alejandro Malaspina's reconnaissance, followed by Dionisio Alcalá Galiano and Cayetano Valdéz's 1792 voyage that came precisely at the time Captain George Vancouver was in search of a northwest passage (and determining the insularity of Vancouver Island). Spain had been at war with Britain from 1779 to 1783, and the rivalry between the two powers had not been quenched thereafter. When San Blas was made operational, it gave a clear indication that a challenge would be made to British aspirations in the Pacific. Oddly enough, when the Spanish under Esteban José Martínez established control at Nootka, they had expected to find Russians there. But John Meares was there instead, and Martínez decided to check this threat. This is the essential background to Meares' voyages.

No name in Northwest Coast histories conjures up more conflicting perspectives than John Meares. Here's an irony of history: Meares Island is named for a person known generally as a scallywag.

PART I The Empire of Fortune

The charge is partly true. Seldom is a place name associated with a person of questionable veracity—honour usually triumphs in such things! Meares Island, however, carries the name of a person who claimed all sorts of geographical discoveries subsequently shown to be false. His "alternative facts" were part of his undoing: truth caught up with him.

At face value he seemed at the time both an officer and a gentleman, as his fellow mariner Charles Duncan attests, but "stabs in the back" destroyed his professions of friendship.[23] On the other hand, as we shall see, he was not so shady as many have claimed. He delighted in literary fights with his opponents, never shying away from a spat. His principal biographer, J. Richard Nokes, entitled his lovely book *Almost a Hero*.[24] That is a worthy title. The most injudicious treatment of him comes from none other than Judge F.W. Howay, who was disinclined to place any great reliance on Meares' writings, which is fair enough. However, Howay regarded Meares' volume as mere propaganda to help him wring a large payment from Spain in connection with the seizure of his ships at Nootka, which is an exaggeration and, more importantly, denies the valuable descriptions of Native persons, ways of life, environments and resources.[25] Judge Howay was no imperial historian and did not understand London's politics.

Many of Meares' actions commend him to us. Not least was his careful policy to win friends among Indigenous allies on the Northwest Coast, measures designed to protect them from undesirable interests. He was ethnographically conscious, too, a great recorder of detail. He was as curious as he was fascinated by what he saw, and he possessed superb skills as an organizer.[26] He was, besides, a man of great initiative and enterprise, and he served his own memory well, wanting to be recognized for his achievements: in short, he was a first-rate propagandist.

He is admittedly a complex figure, and, I say, all the more attractive for that! Many of the world's more compelling personalities are complex in their nature and outlook. You could say the same about his contemporary James Colnett, of whom more later. At Clayoquot Sound, which he got to know so well, Meares was commercially aggressive, friendly in all relations with the locals and, like James Cook before him, altruistic and humanitarian in his dealings.

Meares was not the first to sail to the Northwest Coast following Cook's suggested plan. His enterprise has obscure origins. Likely he convinced some agency houses of the East India Company in Calcutta, trading to Canton (now Guangzhou), to finance a trial expedition. He needed provisioning and supplies from Manila, exchanged for Indian items. He faced many British rivals, some who sailed from India, others from Macau, still others from London. When rivalries presented themselves, he often made accommodations and contracts. But, by right of success, he assumed a position that spoke for others whose interests were threatened by the Spanish, and he gave the exalted appearance that he was the only begetter of trade between America and Asia. He became the national representative of the wronged party who must be vindicated.[27] In London, his star shone brightly over British commercial affairs on the far Pacific shores. In short, he became a crusader for national commercial interests.

At this same time, on the Indian subcontinent, the British were pressing for further commercial privileges. The Mughal empire faced decay, and local rulers could not withstand British and French military power. The Battle of Plassey in 1757 was pivotal in countering the French and giving the East India Company control over Bengal. The Company's financial power and managerial skills expanded mightily, just at the time that Meares was drawn into the orbit of its marine activities. Around Bengal developed an Asian trading system with links to the old ports and new entrepôts of Southeast Asia. Manila in the Philippines, in Spanish hands, had links to North America by way of the annual Manila galleon. Here was a golden link across vast oceanic spaces. Tentacles of power and influence, based on trade and seaborne commerce, stretched out from Bengal, aided and abetted by the powerful and aggressive merchant traders who were seeking new markets and new fields to conquer. In a way they were part of the dramatic liberation of the old order of the East India Company, which is why Meares had so little opposition from the Company and so much support from ministers of the British government.

Meares made two expeditions to the Northwest Coast. In what he calls his "introductory voyage," he sailed from Bengal in March 1786 in the *Nootka*, accompanied by the *Sea Otter*, under Captain Tipping. Provisions were hard to obtain, and the scheme seems slim on the ground, underfunded and undersupplied. Both vessels, to make ends meet, found themselves diverted: the *Sea Otter* to take on opium for Malacca and the *Nootka* to take the paymaster general of the King's forces in India to Madras. In any event, they reached the high Alaskan islands in August, late for coastwise trading, and found themselves surrounded by a fleet of canoes busily whaling. Meares, hearing that rival British vessels were in the vicinity, decided to winter in Prince William Sound, spending much of it ice-bound. Many of his sailors died of scurvy and others of drink.

Captain Nathaniel Portlock of the ship *King George* and George Dixon of the *Prince of Wales*, chancing upon Meares there, charged him with poaching. Portlock, a high-handed fellow, demanded that, after restoring his crew's health and repairing the *Nootka*, Meares leave the sea otter coast, sail to the Sandwich Islands and then make for Canton. This Meares was obliged to do, and with a weakened and smaller crew and a creaky vessel he made his destination. So ended Meares' first voyage to America.[28] He had few difficulties with the various Alaskan Natives, but his quarrels with Portlock and Dixon had commenced, and they dogged him all his life. He had got nowhere near Nootka—or Clayoquot, for that matter—but he had learned that the Russians were well entrenched in Alaska.

Undaunted, Meares made new plans in Canton. In January 1788, with the help of British India merchants, he bought the *Felice Adventurer*, 230 tons, and the *Iphigenia Nubiana*, 200 tons, the latter to be commanded by Captain William Douglas. Both vessels were "snows"—that is, they were somewhat like brigs (two-masted square riggers), but having a square mizzen and trysail set on a separate (or gunter) mast close aft the mainmast. *Felice*, as she came to be known, had a crew of fifty; the *Iphigenia*, forty. These vessels sailed under Portuguese flags. They first called at the Philippines for supplies and trade goods, but the crew was wracked with illness. The two ships parted company in the Philippines, arriving separately on the Northwest Coast. The *Iphigenia* headed for Alaska as planned, taking a great circle route. They dodged typhoons in Japanese waters, which are climactically the world's most unstable. Picking up the Kuroshio—the Black or North Pacific current—the vessels made swift passage in the vicinity of the Aleutian Islands. This same current brought Japanese sea drifters to Acapulco in 1617, the *Hojunmaru* to near Cape Flattery in 1834, and a fishing boat to Puget Sound in 1926; other episodes occurred of Japanese wrecks stranded and picked up in the North Pacific.[29] In any event, Meares reached Nootka Sound on May 11, 1788. He immediately set to work building a house for his men and stores. Half his crew were Chinese, some of whom he was to leave there with others to build a schooner, the *North West America*, forty-five tons, successfully launched that September.

While these projects were advancing at Yuquot, Nootka Sound, Meares raised anchor and proceeded south in the *Felice*. His object was Wickaninnish Sound, so named by Captain Charles Barkley of the *Imperial Eagle*, who had been there a year earlier, trading with Wickaninnish. Historians believe that Meares had Barkley's logbook and charts, so we may say that he was retracing Barkley's discoveries. Meares, rightly, did not claim he was first to bring a ship into the port off today's Meares Island and Tofino; nevertheless, his account is rich and detailed. It is our primary reference.

Two days south of Nootka, the *Felice* was spotted by Wickaninnish and his people. Meares says that he was about six miles offshore when a small flotilla of canoes came out to the ship. Wickaninnish was welcomed on board. Followed by the canoes, Wickaninnish piloted the *Felice* safely through the reefs south of Wickaninnish Island to anchor right in front of his summer village, E-cha-chist. Meares thought it was three times as large as Yuquot in population. For seven days Meares carried out trading there, but then it blew such a gale that he decided to shift to more protected waters at the soonest possible instant. On June 20, 1788, he writes, "In the evening it moderated,

PART I The Empire of Fortune

when the ship got under sail, which was no sooner observed by Wicananish than he came on board, and safely piloted us into the harbor, which we named Port Cox, in honour of our friend John Henry Cox, Esq.—But not choosing to trust entirely to the skill of the chief on the occasion, the boats were sent ahead to sound, particularly on the bar."[30] This proved a prudent measure. Thus it was that the *Felice* passed through Duffin Passage, which is bounded on the west side by Felice Island, named after the ship, and on the east by the Esowista Peninsula of Vancouver Island. In the distance Meares spied a mountain shaped like a "sugar loaf," which is now called Lone Cone and is on the island that bears his name.[31]

In his amusing *Voyages*, one of the most sought after books of early voyaging in the Pacific, Meares provides an admirable first look at the great sea otter chief Wickaninnish and his world of Clayoquot Sound. His account is full of brilliant ethnographic detail. Not least among the reasons why we should look on Meares in a better light is the fact that none other than the distinguished hydrographic surveyor Captain George Henry Richards, RN, when assigning place names in the early 1860s, decided that the island should be named for the person who put it "on the map." But readers will have to decide for themselves—and might prefer the Native name for the island, Hilhooglis.

Let's look in greater depth at this complex fellow Meares. Commander John Meares, Royal Navy, was born in England in 1756, just as the French and British entered the last phase of their desperate struggle for Louisburg and Quebec. Some officer in the navy would have sponsored his admission into the Service, for patronage largely controlled these matters. He passed his examination for advancement to lieutenant on September 17, 1778. By this time, age twenty-two, he had been at sea, first as a volunteer first class, then able seaman and midshipman, for no fewer than six years, ten months, and one day. He was promoted to lieutenant in the navy in 1778, the same year James Cook made his visit to Nootka Sound and Alaska. Unemployed, like so many other junior officers, by the coming of peace after the war of the American Revolution, Meares took to merchant

34

voyaging. He had commercial instincts and adventurous leanings. No moss gathered under his feet. We subsequently find him in Calcutta, forming a company to exploit the northwest America trade in sea otter, which was then the ermine of Asia.

It's easy to dismiss John Meares, and many a historical assessor has done so. Maquinna,[32] the Mowachaht chief, called him "Aita-Aita Meares" or "Liar Meares." This has acquired broad currency by recipients contending that all Native evidence is sacrosanct. The circumstances leading to this epithet are as follows: In his attention-getting *Memorial* to the British government after Martínez captured Captain Colnett's ships in 1789 (see Chapter 3), Meares maintained that he had bought land from Maquinna the year previous.[33] This was accepted by the British ministry of the day. Further, in 1792, during negotiations with the Spanish at Nootka, the mate who had been with Meares, Robert Duffin, attested to the purchase, maintaining that Maquinna had sold an entire cove to Meares. At this time, summer 1792, Maquinna enjoyed excellent relations with the Spanish—especially Bodega y Quadra, the Spanish commissioner—and when Duffin's report was translated to him, Maquinna burst out with the words "Aita-Aita Meares."[34] Other persons wanted to discredit Meares, cut him down to size: Robert Gray and Joseph Ingraham, both Boston traders, declaimed they had never heard of any transfer of land at Friendly Cove to Meares. Others may have done likewise.

Meares is one of the most controversial figures in the history of the British Empire. It has been said that he was "brave to a degree, but tricky in the extreme, his seamanship questionable, his reputed discoveries and 'butter pat maps' as unreliable as they were laughable."[35] He was disparaging of the cartography of the French navigator Maurelle, while Captain Dixon and Mrs. Barkley both questioned his honesty and integrity, in that instance standing square with Maquinna.

Truth to tell, there are as many John Meareses as there are stories about him. He does not fit easily in a box or, from the biographer's point of view, coffin. If you examine all the manuscripts and particularly corporate records and British government files, you will come to

PART I The Empire of Fortune

see him in a larger and more generous context as a formidable trader and agent of commerce, for it was he who first projected a scheme to establish what was called in his day a factory at Nootka Sound, a beachhead of commercial empire. Call him an imperialist, if you will: the world is full of such people. The point is that he wished to establish a solid means to trade with the West Coast peoples, linking Asian ports with North American consumers and traders. Yes, he got into a squabble with the Spanish, who disliked his intrusion—and the whole set off the Nootka Sound crisis and a furious row in the British Parliament. His testimony about events at Nootka in 1789, when Spanish officials seized British vessels and cargoes, became of material value to the British government in forcing Spain to concede its vaunted and well-proclaimed monopoly of trade and navigation in the Pacific Ocean. This was a monumental event.

And Meares holds a particularly important place in Clayoquot Sound history, for it was his favourite trading area. His efforts there drove a secondary wave of commercial interest, this one taken up by none other than Captain James Colnett, who was connected to Meares by commercial arrangement, and whose story is as remarkable as that of Meares. I have thought time and again how easy it is to dismiss these persons of the past; how easy it is for the armchair historians of our age to think them just fools or imperialists or racists.

Meares had a keen business sense. When he sailed from Nootka to Canton in 1788, he had stowed in his ship as many spars as could safely be carried. He knew these would fetch good prices in Canton, where timber was in high demand, especially spars suitable as masts, yards, bowsprits and the like. Meares initiated timber exports to Asian ports, no small claim to fame. In addition, before his departure, he had directed one of the ship's carpenters to go into the woods near Nootka and select "a stick," as they were called by sailors, for a new mast for the *Iphigenia*. A stout party felled and hauled out just such a piece. In addition, various new yards were acquired as replacements or spares for his ships. Meares left Vancouver Island with this lasting impression: "the woods of this part of America are capable of supplying, with these valuable materials, all the navies of

Europe."[36] Meares could foresee the future greatness of these forests in the evolution of shipping and trade, and the availability of spars added to Britain's interest in Vancouver Island as a seat of British naval and commercial power.[37]

This historian marvels at the number of sea miles Meares put under his keel in his voyages to and from the Northwest Coast. From Calcutta, Prince William Sound in Alaska seems almost half a world away. The distance from Canton or Macau to the coast was less, of course, but nonetheless a long and taxing passage. These mariners learned of the ocean currents and prevailing winds and how to exploit them. They knew methods of survival at sea, they prepared for long voyages, and they invariably depended on information gathered from others who had gone before them. Merchant traders by sea were not hydrographic surveyors along the lines of Captains Cook, Bligh or Vancouver, sticklers for scientific detail and comprehensive examination in search of solving geographical puzzles. But merchant traders such as Meares or Colnett or Duncan did add to the knowledge of the far shores. And not only did they share this information between themselves; they also made sure that those persons connected to the British Admiralty were informed of new findings. As an example, Charles Duncan's revolutionary findings of Cape Flattery, Tatoosh Rock and Fuca's Pillar found their way into a January 1790 official chart published by the authority of Alexander Dalrymple, the Hydrographer of the Admiralty. More specific to Clayoquot Sound is Duncan's May 1788 sketch chart of the waters and village site of Ahousat, a copy of which survives in the British Columbia Archives.[38]

It took me years of study and brooding to realize that the merchant mariners were not only a harbinger of commerce but also immensely important in the collection of geographical data. Put differently, I like to think that the commercial sector contributed remarkably to the little-by-little accumulations of the chart. It is not that the official naval expeditions did not do important work in this regard, but when you think of Cook only looking at Nootka Sound and, besides, missing the Strait of Juan de Fuca, supposed to exist according to armchair geographers, you realize that most of the coast, particularly the west coast of Vancouver Island, came into focus on the chart by the evidence provided by the sea otter traders. Meares and Colnett brought naval knowledge to their navigational and trading requirements, and blended this with a spirit of commercial enterprise. As I have said before, with thanks to the lead provided to me by John S. Galbraith, the dean of commercial frontiers of empire, the merchant sector was far more important in the creation of official policy than the statesmen and bureaucrats in offices in Whitehall, London, who are credited with the policy as finally laid down. We see this in Meares' several voyages.

The global nature of trading in Meares' time was new—that is, recent to that later part of the eighteenth century. It was characterized by a web of connection between "country merchant traders," working in conjunction with, but outside the chartered limits of, the East India Company, and foreign agents representing Spanish, Philippine and Portuguese commercial enterprises. Supplying bullion to China and slaves to Mozambique, and acquiring sea otter pelts at Clayoquot formed part of this rapidly expanding global British reach. Macau was the outstation of the East India merchant traders and agents in eastern seas, and the place for the re-flagging of British ships. This is why Meares came to the Northwest Coast displaying a Portuguese flag.

At this time the sea otter was the world's most valuable fur animal. It ranged the coasts of the Pacific Ocean in an almost unimaginably long arc extending from Japan's islands to Baja California. The kelp and shellfish beds of the rocky shores of the northern Pacific Ocean were its essential habitat, and the sea otter could seldom be found in interior channels such as Puget Sound. The otter's lustrous coat was prized, by the large Manchu upper class of North China, not for its warmth but for its beautiful appearance. "A full grown prime skin," recounted an American trader, "which has been stretched before drying, is about five feet long, and twenty-four to thirty inches wide, covered with very fine fur, about three-fourths of an inch in length, having a rich jet black, glossy surface, and exhibiting a silver color when blown open." This marine mammal allowed the British, Americans and others to tap the China market by a seaborne trade directly to Canton via Macau, thus competing favourably with Russian traders of northern latitudes, who were obliged to carry on a commerce with the guarded Chinese by way of the gateway fort at Kyakhta in Siberia. The Chinese accepted the sea otter pelt as a substitute for cash and precious metals, and a direct trade from the Northwest Coast to the Celestial Empire was initiated and flourished.[39]

As it does today, trade to China depended on the vagaries of the market and the concurrence of the Chinese merchants and bureaucrats. In those days, the *fan-kwei*, foreign devils, were denied entry to the country. All trade had to be conducted at authorized houses on the strand, so the island of Macau, six miles south of Canton, under the Portuguese flag, became the offshore place of exchange, storage and communication. Sea otter pelts could be sold from Macau through the agency houses at Canton to the Chinese—until the market became satiated by the mid-1800s.

For 170 years after its discovery in Kamchatka in 1741 by the Bering expedition, the sea otter found itself hunted relentlessly in Aleutian waters. Profits made in the Chinese market were unbelievably high, and the Russians exploited the sea otter grounds unmercifully: they enslaved the Aleuts, pressing them into service to hunt the sea otter and fur seal. Wildlife biologist Karl Kenyon estimated that the unregulated killing of sea otters resulted in a take of half a million, a nearly unfathomable number.[40] By the end of the nineteenth century the North Pacific sea otter populations had virtually disappeared. Since 1911 the taking of sea otters in North American waters has been forbidden by international treaty.

Spain, like Russia, was advancing on the shores of these seas. In Alta California, the Spanish and Russians took many sea otter using rifles or, in the Russian case, the enslaved Aleuts using spears. In 1769 the first mission on the coast of California was set up at San Diego. San Carlos de Monterey was settled in years thereafter, and others followed—all on the same plan though varying in size—

PART I The Empire of Fortune

a square occupied by a Church, administrative buildings, apartments for priests, a guardhouse and places of storage. There were garrisoned presidios (such as San Francisco), or towns, and farms, vineyards and gardens. All this flourished in a warm environment where good soil and water for irrigation could be found. It would not work on the rocky and forested Northwest Coast. Accordingly, supplies had to be shipped in, though at Nootka gallant attempts were made to grow vegetables and keep goats and cattle. The missions and presidios were run by a civic administration; Nootka was run by the Spanish navy, its *real naval*. Acapulco, Huatulco and San Blas were places for shipbuilding and repair and provisioning.

Alta California was a province of the Viceroy of Mexico. The cross and the sword marched side by side in this first phase of Spanish empire in the coastal southwest, and secularization, though authorized in 1813, did not occur until 1833. In short, old Spain ruled in Mexico and Alta California, and this explains why Spanish officialdom kept close eyes on all that went on in distant Nootka and in Alaska. Americans did not arrive as settlers in the Sacramento River area until 1840.

Boston traders came to Alta California too, in the bullock hide and tallow trades, which were ancillary to agriculture and animal husbandry. These facts illuminate how different were the trades of the forested Northwest Coast, where (as in our case) sea otter and timber were dominant in emerging economies. The northern boundary of Alta California was 42° N, and north of that was the "Oregon Country." It will be noted that Drake's Nova Albion had been proclaimed at Drakes Bay, near 38° N, but in an area then unsettled and unoccupied by Imperial Spain.

These were not matters to concern Meares. More important to him was the web of British imperial trade relations as practised and enforced by the East India Company and the South Sea Company. Meares (and his backers) had read the published accounts of Captain Cook's third voyage, which included Cook's visit to Nootka Sound in March and April 1778. These readers comprehended, just as the voyage account had advertised, that vast profits could be

First Encounters

realized if sea otter pelts, said to be the most beautiful of all animal skins, could be sold either through Russian access to Beijing or via the difficult arrangements through officials near Canton. Here was trans-Pacific trade in the making, a critically important chapter in Canadian history. (It is worth remembering that the modern as well as prehistoric history of Canada's West Coast began in Asia, not in Europe.[41] Indeed, a 1794 chart of the North Pacific by Lieutenant Henry Roberts, RN, shows the area immediately north of present-day Whistler, British Columbia, as "Foo sang of the Chinese Navigators about the Year 453." When the Chinese came to the Fraser and Cariboo goldfields in the mid-1800s, they called the country "Land of Shining Mountains," and later "Gold Mountain.")

The reader must understand this: that Meares did not come to establish a colony but a base of operations. A "factory" was the name in those days—the sort of thing the Portuguese and Dutch had here and there in eastern seas. It was a combined house, storeroom, lockup for supplies and equipment, and, in this case, a place for ship repair or ship construction, with a ways running down to the low-water mark. There was little need to fortify it; Meares had no pretensions of being able to defend it from a Native assault or a torching in the dead of night. No, this was not a colony, but it is accurate to say that it was a beachhead of empire. The Spanish did not like it; nor did they like the British ships that arrived there—and this sparked off the Nootka Sound crisis, a story for another time and place.

Maquinna and the Mowachaht and Muchalaht peoples had no objection to Meares being in possession of this small section of beach. They were glad to have the trade. They knew, too, that if Meares came there, and came again in future years, other traders would arrive in their ships. Makúk was a good thing. They welcomed it. Empire was not thrust upon them; they invited it. Of course, they could not imagine the future. Meares and Maquinna lived in the present. Less than a hundred years later, in 1858, a distant queen decreed that this territory on the western edge of the continent would be called British Columbia. Subcomponents Vancouver Island and Meares Island, which is really a tributary to Vancouver

PART I The Empire of Fortune

Island, naturally followed the imperial ordering. Administratively, Meares Island was regarded as a dependency of Vancouver Island.

If the British Empire has long since passed, the hydrographic record it left us is perhaps its greatest legacy. Meares, who possessed the characteristically superb techniques of the mariners of that age, was a fine draftsman and surveyor. His noted *Voyages to the North-West Coast of America*, published in London in 1790, told of his passages in the ship *Nootka* in 1786 from faraway Bengal, India. This was one of the earliest commercial voyages to that part of the world, preceded by James Hanna in the brig *Sea Otter*, from Macau, in 1785.

Meares' book also contains an account of his second voyage to the Northwest Coast, this time begun from Macau. It contains enchanting coastal views—elevations, more correctly—of the coastline in and about Nootka Sound. Meares left for posterity a fine plan of the harbour, entitled "A Sketch of Port Cox in the District of Wicannanish." There is no doubt who possessed this district: Wickaninnish did. And on this same chart you can identify Lone Cone, lying there a little whimsically in horizontal fashion, as if slumbering, and held in embrace by numerous inlets of this wending maze of rock and water and forest.

June 1788 found Meares probing the coast south of Nootka Sound in search of sea otter pelts. On the 12th of that month, he says he "saw a high mountain over the entrance of Wicananish." It was too late in the day to investigate. Moreover, a storm was coming on, all too familiar on this storm-lashed coast. The weather changed quickly, becoming squally and violent, and he therefore ordered the crew to close-reef the topsails. He decided to stand off from the shore in consequence of the advancing evening gale, the customary precaution when sailing off a dangerous lee shore. All that night the vessel kept well offshore, the prudent thing to do while awaiting the morrow.

At daybreak on the 13th he says, "The remarkable hill above Wicannanish appeared very plain in the form of a sugar loaf... As we stood in for the shore, several canoes came off to us from a cluster of islands... in most of which there were upwards of twenty men, of a pleasing appearance and brawny form, chiefly clothed in otter skins of great beauty." Meares marvelled at the great speed of the canoes. He noted, too, the fact that the Native peoples had no fear of coming aboard the trading vessel. There were two chiefs in the group of canoes, Hanna and Detootche. Both he found extremely handsome. The former was perhaps age forty and, Meares said, "carried in his looks all the exterior marks of pleasantry and good humour." The latter was young, beautiful, graceful and possessed of fine qualities of the mind. Then as now the local peoples were hospitable, friendly: "They appeared to be perfectly at ease in our society, shook every person on board by the hand, and gave us very friendly invitations to receive the hospitality of their territory. They were extremely pressing that the ship should go in among the islands." All boded well for future good relations here. These chiefs, as others of the Nuu-chah-nulth peoples, were conscious of self-esteem and how others saw them. Indeed, the acquisition of wealth was a central feature of their existence. Formal recognition by others motivated them to higher degrees of acceptance. As one anthropologist put it, the conscious effort to improve upon one's heritage was the sole kind of rivalry known to the Nuu-chah-nulth.[42] This is a charming revelation, and I have thought long and hard about it. Interestingly, these chiefs came head to head, so to speak, with similarly motivated Europeans, mainly British, and American merchant trading captains.

Meares, driven by commerce—for he had to make his expedition "pay"—was in search of the great chief Wickaninnish and his residence. Like Maquinna in Nootka Sound, Wickaninnish (also spelled Wikianinnish, Wickannish, Huikainanici, Quiquinanis, and other variants in the historical record) was the dominant headman, or chief, of Clayoquot Sound.[43] Other chiefs acknowledged his sovereignty or were otherwise at war with him.[44] But at that time Maquinna stood ahead of him in power and wealth. There may be many reasons for this, but one of them surely is that James Cook's visit had given Maquinna preference in terms of putting Nootka Sound literally on the map. His rising dominance paralleled the early years of the maritime fur trade. Maquinna, as we

PART I The Empire of Fortune

might expect, was quick to exploit this new arrangement with the outsiders, be they British, Spanish, American or other. He had his summer village at Yuquot and his winter residence at Tahsis; similarly, Wickaninnish had his summer village at Wicaninish on the island on the south side of the southeast entrance to Clayoquot Sound and his winter residence at Opitsat.

Wickaninnish, who now enters our story, was a robust and good-looking fellow, advanced a little beyond the prime of life.[45] He was an imposing figure, and Meares was to find that he lived in a state of munificence much superior to any of his neighbours. His name means "having no one in front of him in the canoe." Like Maquinna, Wickaninnish made all arrangements for trade, and he consolidated and enriched his position, for the maritime fur trade brought him unimagined wealth, thus increasing his esteem and influence among his people. He was good at manipulating trade between and among foreign vessels. In so doing the price of furs rose, and his profits increased. Further, situated as he was in relation to inland nations, he served as an intermediary trader and prospered on that trade also, marking up the price of goods for those coming within the orbit of the new coastal trade.[46] It could be that he surpassed Maquinna in wealth and power during the period discussed in this book, and Lieutenant Peter Puget, on Captain George Vancouver's expedition of 1792 and 1793, made bold to style Wickaninnish as "the Emperor of all the coast . . . from the Streights of Fuca to the Charlotte Islands."[47]

Wickaninnish and Maquinna were closely related. For instance, Maquinna's eldest child, a daughter named Apānas (who in 1792 was proclaimed successor to the dominions and authority of Maquinna after his death), was betrothed to the eldest son of Wickaninnish.[48] The intermarriage of their children and kin helped reduce the internecine rivalry that was so extensive on the Northwest Coast.

To find Wickaninnish, Meares shaped a course for the outer islands, or islets, seeking a channel that would lead him into some safe anchorage. From several miles offshore, all he could see appeared as a maze of rock and water with, alas, no discernable

First Encounters

channel. Then canoes arrived from inshore. In them were two chiefs, to whom Meares gave trinkets, a gift offering. The canoes took their leave while Meares gingerly pursued his course toward what appeared to be an opening. But still the way was uncertain. All this changed when, about noon, Wickaninnish arrived in a small fleet of canoes. He undertook to pilot Meares' ship into his harbour. It was now an easy sail; the vessel entered and came to anchor in a roadstead Meares thought wild in appearance. Nearby was a village, and it is shown on Meares' plan. There, upon invitation, the English mariners were treated to a feast of unimagined delicacies. Meares was dumbfounded by what he saw: heaps of fish, seal skins filled with oil, and a fire burning under a vast vat for the making of whale-flesh stew or broth, "that delicious beverage." The house was magnificent, the roof supported by trees "of a size which would render the mast of a first-rate man of war [battle ship] diminutive"— such a lovely imperial comparison. The visitors entered through a decorated door on which was displayed a huge image. Inside stood raised platforms, and uniformly arranged human skulls festooned this royal apartment. Wickaninnish, the supreme host, made every attempt to make Meares happy, and he was successful, for these two headmen, as it were, made a compact that the one would collect skins and the other would return during the next trading season to take in the prize cargo reserved for him. This is one of the first recorded contracts of Northwest Coast trade.

Meares presented Wickaninnish with six brass-hilted swords, a pair of pistols, a musket and powder to seal the relationship. He gave a fine suit of clothes to the chief's brother. Only then did the trading commence, and it proceeded amicably. Meares offered other items, and in return procured 150 fine sea otter skins. All had to go through Wickaninnish. Property was the key thing. Captain Cook had noted in his journal that everything had value to the Northwest Coast Natives: "there was not a blade of grass that had not a seperated owner so that I very soon emptied my pockets with purchasing, and when they found I had nothing more to give they let us cut where ever we pleased. Here I must observe that I have no

PART I The Empire of Fortune

where met with Indians who had such high notions of every thing the County produced being their exclusive property as these; the very wood and water we took on board they at first wanted us to pay for."[49] The trading process also had exasperated Cook. Not only did these people place highest regard on property; they had also, as George Woodcock put it, an "almost obsessive concern over the proper inheritance of titular rights, were much more historically minded than most primitive peoples, and they maintained reliable oral traditions extending back over many generations, so that we can also assume that the way of life the early explorers encountered must have existed unchanged for at least two or three centuries preceding their arrival."[50] There is little to quarrel with here, for cultures rarely take radical departures, and cleave to old ways as long as they can, even clinging to ancient ways of historical understanding and homiletics, or rhetorical patterns.

Meares found Wickaninnish a tough bargainer, and even says that he was probably duped by his trading practices. He does not say cheated, only duped by their cunning—that is, he was outsmarted. Perhaps he was expecting something of an easier arrangement. As well, time was on Wickaninnish's side, for sooner or later his mariner visitors must depart, and he knew they did not want to go away empty-handed or with insufficient cargo for a profitable voyage. As to the people of Wicaninish village, Meares thought them superior in industry and activity to those of Nootka Sound.

Thus it was that this little-known place—the land of Wickaninnish, the chief, the village and the waters in and around Meares Island—was written into the European record as something different from Yuquot and Nootka Sound—a place apart, so to speak, one less travelled, of course, but one dominated by astute traders. Meares had no trouble with these people. He admired them, mixed easily with them. Others, as we will see in the next chapter, had different experiences.

Before closing this chapter, we need to make one observation of importance: Cook called Nootka Sound "King George's Sound." This locale, put on the chart authorized by the British Admiralty, soon became the rendezvous of shipping in these latitudes. And as a place of rendezvous, ship repair, trade, etc., it holds pride of place in coastal history, and, indeed, the history of the Pacific Ocean. However, and this is the central point, by 1792 the great collections of furs were not made there, but rather at such distant locations as Prince William Sound, Queen Charlotte Islands, Nass River and Cape Classet. In the secondary category of trade importance, as the Spaniard Moziño attested in that year, stands Clayoquot.[51] In his view, Nootka only attracted foreigners because there they could supply themselves with water and firewood at no risk; it was also a place to gather news of ships coming and going, and of international affairs swirling about the Sound. Outsiders had come to "possess" Meares Island and adjacent waters as a trading realm different from Nootka, important in its own right—a destination, a collecting place and a location at which to barter away the trade goods of the world for the sea otter skin. How long would this last?

3
Sea Otter Hunters

The previous chapter provided an introduction to the maritime fur trade. In this chapter we dig deeper to examine in more detail the contact and conflict that flowed from the early encounters, when Europeans and Americans sailed into the waters of the Northwest Coast and, more particularly for our point of reference, Clayoquot Sound. Our stories are not unrelated to those of Nootka Sound to the north or Barkley Sound to the south (the southernmost of the big embayments on the west coast of Vancouver Island); nor, indeed, are they unrelated to activities farther north at the Queen Charlotte Islands or on the coast of Russian America, or farther south in the Strait of Juan de Fuca and the Columbia River. All the same, they have unique features, and Wickaninnish features powerfully in them, as do certain British and, after them, American ship captains.

The sea otter, and the trade that developed to exploit that mammal almost to extinction, played a significant role in the international rivalry for this coast and is this chapter's focus. It was an international trade and forms part of a global epic of expanding trade links bringing continents and peoples together. This was made possible by the sailing ship. The Russians dominated northern waters, the Spanish those of California, and the British and Americans vied for control of the central Northwest Coast.[52] These are attractive subjects for the student of history. Still, of necessity, our focus remains Meares Island and its surrounding waters, the inlets and passages of Clayoquot Sound. There are many published histories of the coast and several on the maritime fur trade, but, truth to tell, no history of Meares Island and surrounding waters for our early period. In regards to Meares Island, we focus on Port Cox, Opitsat and Adventure Cove, for they are flashpoints in Clayoquot history and significant in larger measure in coastal history.

Looked at differently, and on the beneficial side, the story of Meares Island and its local waters has a universality all its own. And so we see its history as a microcosm of other such experiences on the coast, from northern California to the Gulf of Alaska. Yet we are bound to remember that such generalities are over-layered by particularities of time and place, and the sea otter epoch, comprising the late 1770s to 1820s, was an unusual and animated time in the history of the area—and indeed of the Pacific Ocean and littoral.

The maritime fur trade, and here specifically the sea otter trade, was ancillary to the trade with China, and it led to competition among traders, whether they were British, American (mainly from Boston) or other. To repeat, this was an international trade, much like the cod fisheries of the Newfoundland Grand Banks. It prompted a nervous Spanish response, described below. Even before the first trading ships arrived, the East India Company claimed exclusive British trading rights in the Pacific Ocean by virtue of its monopoly dating back to 1600, and the South Sea Company claimed the right to control British shipping in these seas. Independent traders of British nationality and British ship owners therefore engaged in subterfuges and used flags of convenience to get around these monopolies.

On his first voyage to the Northwest Coast, John Meares set course from Bengal with the products of India in the ship's hold—guns and ammunition, cottons and brassware, pots and pans, and much more. When the Asian base of operations shifted, as it soon did, to Macau and Canton, the same sorts of items were brought

PART I The Empire of Fortune

to Nootka, Clayoquot and Barkley Sounds, the Queen Charlotte Islands and elsewhere. The British had to export British manufactures under British trade rules. Meares had to work round the controls of the two great trading monopolies, the South Sea Company and the East India Company: that is why he flew the Portuguese flag. The Americans, however, were not so hampered, and Congress gave them free rein. In the circumstances, the natural trading aptitude of the Americans had full scope on the Northwest Coast. The tendrils of the Atlantic world reached out, by way of Cape Horn, to the temperate and forested Northwest Coast. As to trading items, members of Captain Cook's ships' companies had exchanged mirrors, beads, buttons and trinkets—including iron nails—for skins of bear, fox, deer, weasel, mink, wolverine, wolf and, in particular, sea otter.[53] In Alaska they exchanged beads for more skins. It was an incidental or petty trade, not organized on any commercial basis. At Canton, in Cook's day, a sea otter pelt could fetch $120, a huge markup in the value of investment, and it is said that at Canton the crew were on the brink of mutiny for a return to the Northwest Coast to make their fortunes in the peltry business.

In the event, at Nootka, Indigenous people showed keenness to trade, approaching Cook's ships in their canoes, eagerly crying "Makúk" ("Will you trade?").[54] Native demand drove the economy, and the outsiders had much to barter in return. The Indigenous peoples of the coast exhibited sharpness as to buying and selling, conscious as they were about matters of supply and demand. The plan for exploiting this branch of the fur trade was drawn up by Captain James King and published in the official account of Cook's voyage.[55] Meares was one of the first to take it up, as mentioned. Another early trader was John Henry Cox. He and his associate Daniel Beale arranged every British vessel on the Northwest Coast sailing from Canton or Macau, beginning with James Hanna's *Harmon* or *Sea Otter*. Port Cox, adjacent to Tofino, is named for him, and it features on Meares' drawing of "The District of Wicannanish."[56]

In the trade's early years, it flourished in British hands but was soon not without rivals of other nationalities and flags, so many traders wanted to obtain sea otter pelts. In mid-June 1787 (the date is uncertain), Charles William Barkley, in the big East Indiaman *Imperial Eagle,* otherwise called *Loudoun,* a British ship flying Austrian colours so as to circumvent British licensing monopolies, arrived at Nootka. He was fresh from the Hawaiian Islands, where he had taken on foodstuffs. The captain's young bride, Frances Trevor Barkley, had engaged a young girl named Winee, probably from Oahu, as lady's maid.[57] From Nootka the vessel cruised south and east, making remarkable findings along the way. Frances noted in her reminiscences of Clayoquot Sound that she thought it a large sound, and gives as the latitude 49' 20' N, indicative of the fact that the vessel used the sound's northern entrance. Captain Barkley called Clayoquot Sound "Wicananish's Sound." "Wicananish has great authority and this part of the coast proved a rich harvest of furs for us," Frances noted.[58] The vessel continued its voyage of trade and discovery, first to Barkley Sound and then into the Strait of Juan de Fuca, which the captain recognized as that described in the 1625 narrative recounting Spanish discoveries of the pilot Juan de Fuca in 1592.

Meanwhile, yet another scheme was launched from London, by the King George's Sound Company, that in due time brought Captains Nathaniel Portlock and George Dixon to Nootka, but not specifically to Clayoquot. Then, at the same time as Barkley, came James Colnett and Charles Duncan. The redoubtable Colnett is significant in our account. Looked at all together, never was there gathered such a cast of characters with such global seafaring experience, all sailing to Nootka within the space of three years.

The customary plan for trading ships called for them to arrive at Nootka at winter's close in March or April. From there they would sail north or south as required to collect furs. Then in late August, when ships' stores were running low and wintry weather could be expected in a month or two, they would clear Nootka for Hawaii and then China. The next year a return visit to the Northwest Coast might be called for, or, if not, a new ship would be acquired for the purpose. New places for trading in sea otter were found, among them villages

PART I The Empire of Fortune

in the Queen Charlotte Islands, Nasparti and Nahwitti at the north end Vancouver Island, and Cape Classet at the entrance to the Strait of Juan de Fuca. As long as trade proved profitable, the outsiders continued to come. In short, the Native residents could always expect summer visitors. Only the Spanish stood by to upset proceedings, either by interference at Nootka or in general warfare that broke out between Britain and Spain in 1793, also involving revolutionary France. The turmoil in Europe and on the high seas affected British commercial operations in India, China and the Northwest Coast.

From the east coast of the United States came the avaricious traders—"the solid men of Boston"—who eventually came to dominate the maritime trade. Generally speaking, the Aboriginal inhabitants called all American traders "Boston men" and the British traders "King George Men" or, in Chinook jargon, the trade language in wide use on the Northwest Coast, *Kintshautshmen.* Bostonians in their fast and nimble schooners and sloops shifted from village to village as required; they stayed near one village until they had "drained" (their term) it of sea otter pelts, then sailed to the next to do likewise. When possible, they made up a full cargo of pelts, then sailed for Hawaii and Macau, where furs were an acceptable substitute for the usual medium of exchange, silver. The pioneering expedition of trade and discoveries dates from 1787. A Boston syndicate, American pioneers in this branch of commerce, sent the ship *Columbia Rediviva*, 212 tons, and the sloop *Lady Washington*, ninety tons, to trade to the Northwest Coast and China. The former was commanded by John Kendrick, the latter by Robert Gray. Medals of friendship, bearing on one side a representation of the two ships, and on the other the owners' names, were furnished to the commanders. These shiny objects, now numismatic treasures, were "to be distributed amongst the Natives on the North West Coast of America, and to commemorate the first American adventure on the Pacific Ocean."[59] The US Congress and the Commonwealth of Massachusetts patronized the expedition.

The *Columbia* sailed directly for Nootka and reached there safely, but the *Lady Washington*, under Gray, took a different course. On

August 2, in a state of inexpressible joy, Gray sighted the long-looked-for coast of Nova Albion. Passing by a broad sheet of water indicating a great river in this vicinity (the Columbia), one worth examining at a later time (which Gray did), they met up with some Natives who supplied them with berries and other foods, thereby easing the encroachments of scurvy. But a very nasty incident occurred. The shore party, in search of water, was attacked, and the Americans used a swivel gun to fight off the assailants at a place they subsequently called Murderers' Harbor. The schooner sailed north, then entered Clayoquot Sound. It was on this occasion that Gray first met Wickaninnish, and after a brief stay steered for Nootka, joining the *Columbia*.

After long and arduous voyages, these vessels had arrived at Nootka Sound late in the trading season, in September 1788. By this time British trading vessels had already been in the business for three years. The Americans passed a quiet winter in Nootka Sound, for the British had wisely headed to Hawaii for warmth and refreshment. The *Lady Washington* sailed south for Clayoquot on March 16 and was first in the field for the promising new trading year. She arrived next day and spent ten days in the Sound, her men trading, hunting and making a survey of what they called Hancock's Harbour. The thoughtful Robert Haswell, one of the officers, spying out the contorted landscape of mountains, passages and islands, believed a promising inland communication must surely exist, perhaps by rivers. He imagined that what he was looking at was an endless cluster of islands. Did the Northwest Passage lie beyond, to the east? They ventured south toward the Strait of Juan de Fuca, and for a time they even joined in a whale hunt.

The peoples of Clayoquot Sound, like those of Nootka or of Cape Flattery, were whaling people, paddling their canoes far out to sea. Grey whales, then as now, winter in the Gulf of California, then coast north to summer grounds in the Bering Sea, where they feed on Arctic krill. They pass by Clayoquot Sound in April. The "summer village" of Wickaninnish was the base from which they went out in search of a suitable catch. On April 10, 1789, Wickaninnish

PART I The Empire of Fortune

harpooned a whale, the first kill of the season. A large canoe towed it to the nearby beach, with sixteen bladders attached so as to keep it afloat. When the whale was beached, he gave the order to his brother, Tootiscosettle, to strike home the deadly pierce. This was observed by Haswell, on the *Lady Washington*. He was told a custom existed that a slave must be killed and laid alongside the whale's head, which was adorned with eagle feathers. This pleased the gods. Haswell turned away from the scene, choosing not to watch the ceremonial killing of the slave. The American was also told that the whale hunters lacerated their tongues and painted themselves with blood in order that the very large whales would not be afraid to come near the canoes.[60]

Eventually giving up on geographical discoveries, the Americans on the *Lady Washington* returned to Nootka, rendezvousing with the *Columbia*. Repairs were effected and the skippers exchanged vessels. The *Columbia*, now under Gray's command, made for China with furs, then completed a round-the-world voyage, the first vessel to carry the Stars and Stripes in the great circumnavigation. The *Lady Washington*, by contrast, remained in the Pacific, never returning to Boston.

For reasons that need not concern us here, the *Columbia* voyage was not a great financial success. All the same, the Boston merchant syndicate planned a second expedition. It was this one, begun in late 1790 from Boston, that brought the *Columbia* to the Northwest Coast to join the *Lady Washington*, and, central to our interest, to Clayoquot and Meares Island. New motives were afoot to possess Meares Island.

In later years the Americans would come to make the trade almost their own, and after 1803 the British flag was scarcely ever seen on the Coast. One authority says, "When the trade passed beyond the beads-and-buttons stage, these American vessels became, in a way, pioneer general stores, carrying a varied assortment of hardware, copper, paint, clothing, cloth, domestic and culinary articles, arms and ammunition."[61] The traders had to meet Native demands, and the New Englander's natural bent for "swapping," says the same historian, though I think in exaggerated fashion, was a factor in the success achieved. Certainly the Bostonians met the needs and desires of the local markets whenever they could. In 1791 iron collars, produced by the ship's armourer, became fashionable articles of dress. Elsewhere, at the Queen Charlotte Islands, the trader *Jefferson*, of Boston, offered worn-out sails for making women's garments, and bartered for skins with boxes and trunks, seal oil, ship's crockery, carpets, deep-sea lines, ropes and rigging, and anchors.[62] By the time of the second *Columbia* voyage, spirituous liquors had been introduced—West Indian rum brought by the Yankees and brandy brought by the few French vessels that transited the Coast. The first recorded bartering of liquor is that of *La Flavie*, at Nootka in 1792, but the Yankees were not to be outmatched, selling spirits to the Spaniards and seamen there, at a great markup. Explorer-mariner La Pérouse feared that the introduction of spirituous liquor would have fatal effects. Judge Howay, expert on this as on other aspects of the sea otter trade, describes how at Clayoquot Sound preliminaries to barter were warmed by intoxicating liquor: "In 1791, when John Hoskins, the clerk of the ship *Columbia*, of Boston, visited Wickananish, the chief at Clayoquot, the latter expressed regret that he could not welcome Hoskins with liquor, and said that if he had been forewarned of the visit the deficiency could have been met."[63]

This trade formed a powerful influence on the traditional economies of the Indigenous peoples. The Ahousaht, Clayoquot and Kelsemaht, partners in this transformation, put up strong demand for what the ships could bring. Iron tools aided the carving of cedar house posts and other poles. Artistic styles were already established, and the extensive use of metal tools increased production and made larger pieces possible. Copper was always in demand, used for personal adornment such as earrings and also for exquisitely hammered ceremonial shields—true bright displays of wealth. Indeed, the Nuu-chah-nulth delighted in the display of wealth. Conspicuous consumption was exhibited here as in many other places in the world. The sailing ship had changed all. Almost, it seems, in the twinkling of an eye, the insularity of Vancouver Island had vanished, and the

PART I The Empire of Fortune

Nuu-chah-nulth had been brought into a worldwide web, their fortunes subject to its whims and its shifts.

We have already said that Meares gave weapons to Maquinna as presents or to seal a commercial deal. But the arms trade expanded quickly. Captain Vancouver was surprised, in July 1792, to find that every canoe that approached his ships near the Kwakwaka'wakw village at Nimpkish River was armed with a musket and provided with ammunition. In one canoe were three muskets considered to belong to a chief who was under the authority of Maquinna. Maquinna's people kept up a close commercial intercourse with these people. It can be imagined that Maquinna was the arms merchant, or middleman, among the Indigenous people of this part of the coast.

We can imagine, too, that at Clayoquot Sound, Wickaninnish, with close blood ties to Maquinna, and in near proximity to Nootka Sound, also was a middleman in the arms trade. In Clayoquot there were many armed persons, and one informant of the period says that 400 men could be turned out with muskets and well supplied with ammunition. The observant clerk Edward Bell, in Captain George Vancouver's expedition, remarks on the change: "Their former Weapons, Bows and Arrows, Spears and Clubs are now thrown aside & forgotten." Here, as at Nootka, everyone had a musket, he observed, and continued, "Thus they are supplied with weapons which they no sooner possess than they turn them against the donors.—Every Season produces instances of their daring treacherous conduct, few Ships have been on the Coast that have not been attacked or attempted to be attacked, and in general many lives have been lost on both sides."[64] This forms a recurring as well as a sad and depressing theme, and we will return to it more frequently than expected in the following pages.

Although the Boston traders, like the British, were sojourners on the coast and usually wintered in the warm, salubrious Hawaiian Islands (where vegetables and meat were readily available), the *Columbia* and *Lady Washington*, first in the trade from Boston, broke the customary pattern. As mentioned, they spent the winter of 1788–1789 in Nootka Sound. The *Columbia*, on her second

Sea Otter Hunters

voyage, remained during the winter of 1791–1792 at Lemmens Inlet, Meares Island (see Chapter 5). It was this wintering on the coast that brought the outsiders and the locals into close proximity and dangerous contact, to say nothing of the making of trade deals and real estate contracts as hereafter described.

Vessels putting into Clayoquot Sound in the days of sea otter trading arrived searching for Indigenous traders who had time to collect the pelts of the sea otter. The blue-water mariners sailed with care on this treacherous, unsurveyed and unmarked lee shore. From other sailors they had learned coastal navigational secrets and heard about the great dangers. It must always be remembered, in our distant time, that they lacked charts and navigational aids; as such, they were often dependent on whatever Native advice they could obtain for entering port and finding anchorage. The locals were familiar with navigating canoes through shoals and shallow channels, and they could pass undamaged over ledges and deeply sunken reefs. All the same, their knowledge of deep-water passages was limited, and therein lay a problem in the competence of their guidance of deep-sea ships.

No systematic accounting or chronology exists of all the many vessels that called at Clayoquot Sound. But I select two narratives—one Spanish and another British—that throw light on the Native society they encountered.

The Spanish arrived at Nootka on May 5, 1789, under Esteban Martínez, expecting that the dreaded Russians had come south from more northern waters. Martínez was in for a surprise. A week after he arrived, the *North West America*, built by Meares the year previous, and now under command of Robert Funter, came into port. Martínez took possession of her, gave José María Narváez command of the vessel, then issued orders to send the vessel to search for a strait in more southern waters. Already Martínez had tangled with Englishman James Colnett, seizing ships, crews and cargoes (mentioned in Chapter 2, with details later in this chapter). The further seizure of the *North West America* increased what the British regarded as outrages against commerce. The British wanted free navigation, fair and square. The imbroglio that developed, now known as the Nootka Sound crisis, is a celebrated event in world history. All of a sudden the international rivalry for rights of trade in the Pacific attracted the chancelleries of Europe and also business circles in Boston and New York. Martínez, on his own initiative, had seized Colnett's *Argonaut*, its companion vessel *Princess Royal* and the *North West America*. Spanish authorities backed his decisions. Serious consequences would result from these actions, and discoveries of these islands and straits would become of major importance. Here was the beginning of a collision of empires.

Next year, 1790, the observant young ensign Manuel Quimper undertook a somewhat similar mission to Narváez's—that is, extending Spanish knowledge of Vancouver Island even farther south and into the Strait of Juan de Fuca. For us, he provides authoritative data on Wickaninnish and the flourishing Indigenous life in this unique collection of islands and passages. In fact, we are astounded, delightfully so, at the rich details he provides, first, in his letter to the Viceroy and, second, in his day-to-day report of proceedings, noted below.

Quimper, on short notice, sailed from the Spanish base at Nootka on May 31, 1790, in command of the captured and renamed sloop *Princesa Real*. That vessel, designated a bilandra by the Spanish, had a complement of forty-one men and nine soldiers, with Gonzalo López de Haro as first pilot and Juan Carrasco as second pilot. Quimper had instructions to explore the Strait of Juan de Fuca, making inquiries as he sailed south and east.

Quimper sailed into Clayoquot Sound on June 1. The most recent trader had just left. The labyrinthine waters of the sound, leading from one island to another, one village to another—with a cul-de-sac or two thrown in for good measure—could not easily be examined in one or two days. Quimper's recounting of his days in Clayoquot Sound shows that these were waters and islands accessible to international shipping of that age.

He visited Opitsat where, to his surprise, he found Maquinna living, a refugee from Martínez. A year earlier, in the midst of the uproar with Colnett, Martínez had shot and killed Callicum, one of Maquinna's kinsmen.[65] Quimper was taken aback, but realizing the implications of Maquinna's self-imposed exile, he gave the famed sea otter chief every assurance of Spain's friendly intention.

Quimper's diary is full of treasures. Take, for instance, what he recounted on June 2: "The day dawned clear and calm. At sunrise canoes full of Indians, men and women of all ages, began to come, asking for something with the word 'pachito,' and on not receiving anything called us 'pizac,' meaning 'bad people,' giving us to understand that other vessels which had come to the port had given presents to everybody."[66] This posed no problem: the captain promptly had the caulker cut up sheets of copper into small pieces as presents, tokens of friendship that might initiate trade and a reciprocated warm welcome. Good results were obtained. At eight that same morning Wickaninnish—Quimper spelled it Huiquinanichichi—sent out canoes requesting him to come ashore. Quimper, fearing ambush, refused. Wickaninnish insisted. Now it was Quimper's turn to budge. So, taking the armed longboat, with the pilot and a squad of six soldiers, he landed at the beach where the brother of the chief guided the Spaniards to the house. It was then that Quimper found Maquinna.

When Quimper met Wickaninnish, he presented him with three yards of scarlet cloth, the same as the King of Spain's royal crimson. Quimper admired the great house, with its huge supporting posts and beams, columns of huge carved figures, and the entrance a great figure whose mouth was the door. One hundred people could live in this house, and in regards to the population of the village, Quimper thought it might reach a thousand or more of both sexes and all ages. Quimper's invitation to the chiefs to come to the sloop where he could entertain them thoroughly was accepted, and at 3:30 in the afternoon they came in canoes. They were presented with copper sheets, and there was a further gift of Spanish presents. Still Maquinna was doubtful, even asking the seamen if the heavy-handed Martínez was in command of the frigate at Nootka or whether it was Francisco de Eliza. Maquinna's fear ran

PART I The Empire of Fortune

deep. He had been offended fully. When Quimper reassured him once again, Maquinna embraced the Spaniards with much joy saying, "Amigo amar a dos" (Friend, love is here between us.) words he had learned in Nootka. "At sunset they returned to their settlement and I ordered a small gun fired for them all to go away. On shore they fired two muskets. Night fell with the weather fine and calm and nothing more to relate."[67]

What extraordinary material Quimper's diary provides. We learn that the Natives, one and all, wanted their share of presents as preliminaries to exchange. They were fearsome, keeping visitors on their guard. For this there was at least a partial explanation. Quimper learned of Maquinna's deep-seated fear of the Spaniard Martínez, which had obviously made him suspicious of Spanish friendship. In his wisdom, for he had met many Europeans by this time, going back to Juan Pérez (who passed through in 1774) and Cook, Maquinna feared the violence and cruelty that the visitors might inflict on him and his people, upsetting his power, subverting his influence. He obviously hoped that Martínez had gone away, and Quimper reassured him of this, restoring friendship and mitigating fears. We see the ceremonial use of guns on both sides. We see in various pages of the diary the trading that went on, with the officers, sailors and soldiers of the Spanish king. Here was an invitation to better friendship, for exchange on this coast was important. Makúk—will you buy, will you sell—this was the essential aspect of equitable friendship. I recall what Captain Cook had said about the Nuu-chah-nulth: they put a value on all property. They only stole trifles.[68] Quimper completed the trade in sea otter skins that he had been ordered to undertake, exchanging the King's copper for the pelts.

Passing out of the Sound on June 10, he steered south and east, toward the Strait of Juan de Fuca.[69] Quimper preferred to conduct his inshore explorations in small boats, a prudent measure. He had, for himself, his longboat. But realizing he would need other craft for the complicated assignment at Clayoquot Sound, he acquired two large cedar canoes in exchange for four large sheets of copper, and twenty-eight paddles for two sheets of copper.[70] In other words, Native watercraft were used to aid European discoveries. In his words, "I made sail continuing my course for the inside of the strait [of Juan de Fuca], towing the longboat and two large canoes which I purchased with the King's copper, having in view their usefulness in the exploration, as they would serve as efficacious adjuncts in his examination, and at Royal Roads took possession in the name of the King of Spain." He then crossed the strait, undertook an act of Spanish ownership, visited Discovery Bay, shifted back across the strait, made examinations of southern Vancouver Island as far as Gonzalez Point (today, the southern reach of Victoria Golf Club), could not reach Nootka on account of storms, so shaped a course for San Blas, where he arrived on November 13, 1790. In all, his had been a marvellous reconnaissance, and in coastal and inshore waters those two prized canoes proved highly useful, repaying the investment.[71]

Our second narrative is by the American sailor John Bartlett, a highly literate fellow. In late November 1790, the snow *Gustavus III*, 152 tons, owned by John Henry Cox—or "Squire Cox," as Bartlett fondly called him—set sail from Lark's Bay near Macau, bound for the Northwest Coast. Previously named *Mercury*, this vessel from London now flew the flag of the King of Sweden as a flag of convenience. The reason was to get around the monopoly requirements of the two British chartered companies already mentioned, and perhaps to mollify Spanish authorities known to be clamping down on British trading vessels at Nootka and on the Northwest Coast. Bartlett had received two month's advance pay, and the vessel was well stocked with fresh Chinese pork (disagreeable when compared to American, he said) and salt beef. The ship's company was multinational and multi-ethnic. There were thirty-one on board, all in good health, though the sole Hawaiian in the crew would later die of scurvy. The skipper, Thomas Barnet, was English, as was the sailmaker; four Irishmen were mates or seamen; four Welshmen served as gunner, carpenter, seaman and chief mate; seven Americans, one Swede (captain of the colours), seven Portuguese, a Manila boy as cabin steward, a Goan cook, three Chinese and the Hawaiian.

PART I The Empire of Fortune

We learn from these particulars that this was essentially an Anglo-American crew, with Asians, Portuguese and others brought in to fill up the complement, many to do the heavy lifting or the menial tasks. This sort of mix was typical of the "English" ships that came to Clayoquot in those years.

Gustavus III was a fine vessel and well equipped; even so, the voyage across the Pacific had consumed a tedious seventy days, with gales and dirty weather most of the time. The intention had been to arrive at Barkley Sound in early March 1791 and begin trading at the prosperous outset of the season, then work northward as required. In the event, a good anchorage could not be found near the entrance of Barkley Sound, for the sea bottom fell off steeply there; accordingly, the captain ordered a coastwise route north in search of something better. We now take up the sprightly narrative supplied by the observant American sailor John Bartlett, who was not, we find, at all keen on Indigenous capabilities to pilot a vessel the size of the *Gustavus III* to a safe haven:

> After sailing along shore for several days we at last found the harbour of Wickanninish which was pointed out to us by an Indian named Captain Hannah [Cleaskinah, who exchanged names in token of friendship and trade links with Captain James Hanna, of the *Sea Otter* in 1786] who came on board not long before. Near the entrance was an island that had three trees on it that appear like a ship in stays and is called Ship Island. At four p.m. we saw the smoke at Wickanninsh [Opitsat, Meares Island]. Captain Hannah [had been] in this harbour but once before but we sailed according to his best judgment. Before long the natives on shore began to make signs to us to steer more to the northward which were not regarded by our captain and soon we landed on a ledge of rocks and came near losing our vessel. We hove all sails back and fortunately she fell off the ledge into twelve fathoms. A boat sent to sound for the channel soon discovered the entrance between two islands and at five p.m. we came abreast of Wickanninish town or village, which contained about two hundred houses or long huts of square form, built about twenty yards from the water.

> We were soon honoured by a visit from their chief whose name was Wickanninish. He was a tall, rawboned fellow who came attended

by thirty or forty canoes with fish and furs to sell. Several of them were bound out for whaling with gear in the canoes. Their lances and harpoons were very curious being made of bone neatly polished. Their lines were made of animals' hides and their drags were made of skins blown full of wind in the form of a winter squash.

Early the next morning we weighed anchor and ran up to Cox's Harbour with the boat sounding ahead of us. The tide was running very strong at the entrance of the harbour and we were swept in amongst some rocks and so near the shore as to rack the limbs of the trees with our yards and very near being cast away a second time. In this harbour we lay moored for several days as it was landlocked and a safe place in which to overhaul our rigging. One day the boat went ashore to kill geese which were very plentiful.

On Saturday, March 15th, the boat was sent with the carpenter [William Howard] and Charles Treadwell [American seaman] to cut wood at a point about a mile from the vessel and out of sight of her. Late in the afternoon the boat went to get the men, and just as she went ashore three canoes put out from where our men had been cutting wood. They had stolen a large iron maul and threatened to pick out the carpenter's eyes with their arrows when our boat just at that time saved their lives. The next day, at 10 o'clock, our second mate died of the scurvy having been sick for some time. He was born in Cork and was twenty-eight years old. We did not bury him until the sun was down and it was so dark when our captain was reading prayers that he began to damn his eyes because he could not see the print plainly.

We remained at this village until the 26th when we got under way at four p.m. bound to the north on our trading voyage. In all we bought forty skins at this place. [They then sailed for the Scott Islands, lying off the northwestern extremity of Vancouver Island, then for the Queen Charlotte Islands.][72]

And so closed Bartlett's insightful narrative of late winter 1791—detailing the perils presented to a vessel of this draft sailing these waters, the lack of charts and sailing instructions, Wickaninnish and the village of Opitsat, and the adventure of the Natives seizing the shore party that was cutting ship's timbers. This last was an

PART I The Empire of Fortune

episode that fortunately did not end in tragedy; it throws a sidelight on Native behaviour, but is an incident into which we might not read too deeply, perhaps.

Twenty-two days after the *Gustavus III* hauled for northern waters, two warships made the entrance and came to anchor in Clayoquot Sound. They flew Spanish colours and were, respectively, the two-decker *San Carlos* and the schooner *Santa Saturnina*. Meares Island does not feature here specifically (and the Spanish never proved its insularity), but the exploration of the Sound throws light on Spanish inquiries and motives.[73] This was the first scientific examination by any nation of the complicated and mysterious passages of Clayoquot Sound.

The Spanish claimed all this territory as part of the Spanish Empire by virtue of the doctrine of discovery (something the British would not admit to) and by the Treaty of Tordesillas and papal sanction of same. Meares Island fell within this claim, so was now possessed by the King of Spain. The Spanish, thinking in broadest terms, were also in search of a northwest passage, which the pilot Juan de Fuca claimed to have found in 1592, and which Meares had also alleged to exist.[74] As of 1791, the thinking of the Spanish was that it might lie to the east of Vancouver Island. By this date they knew of Clayoquot Sound, for Manuel Quimper had been there the year before. Now a new plan was brought forward on Eliza's advice: as part of the Spanish search for the alluring channel to the Atlantic (if, indeed, one existed), a further examination of harbours and waterways was called for, and one of them was Clayoquot Sound. Thus it was that Eliza in the *San Carlos* and Narváez in the *Santa Saturnina* sailed in company from Nootka, which had recently been refortified and garrisoned against any untoward development—in other words, a British takeover.[75] The date of departure was May 3, 1791.

Reading between the lines, the Spanish were approaching Clayoquot not just for exploration but for trade—and perhaps to save a few souls for Christ. For all their flowery arguments, repeated by historians, that they were mapping the unusual reaches and recondite places of the coast, they also wanted to be part of the lucrative sea otter trade. Then again, they were in the employ of the King of Spain. A conflict of interest, or profiting at the Spanish navy's expense, must surely have crossed their minds. Eliza placed the discovery of a passage to the Atlantic Ocean to be of the highest priority.[76]

Four days out of Nootka, in the afternoon of May 7, 1791, the two vessels dropped anchor in the outer harbour, or southeast entrance, to Clayoquot Sound. "The Puerto de Clayocuat," writes Eliza, "is formed by various islands and although open to the SE, S and SW winds the sea is not troublesome, as the numerous flat islands at the entrances form a barrier. The anchoring ground or bottom is all very clean and of fine sand."[77] He had come on a particularly fair day for weather, we note with amusement. Wickaninnish with his sons came out in a canoe to visit the ships. By sunset, fifty-eight canoes of all sizes were crowding alongside the packetboat. The next morning eighty large and small canoes could be counted alongside, bringing sea otter skins and a great abundance of crabs, larger than usual.

Later that afternoon, on Eliza's orders, the *San Carlos* shifted to the secluded anchorage inside—that is, to Meares' Port Cox, adjacent to today's Tofino. The low peninsula afforded shelter from strong winds outside; in addition, a small creek had reliable drinking water, and casks were filled here. Eliza in the *San Carlos* rode at anchor until the 22nd; during these days he deployed Narváez in the *Santa Saturnina* and an armed longboat to examine the labyrinth of inlets to the north of the anchorage and later to the northwest as well as to the east—in other words, the various navigable channels in and near Meares Island. The work was best accomplished in small boats. Observations were made at Puerto de San Rafael and again at Puerto de Clayocuat, the latitudes established and the longitudes similarly west of San Blas. Like other mariners before them, the Spanish were bringing empirical science combined with surveying technique not only to mark their base points for future triangulations, chart making and explorations, but also to give exact places on the globe that other mariners could find if so inclined, all matters of navigation and sailing being properly attended to, of course. We often forget that mariners faced a plethora of difficulties and a host

PART I The Empire of Fortune

of challenges just to reach a location safely. Clayoquot Sound was no different, and on the outside it was a storm-tossed coast.

In any event, at the end of the reconnaissance taken under Eliza's direction, Lieutenant Narváez and the pilot Carrasco drew a plan of the Archipelago de Clayocuat entrance and port proper. Jim McDowell reprints this plan, on which had been traced the respective routes taken on survey duties by Narváez and pilot Juan Pantoja.[78] The Spanish called Clayoquot Sound "Puerto Narváez," and from it, according to the authority Henry R. Wagner, who pored over all the documents, "it appears that the port was between Wakennenish Island and Meares Island to the east." A favourite port of call of fur traders, the Americans knew it generally as Company Bay, or Hancock's Harbor.

The Natives were numerous, friendly and keen to trade. Eliza says there were five large villages in this archipelago embraced by the Sound. Of these, he says, four might contain 1,500 persons while that of Wickaninnish might have 2,500. These are large numbers, putting the total number of men and women at 8,500 as a guess, but who is to say? On arrival, 600 entertained the Spanish with a great dance in Wickaninnish's big house. Eliza, engaged in private commerce, tried to barter copper for sea otter skins but with poor success, other traders having pre-empted him. The Natives wanted Monterey shells, the fabulous abalone shells, which were used for personal ornament.

The survey completed to the commander's satisfaction, the Spanish visit to Clayoquot Sound ended, and the Spanish vessels sailed away to continue their examination south and west to Cordova (now Esquimalt). From there they engaged, though separately, in subsidiary quests to Haro Strait, Saturna Island, the northern San Juan Islands, New Dungeness and elsewhere.

Amused by the complicated geography of islands, passages and inlets, the Spanish speculated about the possibility of a passage to the Atlantic, in part because of the large number of whales they had seen. Port Angeles and Neah Bay were visited, then the *Santa Saturnina* headed for Monterey, California, and the *San Carlos* back to Nootka, having concluded the year's explorations. The comprehensive chart produced in consequence of these extensive examinations contains several inserts, including one of especial interest to us: Puerto Claycuat. The Spanish preferred to keep their information to themselves. Thus it was that this chart did not appear in published form, for universal appreciation, until 1872, when it was filed by the United States government as part of the San Juan Boundary arbitration disclosures.[79]

To this point, European relations with Indigenous peoples at Clayoquot Sound had been mostly peaceful. This did not last. The Clayoquot, Ahousaht and Kelsemaht peoples, like all Nuu-chah-nulth nations, were militant societal groups, which should come as no surprise. Inter-village and inter-tribal rivalry was a feature of existence on the coast long before the Americans, British and Spanish arrived. Trade in arms and ammunition (black powder pistols and muskets, and possibly small cannon) was a feature of early contact history. However, as Robin Fisher has shown, Indigenous peoples of the coast preferred hand-held weapons; firearms may have been superior weapons, and much admired by the chiefs, but when it came to combat, traditional weapons were used.[80] For one thing, gunpowder, once expended, was not easily replaced.

It must always be remembered, too, that the Europeans and the Americans also came well-armed and experienced in, and possibly anticipating, "frontier warfare." Particularly experienced were the Bostonians, who had fought the British during the Revolutionary War and, like most men in eastern North America, were familiar with "forest actions." The trading vessels all had mounted cannon of one sort or another, which were sometimes used in a display of power (as we will see in the Colnett case, below). In addition, such vessels were well equipped with swivel guns, blunderbusses and various firearms and, doubtless, cutlasses and perhaps pikes. They also had boarding nettings to prevent surprise attacks from canoes at night.

In short, trade readily occurred. It always began with gift-giving by the visitors, and sometimes an exchange of presents—with the promise of a larger exchange the next day. When the trade was brisk, there was less noise and uproar than usually occurred.[81] But the visitors—and probably the locals as well—were always on the alert for anything that might lead to violence.

It will always be a matter of argument as to the extent of the violence between Natives and newcomers. Violent incidents are a matter of record, but I prefer to see them as isolated or standalone episodes, a reaction to specific events; they were not demonstrations of organized warfare. Still, they exist and cannot be set aside. However, the documentation on these incidents is sparse, and in many cases we have only one testimonial or written piece of evidence. Unsupported accounts are always limited in value. The Native side of the evidence is conspicuous by its absence, as the anthropologist Drucker attests. We have to remember that the First Nations of the Northwest Coast had an oral rather than a written culture. Historians can explain their motives and actions only through the descriptions given by European and American outsiders, and then, must weigh the evidence and make the best judgment they can.

In his own time, James Colnett was famous among British mariners. He was a great seaman and navigator, but his fame, or notoriety, arose because of what transpired at Nootka in 1789, when he was imprisoned by the intemperate Spanish naval officer Martínez. Colnett became known as a central actor (second only to Meares and Martínez) in the drama unfolding on the far side of the world. He was by no means blameless, but he did have the doctrine of freedom of the seas and freedom of navigation on his side. He also had an excellent propagandist in the form of John Meares, who broadcast the iniquitous actions of the Spaniard throughout the British Empire. Colnett survived all this to become a formidable part of the European story of Clayoquot. Accordingly, a mountain on Meares Island bears his name.

Colnett, a midshipman during Cook's second Pacific voyage, earned his commander's approval as "clever and sober." He gained expertise in gunnery. Promoted to lieutenant, he eventually found himself on half pay when the Royal Navy no longer required his services. He obtained Admiralty permission to command the *Prince of*

Sea Otter Hunters

Wales, with the *Princess Royal* as escort, for Richard Cadman Etches & Co.'s trading expedition to the Northwest Coast under licences from the South Sea and East India Companies. He was on the coast in 1787, wintered in Hawaii, sailed for Canton, and there formed a new company with Meares, the Associated Merchants Trading to the Northwest Coast of America. The *Prince of Wales* freighted tea home to England. At this stage, Colnett took command of the *Argonaut*. He sailed for the coast in April 1789, taking with him twenty-nine Chinese artisans, along with materials for building coastal vessels and establishing a permanent settlement in Nootka Sound. Such a base would be a trading post, a point of collection for furs, a repair depot and a headquarters of ancillary posts.[82]

However, the scheme to establish this foothold of empire fell afoul of a Spanish naval officer hell-bent on exercising his authority to gain personal renown. Colnett found he had been forestalled by the Spanish at Nootka. Merchant sailors are an independent lot: they do not like to be interfered with, and after a violent drunken argument with Martínez, Colnett found himself in irons and his vessel seized. The *Argonaut* and the *Princess Royal*, plus their cargoes and stores, their commanders, officers and crews, and the Chinese artisans, were sent to the Mexican port of San Blas as prize vessels and prisoners.

This event nearly ended in war between Britain and Spain, and the bullish British used the threat of naval action to convince the Spanish to back down and accept the Nootka Conventions, permitting British trade and navigation. The international legal tangles of the conventions, and the diplomatic pressure on Madrid, as fascinating as they are, cannot detain us here.[83] The main point is that the Nootka Convention of October 28, 1790, changed this state of affairs.

Meanwhile, in fever-ridden San Blas, local Spanish authorities released the *Argonaut* and Colnett from captivity in the summer of 1790. A long voyage lay ahead to get back to Nootka, and the vessel was only half-provisioned. November's gales posed high risks for any sailing vessel making for Nootka, but Colnett had no choice. The weather-battered *Argonaut*, lashed by winter's furies and

PART I The Empire of Fortune

suffering much damage to spars and rigging, could not make Nootka but found welcome refuge in Clayoquot Sound. She came to safe anchor and was suddenly enveloped in a pea-soup fog. Her successful entrance can be credited to Mate Thomas Hudson, who had been there before. Local knowledge was of greatest importance. Later the vessel shifted to much-favoured Port Cox.

From Colnett's manuscript we pick up the story of what transpired at Port Cox. Nootka Sound was his ultimate destination, but, he recounts, gales were either coming straight out of Nootka bound for Clayoquot or the other way round, preventing the *Argonaut*'s passage to Nootka. In the circumstances, Colnett sent Mate Hudson and crew in the jolly boat to Nootka with messages that he was at Clayoquot and in need of assistance for repairs to his ship. The unfortunate jolly boat came to grief on the rocks just south of Nootka with loss of all hands.

Meanwhile, at Port Cox, the ship's carpenters made repairs to the rudder of the *Argonaut* and replaced the rotten bowsprit. Colnett wanted to lay the ship on shore for the repairs, but there was nowhere he could protect his stores from the Natives, "who were moving their habitations near us, and were very numerous also, having as many fire arms as myself and perfectly acquainted with the use of them."[84] All the same, the necessary general refit was completed. Shore parties gathered wood and water. Whale and dogfish oils were purchased for the ship's lamps—another local source aiding the ocean-going mariners.[85] All was nearly ready for departure. But outside, on the outer coast, the gales struck with unrelenting fury.

Colnett helped Wickaninnish rig and sail two canoes after the manner of the British longboats. Much trading took place, too, but other storm clouds were gathering. The Natives were numerous, and Colnett thought them increasingly warlike in their preparations:

> This reciprocal Friendship continued until the 31st, when at Supper and only one Man left on deck, was alarm'd by his calling for Assistance on deck, that the Indians was going to Board us in large Canoes. Arms being at hand, everyone seiz'd them, and were soon on deck, when I observed 3 or 4 Canoes lash'd together. They were

dropping on board with the Ebb tide, but we soon made them Shift their route by keeping a constant fire of Musquetry, as long as a shot would reach them. Being within Gun shot of the Village [of Opitsat] I pointed one of the Cannon myself, and fired into it, that they might know if they made such another attempt, it was in my power to annoy them considerably. On discharge of the Gun They set up a Hue and Cry, and return'd it with several Muskets but, if with Ball in, they did not reach us.[86]

Colnett concludes his extended discussion of this incident thus: "Indeed our Confidence in each other was entirely lost and in the morning January 1st [1791], the wind proving favourable sail'd and by Noon was clear of this Port which gave me no little Satisfaction."[87]

The *Argonaut* reached Nootka Sound in early February and soon sailed for Hawaii and China, arriving in July 1791. Colnett became famous: "Everyone has heard about Colnett," wrote Patrick O'Brian in *Far Side of the World*, and so it was at the time among persons concerned in the merchant trades and naval matters. The Clayoquot had reasons to remember him too, though not kindly. Looked at differently, the Nootka seizure did him no harm in high places; rather the opposite. He found himself high in Admiralty favour. London whaling companies thought him just the right sort of fellow to undertake a voyage to the Galapagos and other islands to find places of rendezvous and refit for the extensive British whaling fleet working the waters beyond Cape Horn. In consequence, he sailed in the small ship *Rattler* to the Galapagos and other notable islands of the eastern Pacific.

There was also a scheme promoted by some British persons to establish a convict settlement at or near Nootka, along the lines of the one in New South Wales. That came to naught as there were enough places in Australia for this sort of thing. Another scheme imagined Hawaii as a mid-Pacific base of operations under the Union Jack, with communications to Nootka Sound and Macau. Many of these schemes seem wild, but the one that made eminent good sense was the one brought forward by John Meares, which Colnett attempted to carry out: to set up a base of operations at Nootka

Sound. To this end, Colnett had a detail of Chinese labourers on board the *Argonaut* to assist in the project. The Spanish put a stop to these intentions. Who knows what would have happened if Colnett had not been arrested, and his vessels and cargoes seized, by Esteban Martínez.

The trade continued despite the absence of the factory. At the end of the process, when the sea otter had almost disappeared and the trade become of no value to the British, Americans and others, the Natives were left alone. They entered a quiet period, and it was not until the 1860s that the outsiders came again, this time looking for timber and forest products. During this quiet period, the riches of the outside world were essentially cut off, and the local nations developed internal, inter-tribal trades; this was a time, too, of rivalries, slave trading and internecine warfare.

As an aside, timber was not only of interest in the later period. Captain Cook, we are reminded, replaced various damaged masts and yards when he was at Nootka, and when Meares was there in 1788, he freighted spars (for masts) and deal (sawn boards) to China, for there, he declared, "spars of every denomination" were in constant demand. He left Vancouver Island with this lasting impression: "the woods of this part of America are capable of supplying, with these valuable materials, all the navies of Europe."[88] How many vessels in the sea otter trade freighted spars and deal from these waters is not known, though there are incidental cases: *Mentor*, in 1816, with spars for China, and *Arab*, in 1819, with spars for Chile.[89]

In short, the Natives of Clayoquot Sound had met with outsiders on numerous occasions in the course of the trade in sea otter pelts. Vessels on discovery missions had also called there, but the real attraction was trade. Clayoquot Sound, and Port Cox, became an important nexus of the sea otter, or maritime, fur trade of the Pacific. The Natives now participated in global markets. They wanted iron, copper and abalone shells, and for these they traded sea otter pelts. This was makúk, pure and simple. Connections with the wider world developed from local demands.[90]

Although it may appear that the Europeans and Americans came with aggressive intent, we need to be careful in our judgments and more discerning when it comes to the wild generalizations that seem to be made these days in regards to race relations. Perhaps we can put some of the British traders in the camp of the evil-minded and evil-intended. However, we know from the documents that John Meares pursued a clearly defined policy, in keeping with investors' demands, to win the confidence of the Natives of the Northwest Coast. In consequence of his own experiences in trade, and on the basis of other information he had received, moreover, necessity dictated good relations with the locals, and no harm was to be done to them. Rather, friendships were to be cultivated. He himself had been circumspect in his dealings with the First Nations. Thus he instructed Captain Colnett in April 1789 to observe the following in future dealings with the Natives: in view of "reports having been spread of great Acts of Cruelty and Inhumanity being committed by the Crews of various Vessels on the Coast of America, in their Commerce with the Natives," Colnett was warned to intervene to stop any such acts, and to "seize the Offenders, and put them in irons, and send them to the [Company's] Agents in China" for punishment. Furthermore, Meares recommended a policy of forbearance: "We are here necessitated to dwell on this Subject, from the strong Reports of such atrocious Acts being committed, which are at once not only destructive of the Commerce, but of every sentiment of Humanity; we recommend a steady Pursuance of a mild Conduct, as the only Means to cultivate the good Will of the Natives, and draw them within the Verges of civilized Life."[91]

These words sound high-minded and altruistic, and in this age we may find them hard to accept at face value. But they speak to a growing British awareness (not shared by all European peoples and certainly not by the Americans) of the imperial mission, which grew into a Britannic peace. In a sense, Meares and Colnett were following what we might call the official line with regards to conduct to be observed. After all, this represented fully James Cook's instructions for all his voyages to the Pacific, and notably, in our case, his third voyage, the one that brought him to Nootka. The British regarded

PART I The Empire of Fortune

trade as their vehicle of friendship, and the British were traders extraordinare. Thus Meares' instructions to Colnett recommended forming treaties with various chiefs, "particularly near Nootka." Meares ordered Colnett to gain "the Confidence of the Chiefs, who are known to manage the Commerce of their Subjects." This is a telling observation on the power of the likes of Maquinna and Wickaninnish. In order to secure their confidence, Meares regarded it as necessary to negotiate an explicit understanding involving protection. In Meares' words, "so anxious are we to have a good Understanding, and the perfecting a Treaty, that we authorize you to take under your Protection all our Allies, and protect them from Insult from all Persons whatever. Our Sentiments on this Head you will make known to all Persons whom it may concern, in order that they may govern themselves accordingly."[92]

Colnett's actions at Clayoquot Sound and elsewhere, though interrupted by his incarceration at the hands of Martínez, stand in sharp contrast to those of John Kendrick and Robert Gray, to which we now turn. The visits by these captains and the ships they commanded are important in Meares Island history for two reasons: the first is the use of a cove at Meares Island as a winter sanctuary for the traders in 1791–1792; the second is the relationship of Wickaninnish to Kendrick, and the fur trade transactions entered into at that time.

4
Buying and Selling Clayoquot

In late summer 1788, we are reminded, the American ship *Columbia Rediviva*, sailing out of Boston, arrived on the Northwest Coast. Her master was John Kendrick, born about the year 1740 in Harwich, Massachusetts. One of the officers, Robert Haswell, a person of discriminating views, recounted that early on the very pleasant Sunday morning of August 31, 1788, while easing into the southeast entrance to Clayoquot Sound, a great many inhabitants came out to the ship in canoes, bringing an abundance of skins. Prospects of trade seemed fair, "but greatly to our mortification there was nothing in our vessel except muskets." The Clayoquot were ardent for copper: "copper was all their cry." In conversation with the Americans, Wickaninnish and other chiefs mentioned several traders—Meares, Barkley, Duncan, Hanna and Douglas. They remembered them all as recent visitors. However, communication was limited: what they said of these traders the Americans could not fathom. The language barrier presented further possibilities of misunderstanding, and there was no interpreter on board the ship. Such knowledge of their language as was possessed by the Americans, the locals could not comprehend.[93]

PART I The Empire of Fortune

Kendrick has black marks after his name for his violent and shaming treatment of Koyah, Haida chief at SGang Gwaay Llanagaay (Red Cod Island—now Ninstints on Anthony Island, Haida Gwaii) a year later, in 1789. The "Kendrick-Koyah affair" is regarded as a shocking violation of Haida cultural mores, for by taking Koyah prisoner and locking him to a gun carriage, Kendrick shamed the chief before his own people. Koyah spent several years attempting to regain his status among his own people by showing that he was not a slave of white traders, and he led several attacks on British and American merchant shipping, the last one likely fatal to him.[94]

At Clayoquot the story was different: Kendrick got along well with Wickaninnish and his people. To further trade, his intention was to set up arrangements with the respective head chiefs of the many villages in and near Nootka, most notably Clayoquot Sound: these embayments were the focus of the bountiful maritime trade in these latitudes. He intended subsequent voyages, building on the success of the initial trade.

To Kendrick can be accorded the odd distinction of being gunrunner to the Clayoquot. He initiated the trade in firearms. Not only did he give Maquinna a swivel gun, but he also furnished Wickaninnish with more than 200 muskets, two barrels of powder and a considerable portion of shot. In a flash, the world had been transformed. As Vancouver's clerk Edward Bell said, quoted in Chapter 3, "Thus are they supplied with weapons which they no sooner possess than they turn against the donors."[95] This was written at Nootka in October 1792. A Spanish authority supports Bell's charge of Kendrick's influence in the trade in firearms. However, there is widespread discussion and much dispute about the role of firearms in relation to violence (against other Indigenous persons and against European and American visitors), and so we take Bell's comments with caution.[96]

Why not, Kendrick reasoned, enter firm arrangements with certain Northwest Coast chiefs so that exclusive trade would exist when his ship returned to their locales? This Yankee, in many ways like Meares, was shrewd and forward looking. He intended to take

Buying and Selling Clayoquot

control of the locus of the trade. Thus he had his eye on all of Nootka Sound and, as if that were not enough, even cast a glance widely south to Clayoquot. His empire building differed from that of the Spanish. The Spanish pressed their claim to Nootka, and especially Yuquot, tearing down Native structures and putting up their own buildings—a hospital, garrison, church and fortifications. They intended to stay. Kendrick wanted what we might call "soft empire"— that is, a place of convenience and a promise of trade in the future. For their part, the chiefs had proffered friendship to Kendrick. They wanted close business connections for the two-way traffic of assured imports and sea otter pelt exports, all at good prices of exchange. Thus it was that in Nootka Sound, Kendrick got busy forming firm bonds of friendship. He entertained with Chinese fireworks at night. He offered sailcloth and black powder as gifts and favours. There was feasting. These formed the preliminaries. He prepared for more serious arrangements. For their part, the chiefs of the Indigenous peoples on the coast saw it as perfectly within their rights to sell whatever was theirs.

With the necessary groundwork completed, Kendrick swapped ten muskets for a harbour known as Chastacktoos (Mahwinna, Maweea or Moweeena; now known as Marvinas Bay), an excellent place for ship repairs to be carried out, as it was safe from all winds.[97] That was where the *Lady Washington* lay at anchor. To this was added all lands and waters within nine miles north, east, south and west of that harbour. Maquinna expressed delight, for the terms of this treaty, signed July 21, 1789, attested that he could live and fish in the above-mentioned territory forever, as could his heirs, executors and administrators. The American captain, for his part, also acquired freedom of passage and navigation throughout the land of Maquinna.[98] No Spanish warship could upset his trade now. The centre point of the purchase came to be called Safe Retreat Harbour.

Here was a prodigious gain, and a mighty transaction. The eighteen-mile square embraced 324 square miles. Maquinna, jubilant, had already shown his pleasure by climbing the rigging of the *Lady Washington* and pointing to the four directions. Presumably

PART I The Empire of Fortune

Kendrick was under obligation to provide him some sort of protection as an ally, as well as to engender trade. Perhaps, too, Maquinna and the other chiefs hoped that the rival British and Spanish could be kept out. From our time it seems all very fuzzy as to intent, but it makes clear that the head chief and his subordinate chiefs could do just as they chose: no elected tribal or band council offered countering opinions or raised objections. There was no land registry office and no colonial government.

Kendrick did not stop there and made three other purchases in Nootka Sound. The opinion of Kendrick's biographer is that this was a brilliant defensive move to block the claims of the British and the Spanish. I find his argument conclusive. Moreover, these properties had valuable fishing grounds, good harbours and land where gold would later be found. This was done by deed and not by treaty (which involves mutually recognized nations or states).[99]

Empire-builder Kendrick now looked southward to expand his trading sphere. If Clayoquot could be added, he would have in total more than a thousand square miles of Vancouver Island. Thus it was that at Clayoquot on August 11, 1791, Kendrick signed a deed conveying to him "a territorial distance of eighteen miles north, eighteen miles south, eighteen miles east, and eighteen miles west of the village called by the natives Opsitsa, which village is to be the centre of the said territorial distances, with all mines, minerals, rivers, bays, sounds, harbors, creeks, &c., and all the islands, with both the produce of land and sea within the limits of said territorial distance. Opisita being the centre is situated in latitude 49° 10' north, and longitude 126° 02' west from the meridian of London."[100] Wickaninnish and five others—Tootiscosettle, Yeassluar, Tatootchtheatticus, Yackgulgin and Hycreguis—signed the deed. These were chiefs, sons and close relatives of Wickaninnish. Now where is the *original* of this extraordinary contract? Would that we could find it! It has been lost. Can we content ourselves with a printed version, for that's what has come down to us.

By good fortune the deed survives and can be found on page 8 in Hall J. Kelley's *Discoveries, Purchases of Lands, etc., on the Northwest*

Coast, Being a Part of an Investigation of the American Title to the Oregon Territory (Boston, 1838). When I first chanced upon this rare book, I realized it was an example, pure and simple, of that boisterous "Oregon fever" that beset American businessmen and land seekers desirous of getting their hands on the far Pacific coast of North America, and using any logic that would help their case. At the time, the Oregon Country stretched from present-day Oregon north to the border with Russian America at 54° 40' N, and south to Mexico. By the mid-1820s, Britain and the United States remained the sole contenders for the territory.[101]

The Clayoquot deed signed by Wickaninnish and the other chiefs is similar to four others we find in Kelley and elsewhere, except that it did not include the clause of the Nootka document, which reads "only the said J. Kendrick does grant and allow the said Maquinnah to live and fish on the territory as usual."

We know that the deeds were in Canton as of May 11, 1795, in the possession of Kendrick's clerk, J. Howell. Further, they were registered in Macau in December 1796. The originals were sent to Boston, with authenticated copies to follow by subsequent conveyances. However, through the all-too-familiar occurrence of envelopes and packages being lost in the mail, these subsequent shipments did not find their way to their destinations. But for legal history enthusiasts there is a bright light. Kendrick's own copies found their way to Thomas Jefferson, US Secretary of State, under cover of a letter dated March 1, 1793.[102]

We now move to the key substantive issue, as Kendrick saw it. Under these deeds Kendrick wrote, "tracts of land, therein described, situated on islands in the North West Coast of America, have been conveyed to me and my heirs for ever, <u>by the resident chiefs of those districts, who, I presume, were the only just proprietors thereof.</u>"[103]

Empire followed trade in Kendrick's logic. His beachhead of forged alliances and commercial connections on Vancouver Island's west coast were to him only made more secure if the US government acknowledged and even registered these claims. But this was not American sovereign territory, though it was claimed as such.

PART I The Empire of Fortune

In any event, Kendrick asked Jefferson to get the United States to recognize his ownership of territory. He noted in particular, so as to appease Jefferson (who worried about foreign entanglements), that the Spanish at Nootka had acknowledged his purchase: "My claim to these territories has been allowed by the Spanish Crown, for the purchases I made at Nootka were expressly excepted in a deed of conveyance of the lands adjacent to and surrounding Nootka Sound, executed in September last, to El Senor Don Juan Francisco de la Bodega of Quadra, on behalf of his Catholic Majesty, by Maquinnah, and the other chiefs of his tribe, to whom those lands belonged."[104]

Kendrick thought in imperial terms. He pressed the point that the value of the maritime fur trade to US commerce meant that a base of operations there—a settlement, if you will, under protection of the US government—would be advantageous to the nation. The future-thinking Kendrick intended that the lands he purchased would be of use to the government in some future plan.[105] He held that when he made these purchases he did so under the impression that the United States government would sanction them. He believed that the Spanish crown allowed his claim to those same territories; he specifically maintained that Bodega y Quadra, the Spanish authority at Nootka, accepted the deed of conveyance as legitimate in regards to the Maquinna document. Kendrick spoke of the five deeds as forming one property. Might what he had in mind be a toehold of empire, the first step to a transcontinental America in these latitudes? All would be to his gain, too. Interestingly, he was writing in these terms just as Alexander Mackenzie was making last preparations at Fort Fork, Peace River, for his crossing from there to Dean Channel on the Pacific. Imperial designs were intersecting on the far side of the world.

Kendrick fully expected to be compensated for these private purchases. He also expected that much would come to him as a pathfinder of empire. Who knows what might have eventuated in the next few years, as tensions increased regarding the future sovereignties of the Northwest Coast, had he not been killed, perhaps accidentally, perhaps due to negligence, on December 12, 1794, in

Honolulu. Kendrick's cause was taken up by friends and interested persons, of which more will be mentioned below.

Reverting to the Kendrick deeds, as they are called, the question raised by interested parties is this: did Wickaninnish sign the deed with Kendrick? Or, put differently, was he a party to the transaction? Evidence is found in two places. John Young, sometime prime minister of Hawaii, saw the deeds and testified in 1835 that he distinctly recollected seeing the names of Maquinna and Wickaninnish.[106] And we should not discount the oral evidence of Bostonian Samuel Yendell, of the *Columbia*, who wrote in 1838, "while at Clyoquot, on that coast, in the village of Wickanannish, I heard it often said that the Indian chief Wickanannish had sold to Capt. John Kendrick his territory."[107]

If we take this as credible, Kendrick had bought Opitsat and much else in the territory, extending eighteen miles in the four cardinal directions. Doubtless Wickaninnish and the other signatories were interested in trade prospects, not territory sales. But when the Anglo-American contest for sovereignty on the Northwest Coast increased in alarming strength, drawing forth many tensions on the international scene, these same Kendrick deeds were gathered as evidence of American toeholds of empire and embraced by Americans in the process of bolstering their case for control of the Oregon Country from Alta California at 38°N to the Alaskan panhandle, 54° 40' N. None other than Robert Greenhow, translator and librarian to the Department of State, published extensively on this topic. He used Kendrick's deeds as undefiled evidence of US interests in sovereignty.[108] Greenhow was far from disinterested. In consequence, the view of official scholarship from Washington, DC, had now come to possess Meares Island as part of a sort of proto-empire on the Northwest Coast, the first step to acquiring complete sovereignty as recognized by the comity of nations. We also observe that for the first time a location on Meares Island, Opitsat, had been possessed by geographical science and the calculations of latitude and longitude. Kendrick gave it this measurement on the earth's surface, giving Opitsat a spatial relationship in regards to the rest of the world.

PART I The Empire of Fortune

If, we might reasonably ask, Clayoquot Sound had been part of the United States, would Kendrick, Gray and their successors forever have owned the land? An interesting question, to which we have an answer in American law. The Kendrick and Gray deeds, we find by our study of land purchase law in the United States, would have been null and void at the time. "The prohibition of private purchase of lands from the Indians, which had been part of the colonial and imperial policy [of Great Britain], continued as a fixed policy of the United States," according to a leading authority on American Indian law (here I use "Indian" as per the custom in the United States). The first Congress under the Constitution incorporated this into the Indian trade and intercourse act of 1793.[109] At face value, this meant that US commissioners had to treat with Indians for their lands; Congress appropriated funds for compensation to Indians. But Clayoquot Sound was not in US sovereign territory in any case. No further comment need be made here about the general tendency in the history of the American frontier to seize, capture and rob Indians of their lands, and many a book has been written on that subject.

Looked at from Wickaninnish's perspective, he had every right to sell what he wished in the way of land or other resources. He wanted the promise, the security of future trade. I like to think of the Kendrick deeds as demonstrating his personal claims as of 1791. These include his right to sell property as he wished, and with other subordinate chiefs' consent (and their marks on the document). It demonstrates, undoubtedly, his status as of that date. It shows, too, his willingness to enter into contractual arrangements as of that time, for other considerations beneficial to him. It shows that he was not duped, and that he enjoyed a one-on-one relationship with Kendrick. Further, Kendrick's nationality was not a consideration here. Certainly it was not a release of sovereignty; rather, it constituted a real estate transaction and a trade alliance. Wickaninnish, in short, was sovereign lord, master of all he surveyed. This is borne out by the insightful remarks of Bell, the clerk of HMS *Discovery*, with which we conclude discussion of this particular matter:

Buying and Selling Clayoquot

Though Maquinna is the greatest chief in the neighborhood of Nootka Sound yet Wicananish who resides at Clyonquot seems to me to be the Emperor of the Sea Coast between Defuca's Streights and Woody Point, an extent of upwards of a degree & a half of Latitude, and the most populous part of the Coast (for its extent) but Maquinna is not tributary to him nor does he allow his rank to be inferior to Wicananish's. Their families are united by Marriage which of course unites their Politicks. Wicannanish's property is very great and . . . is possessed of about 400 Muskets. With such a force no wonder that small vessels are afraid to enter the Port. He attempted to take the Ship Columbia while she was wintering Clyonquot but I cannot bestow much pity on those who have been attacked when I recollect that they themselves have put the very weapons in their hands which are turn'd against them. Notwithstanding this treacherous piratical disposition the Chiefs behave with some degree of honor to those with whom they make bargains.[110]

5
Fort Defiance and the Destruction of Opitsat

At this point it is worth considering the importance of personality and character as agents in historical process. John Kendrick, though not free from engagement in violent episodes on the coast, was on the whole more amenable to Indigenous peoples than was Robert Gray. The latter was difficult, vengeful and self-interested to a fault (giving his ship owners concerns that he was not acting fully in their interests). He was resolute and self-reliant, and although of kindly disposition was prone to outbursts of temper. Kendrick, with all sorts of experience in making real estate deals there and elsewhere, believed in fair compensation for items traded with the Northwest Coast peoples. Perhaps he feared what might happen when Gray got into Clayoquot. His orders to Captain Gray are instructive: "Treet the Natives with Respect where Ever you go. Cultivate frindship with them as much as possibel and take Nothing from them But what you pay them for according to a fair agreement, and not suffer your peopel to affront them or treet them Ill."[111] Such were Kendrick's

Fort Defiance and the Destruction of Opitsat

pronounced intentions, and his orders to Gray. As so often happens, matters turned out differently.

As mentioned in Chapter 3, Gray made his second voyage from Boston in 1790, this time commanding the *Columbia* (his ship on the first voyage had been the *Lady Washington*). He reached Nootka Sound on August 28, 1790. The speed of these global circumnavigations catches our imagination and wins our admiration.

From Nootka Sound, Gray coasted southward in the *Columbia* with confident expectation of reaching Neah Bay, near Cape Flattery. There he intended to winter and construct the schooner he had brought out from Boston in frame. Fog shrouded the coast; strong currents persisted; roaring surf warned of the dangerous shore. Clouds prevented any observation that would have given them a position. Once again stormy conditions ruled the day, and a southwesterly gale drove him back toward Nootka. Gray now had it in mind to winter in Nasparti, or Columbia's, Cove in what he called Bullfinch's Sound—now Nasparti Inlet or, the Nuu-chah-nulth name, Quin-ecx. This is on the Brooks Peninsula, Vancouver Island. First Mate Robert Haswell, realizing that this destination could not be achieved, suggested Clayoquot as an alternative. The captain agreed that this would be the best place they could winter if, as Gray made clear, "proper wood could be found to saw into plank."[112] It took two attempts but on the second, September 18, Gray steered safely through the dangerous southeast entrance, lost an anchor in a stiff breeze, and just after midnight found welcome refuge in Clayoquot Sound, coming to anchor in Port Cox.

The young mate, John Boit, Jr., takes up the story: "This day anchor'd in our Old Station in Clioquot Harbour . . . At this Harbour Captain Gray had determin'd to Winter, if he cou'd find a suitable place to build a sloop of 45 tons . . . The stem and stern post with part of the floor timbers had been brought from Boston for that purpose."[113] Ship's boats were sent out on reconnaissance, and they found a commodious and snug cove completely suitable to

PART I The Empire of Fortune

their needs on the east shore of what is now Lemmens Inlet, about three miles north and east of Opitsat, the perfect location on a rugged coast, free from winter's ravages and blessed with many other advantages.

Before the *Columbia* shifted to the cove, Gray had a happy meeting with Kendrick, in the *Lady Washington*, who had anchored nearby at a small island he had fortified and named Fort Washington, after the US president (exact location unknown). Kendrick was about to sail for Hawaii. That evening the two ship's companies visited each other, swapping accounts, tales and stories. Many must have recounted their departure from Boston all those many years and months ago, and all the experiences they had had in the Pacific since then. Nothing is known of what they said about Clayoquot Sound and its peoples.

After Kendrick's departure, the *Columbia* moved to the cove. Upon arrival, no time was to be lost as the season was fast advancing. The first necessity was shelter ashore. The *Columbia* arrived at the site on September 21, and that same day carpenters and other artisans, as well as regular sailor hands, started clearing the land and constructing a fortified log shelter. This was designed to contain a boat builder's shed and a blacksmith's shop with forge, along with several lodging rooms, "the whole well armed, two cannon mounted outside and one inside of the house through a port, and in every direction loopholes for our small arms and pistols, of which we have a tolerable plenty, and our party is augmented to ten in all."[114] From a pole at the front apex of the roof flew the Stars and Stripes. Two saw-pits were in use frequently to cut plank sheathing from logs towed to the spot. The place had the appearance of a "young" shipyard, reported Boit.[115]

"I am daily visited by some one or other of the Chiefs," wrote Haswell in his log, "who express great admiration at our artisans. The sawing of plank, the smith work, and the dexterity with which our people cut down and hew trees strikes them with wonder. They almost always when they come sell a few skins, and generally bring a few wild geese and ducks for sale."[116] The water being shallow there, the Americans cleared a small channel so the vessel could be

Fort Defiance and the Destruction of Opitsat

extricated from the shipways; it would be used at launch time. On October 3 the keel of the sloop was laid, "every person busily employed."[117] Meares Island's forest provided the ship's carpenter with what he needed: a shore party cut planks for the sloop's decks. Trees could be felled near to where they were required. Haswell wrote tellingly of the forest: "It was as compact a thicket as ever grew, few of the trees were less than two fathoms [12 feet] round and many of them four [24 feet]."[118] Weather proved favourable to their work—that is, it was not too rainy—but daylight hours were shortening, made even shorter by the height of the trees, which obscured the sun. Many of the Europeans were confined with severe colds and rheumatic pain, resulting from cold wet weather, but the forest also met every requirement for warming fires.

The location became known as Adventure Cove (sometimes Winter Cove)—Hoskins says the Indigenous people called it *Clickelecutsee*—and the shore establishment Fort Defiance. It mounted four cannon, and had forty muskets and several blunderbusses. The cove not only gave the *Columbia* shelter from winter storms but also offered a beach where they erected the shipways. A stream afforded drinking water. The *Columbia* was kept berthed abreast a sheer (and natural) rock face in the north, sheltering, arm of the cove. This unusual geological formation was called Rock Bluff, and is described in Boit's log as "a bluff point of rocks, where she [the *Columbia*] lay'd as to a wharfe not even touching the ground at low water."[119] Again, nature provided benefits. The *Columbia* remained there for a time and then was shifted across the cove and brought to anchor beside the ways and near the house. This move was made to give defence against impending attack.

Fort Defiance was a temporary structure sufficient for the occasion, but was perhaps built with the thought that American traders might come again in some future year. On October 12, Wickaninnish and one or two of his brothers visited the place: "They gazed with much admiration at our house and vessel and expressed much wonder."[120] And well may we ask if they had also begun to think that the Americans might not go away. Perhaps they had become uncomfortable with the lingering presence of strangers. Events were turning decidedly uncordial.

On March 25 the *Adventure* was hauled down the ways. She was then fitted for sea and supplied for a four-month cruise among the Queen Charlottes under Haswell (and a crew of ten). Meanwhile, the *Columbia* had been re-rigged and stowed with the items kept safely ashore. She was ready for sea again. The two vessels left Adventure Cove in company. They passed down Lemmens Inlet, probably under tow of their boats. Adverse winds delayed their outbound progress. They eventually passed through Templar Channel and out into the wide Pacific's swells.

Before they left, however, on March 27, 1792, John Boit, under instructions from Captain Gray, took three boats, well-armed and manned, to destroy Opitsat village. He used the word "destroyed," and we may wonder if he means that the boat landing parties set fire—put the torch—to what was likely the main house and other buildings, some with carved and painted fronts. "It was a Command I was no ways tenacious of," he wrote in his log for that day, with regret, "and am grieved to think Captain Gray shou'd let his passions go so far. This village was about half a mile in Diameter, and Contained upwards of 200 Houses, generally well built for Indians. Ev'ry door that you enter'd was in resemblance to an human and Beasts head . . . Ther was much more rude carved work about the dwellings some of which was by no means innelegant [sic]. This fine Village, the work of Ages, was in a short time destroy'd."[121]

After they left Clayoquot Sound, Gray dispatched the *Adventure* to barter for furs in the rich Queen Charlotte Islands. Gray himself, meanwhile, sailed south toward Cape Flattery, looking for trade and the glories of discoveries. He sailed south almost to the California line, then hauled to the north, seeking bays and estuaries suitable for trade. Once again weather determined action: winds and currents obliged him to beat offshore for days. Then, in the vicinity of 46° 10′ N, Gray noticed evidence of a large river. The outflowing current was too strong to chance an entry, but Gray would return presently to what we now know as the Columbia River.

Fort Defiance and the Destruction of Opitsat

As the *Columbia* was working in squally seas off the coast of present-day Washington State, two British warships, the *Discovery* and *Chatham*, under Captain George Vancouver and Lieutenant William Robert Broughton, were approaching the coast of Nova Albion. In mid-April they raised land near Cape Mendocino, California, and were making their way to Nootka, surveying the coast as they went, investigating the possibility of a northwest passage. In their possession the officers and midshipmen had copies of Meares' *Voyages*, published just two years previously. When fabulous Mount Olympus (7,915 feet) came into view, they were delighted to see the majestic peak just as Meares had reported it in his writing. On board the vessels, many doubts were held about this strange, uncharted American continent. So many geographical mysteries presented themselves. It was the mission of this naval expedition to solve these mysteries. The skeptical Captain Vancouver, taking James Cook's opinion as a given, could not imagine that a Strait of Juan de Fuca existed. But, as Homer says, after the event any fool can be wise.

Late that same month, early on April 29, 1792, lookouts posted aloft spied a strange sail. This proved to be the *Columbia*, flying the Stars and Stripes. This chance encounter occurred south of Cape Flattery. In the circumstances, mutual suspicion reigned. Vancouver, we are reminded, had the dual purpose of completing Cook's survey between 50° N and Cook's River (now Cook's Inlet) and receiving restitution of territories from the Spanish, but Captain Gray of the *Columbia* could not believe the British were on an official expedition of geographical inquiry. He preferred to regard the British as rivals in trade, and, mused Vancouver's surgeon Archibald Menzies, "this is conformable to the general practice among traders on this Coast, which is always to mislead competitors as far as they can even at the expence of truth."[122] In any event, the vessels hove to, lying near one another, all the time rising and falling with the swells of the sea. Vancouver sent Menzies and Lieutenant Peter Puget across in a boat to talk to the American captain. Vancouver wanted to find out from Gray if it was indeed true that the *Lady Washington* had found an interior channel (thus proving the insularity of Vancouver

PART I The Empire of Fortune

Island) as Meares had stated in his *Voyages*. No, said the astonished Gray, none of that was true: in his 1789 voyage he had sailed into the strait only a distance of seventeen leagues—about fifty-one nautical miles—found no trade there and returned to the wide Pacific.

And what about Clayoquot and Opitsat? Surgeon Menzies has left an account of what Gray said, and Vancouver did likewise, including his in the official voyage account. Vancouver wrote: "Whilst he [Gray] remained at Clayoquot, *Wicananish*, the chief of that district, had concerted a plan to capture his ship, by bribing a native of Owhyee [Hawaii], whom Mr. Gray had with him, to wet the priming of all the fire-arms on board, which were constantly kept loaded; upon which the chief would easily have overpowered the ship's crew, by a number of daring Indians who were assembled for that purpose. This project was happily discovered, and the Americans being on their guard the fatal effects of the enterprise were prevented."[123] It seems entirely possible to me that the "preventive" measures taken may have fallen under the heading "the best defence is attack," and this may be why John Boit was sent with the boats to burn Opitsat, but Gray did not talk about this attack, or if he did, Menzies and Puget did not mention it.

After his meeting with the British, Gray continued his journey down the coast. On May 11 he carefully guided the *Columbia* across the treacherous bar and into the river whose presence he had noticed twice already, finding safe anchorage inside. This was the first entry of what an earlier land-based explorer, Jonathan Carver, had imagined as the River Oregon,[124] and others had speculated as "the River of the West." Gray named the river Columbia after his ship. The trading, however, proved a disappointment, and Gray left his great "discovery." He traded on the coast, then sailed for China. He returned to Boston on July 20, 1793, having circumnavigated the globe a second time. He died of yellow fever and was buried at sea in 1806. He is less well known in Clayoquot and Canadian history, but his finding of the Columbia River was of monumental importance to the United States: it stimulated further efforts to get a foothold on Pacific shores and was a factor in official

Fort Defiance and the Destruction of Opitsat

decisions to send Lewis and Clark there. His discovery of the great river gave the United States a tenuous claim to these parts of the Pacific coast.

As for the little *Adventure*, the first sailing vessel built in Clayoquot Sound, and the second on the Northwest Coast (Meares' *North West America*, at Nootka, being the first), she made an extensive cruise around the Queen Charlotte Islands and collected a handsome 500 skins. At Nootka she rendezvoused with the *Columbia* and transferred furs to her. The vessels sailed in company for the Charlottes and completed their profitable trading. They returned to Nootka. There the swift and nimble *Adventure*, of great value in the coastal trade but now expendable, was sold to the Spanish for seventy-two prime sea otter skins.[125] Renamed *Horcasitas*, after the Viceroy of Mexico, she sailed for Monterey in October and was sent back to Nootka with dispatches, returning in December. She proved her worth as a dispatch vessel, but eventually disappeared from the record.[126]

It will always be a subject of mystery—and disappointment to Canadians—that Captain Vancouver did not discover the river (though Broughton, of the *Chatham*, made an act of possession upriver in October of that same year). It is also a matter of dissatisfaction that the Canadian fur trader David Thompson, travelling overland, did not get to the mouth of the Columbia River sooner. I discuss these matters below.

Before we leave Captain Vancouver, whose voyage account gives us instructive insight concerning Captain Gray's strong and undeniable views about the treachery of the Clayoquot and the reason for his ordering the wasting of Opitsat, as recounted by Boit, we have one further and final window on this world of sea otter traders. Again, we cite the British naval captain as our authority. When at Nootka, Vancouver was told by American traders that a British captain, James Baker, of the merchant vessel *Jenny* of London, 78 tons, had fired on the people of Clayoquot Sound and had committed an act of piracy. This must date from 1792. Vancouver was suspicious of this report; he thought the Americans were seeking "the prejudice

PART I The Empire of Fortune

and dishonour of the British subjects trading on the coast."[127] This may well be true but is not conclusive. Little love was lost between the two nationalities. The Spanish sometimes felt themselves in between, and the Muchalaht and Mowachaht at Nootka were at the whim of these rivalries swirling around them.

As for Fort Defiance, whatever shore structure the Bostonians left behind fell into disuse. The relentlessly growing forest and impenetrable salal soon reclaimed the site. As a *Canadian* historical site it counted for next to nothing because it originated in American activities, but the quest to find it was kept alive by certain individuals interested in the history of trade and exploration. Perhaps someday, they reasoned, someone would chance upon the bricks that were used in the hearth and chimney. The hunt to find the location consumed many years and attracted many residents of Vancouver Island, notably those of Tofino. But, as might be expected, it was Americans who first sought to find the site in order to close an amazing chapter in their oceanic endeavours.

Captain Gray and the *Columbia* hold a unique place in US history as the first to carry the Stars and Stripes around the world. Boston had a solid interest in the story, and over the years the Massachusetts Historical Society acquired several logs and journals of Boston mariners who had been involved. One by one these appeared in published form, and some years before F.W. Howay, that unequalled pioneer of sea otter trade history, edited the logs of the *Columbia* for publication by that society (1940), the key facts were made known about where a search might prove effective in locating Adventure Cove. It was propitious that none other than Samuel Eliot Morison, the famed Harvard scholar and a seasoned mariner, should interest himself in the matter, demonstrating yet again the roles of sailor-historians in the preservation of sea history. Morison, who had written the seminal *Maritime History of Massachusetts, 1783–1860*, first published 1921, knew the history of the Bostonians in the trade at Nootka, Clayoquot and the Queen Charlotte Islands, with connections to Hawaii and China and thence around the world. He wanted to find the Boston pioneering spot on the Northwest Coast. In the

Fort Defiance and the Destruction of Opitsat

mid-1930s he solicited the help of Edmund Hayes, a Portland, Oregon, timber baron, himself a yachtsman and a keen student of coastal history.[128] Hayes had his own sailing vessel, the ketch *Seaway*, and he had deep pockets. Curiosity ruled his world, but he also had a particular nationalistic interest in the matter, for as he mused, "The sovereignty of the states of Washington and Oregon was undoubtedly determined by the discovery in May, 1792, of the Columbia River by the ship *Columbia* of Boston."[129] Hayes was fascinated by all things connected to this famous ship, including the destructive episode at Adventure Cove. Thus, sailing from the Columbia River on their quest, Hayes and Morison began the search for Gray's winter headquarters. They had the records of Boit, Hoskins, Howay and others at their disposal. They also had in their possession photographic copies of inspiring, sprightly watercolours executed by George Davidson, a carpenter on Captain Gray's ship in 1792.[130]

Morison and Hayes knew they had to search for a sheltered cove, one where the *Columbia* could moor to trees on either side, and where the entrance was not more than one hundred feet wide. Further, the cove must bear east by north from Port Cox, the anchorage off the village of present-day Tofino. There were many possibilities. Just south of Morpheus Island they thought they had found the site but were wrong—and later Hayes stated that the search had been somewhat superficial due to time constraints. All the same, you cannot blame Morison for waxing poetic: "It was quite a thrill for a Bostonian like myself, who has followed the history of the northwest fur trade, to visit the site of the lively scene depicted by the brush of Davidson and described in the *Columbia*'s log. We all wished that we had time to search among the salal and the fir and cedar that have grown up since 1792 for bricks from Fort Defiance's chimney and other relics of that busy winter. When we visited the place no vestige of human life was visible; the place had reverted to its original state, and some fresh elk track on the beach showed that the game had come back too."

He also remarked on the large trees there. Some of the cedars were 250 to 300 years old, so in *Columbia*'s day they would have been

PART I The Empire of Fortune

mature trees. "The sight of many great gnarled cedars that had been old when the *Columbia* came made us feel that mankind was still but an intruder and temporary occupant in this northwest coast of America."[131] That was the view of the newcomer.

Kenneth Gibson of Tofino, contractor and keen local history enthusiast, had been gathering information on the site for some considerable time as well. He got to know Hayes, who made several trips to Tofino in search of the *Tonquin* wreck (of which more below). Hayes, who had studied the trader narratives, the Native traditions at Clayoquot, and the several writings of Judge Howay and other publications, provided Gibson with additional historical information on the lost cove, including two old drawings on glass by George Davidson.[132] In 1966 the *Vancouver Sun* printed an article by Major George Nicholson of Victoria, veteran west coast historian and sometime postmaster at Opitsat, announcing the renewed quest for Adventure Cove undertaken by Gibson.[133] When Gibson found brick rubble about one foot underground, he knew at once that this was probably Gray's Fort Defiance. But he needed to test the bricks, and with Hayes' help the bricks were identified as some of the two thousand that had been sent out from Boston for the purpose. A small axe, similar to a lathing axe, was found. When the site was compared to the illustrations and to all the extant logs and journals, the case was proven beyond a shadow of doubt. Hayes credited Gibson with the discovery, rightly so, and recognition was also owing to Nicholson, the chronicler of the coast.

On December 9, 1966, the British Columbia government, by order-in-council, declared "that the remains of Fort Defiance, the winter quarters of Robert Gray in the years 1791–1792, have been located on lands situated in the west coast of Vancouver Island in the vicinity of Lemmens Inlet." The site was designated by the provincial cabinet under the Archaeological and Historic Sites Protection Act, which gave protection to 135 acres to keep souvenir seekers away until archaeologists could probe the find. Willard Ireland, the Provincial Archivist, interested the Government of Canada in having the Historic Sites and Monuments Board, Department of Natural

Fort Defiance and the Destruction of Opitsat

Resources at Ottawa, provide assistance in clearing the site. William Folan undertook that site visit for the Department of Northern Affairs, and Dr. Donald H. Mitchell, University of Victoria, began archaeological examination of Fort Defiance. The site was verified, and later excavations were made and reports published in the scholarly *BC Studies* in 1970 and 1972–1973.[134] Dr. Mitchell's work stands as the first scholarly treatise on Fort Defiance. Meares Island, or a fragment of its history, had now been possessed by archaeology.

To Hayes goes the last word, for he had pressed the search for years and delighted in the final result. He could see the larger view. He wrote:

> Adventure Cove was an important base for the *Columbia*, from which she sallied forth in March 1792, to carry on her trade, but more importantly, to discover the Columbia River. Captain Cook (1778) and Captain Vancouver (1792) both missed this river, although well-equipped, for those times, with splendid vessels and crews. The Northwest Coast in 1792 was uncharted, except for Nootka Sound (Cook, 1778), and an almost unknown region of the world. Explorers were still seeking the mythical Straits of Anian. It was not unlike Little America in the Antarctic of today. The accomplishment of Captain Gray, in the *Columbia*, in establishing winter quarters and building a vessel, the *Adventure*, was an outstanding feat. It is for this reason that the finding of the exact site is historically important.[135]

We retrace our steps. We must now return to the few days before the *Columbia* and the *Adventure* made their exits from Clayoquot Sound. Specifically, we examine what happened on March 27, 1792: the destruction of Opitsat village.

When I composed my Meares Island historical account for the legal team, I left Boit to speak for himself. What he says of the attack on Opitsat is part of the record. It cannot be wished away. What else could I do? But no other evidence from his contemporaries supports his story. Haswell and Hoskins, there at the time, do not mention it in their narratives. This is odd. And Gray's own account does not survive.

History "in the dock," so to speak, takes on added meaning. And unsurprisingly, when the *Meares Island* case came to trial in 1993, the

PART I The Empire of Fortune

burning of Opitsat, as recounted by Boit and by nobody else, came up for close examination. I had no doubt it would. Mr. Woodward questioned Dr. Barbara Lane, the anthropologist and ethnologist of our team of experts, on the matter. She made the point that the weather had been very wet at that time. Using flint to start fires would have been difficult. Further, many of those persons who lived at Opitsat had relocated to other sites at the end of the herring season. That would explain, incidentally, why Boit does not mention any damage to persons. Dr. Lane did not discount the difficulties that existed between Wickaninnish and Gray; nor did she shy away from the fact that war and vengeance were possibilities. But on the basis of what she knew about the documentation, she did not think Boit's written appreciation of the episode credible.

I have my doubts about this. Why would Boit lie? Did he write his account to do damage to Gray's reputation? No. Had he had been overlooked for promotion? No. Maybe Boit exaggerated the damage caused. If the attack were as destructive as Boit says, surely Hoskins and Haswell would have mentioned it. Or maybe not: perhaps it was all in a day's work.

So what did happen on Meares Island more than 225 years ago? And why? Over many years I looked elsewhere for confirming evidence and came up with three accounts from the time that provide a plausible explanation of Gray's motivation.

The various diaries and journals of the American officers and mates that survive from this date in history tell of growing, unmistakable tensions between the Clayoquot peoples and the Americans. The former, quite naturally, wondered if the Americans were going to take up permanent residence, which must have given them cause for alarm. The Americans found themselves placed on the defensive, which was their natural inclination, given that they were in the lands of a very populous people of warlike propensities. Besides, the Americans would have known of other encounters in those very waters, or on the Northwest Coast more generally. Fresh in their minds was the violence on the coast north of Cape Mendocino (mentioned in Chapter 3), where in August 1788 they

Fort Defiance and the Destruction of Opitsat

had met canoes of fierce and warlike bands addicted to thieving. At or near Tillamook Bay, thirty miles south of where the Columbia River enters the Pacific, the Americans used muskets and swivel guns to drive off the canoes intent on piracy. A Black sailor from Madeira, isolated from the ship, was killed ashore. The name Murderers' Harbor was given to this place.[136]

Near Adventure Cove, Native military and political power was being exercised. Wintertime demonstrations intensified. On January 18, 1792, an attack was made on the *Columbia*—mainly a demonstration of force, it included profuse verbal declarations or, as Boit described them, "a most hideous hooping . . ., and at every shout they seem'd to come nearer." One of the Americans saw "many large Canoes off the entrance of the Cove." All hands were brought to arms in preparation to repel an attack. "After this," Boit writes, "no more of the Natives visited Adventure Cove, except some old women and young girls, who brought us berries and fish—and most probable they was sent as *spies*."[137]

We may imagine that Gray's destruction of Opitsat, described by Boit, was designed to check the Natives and destroy their military power. It could be classified as a reprisal combined with a pre-emptive raid, and was a premediated act, not done in a fit of anger or fear. New Englanders were old hands at this sort of "forest diplomacy." So here we have a plausible motivation for Gray, and this incident is corroborated. Haswell also writes that on February 20 there were 2,000 well-armed men in Opitsat village. Informants said the Opitsat men intended to attack the "Highskaht" (presumably the Hesquiaht), but Haswell and others regarded this as a pretext—their real intent was to attack the Americans.[138]

Searching further, examining the various narrative and journals of Captain George Vancouver's visit to the Northwest Coast, I found a general description given by Captain Gray on April 29, 1792, that is 33 days after the Opitsat event, as to why the Americans might be moved to such an act of revenge. This is to be found in the journal of Archibald Menzies, surgeon and naturalist in Vancouver's expedition.

PART I The Empire of Fortune

As mentioned earlier, on the 29th Vancouver sent Menzies and Puget in a boat across to the *Columbia* to determine what Gray knew about the prospects of a northwest passage. After expressing his astonishment at Meares' claim that he had discovered such a seaway, Gray turned to the matter of Clayoquot Sound. My opinion is that it was a matter of some consideration to the American captain, otherwise he would not have mentioned it.

Here is what Menzies recalled of the conversation:

> He further informd us that in his present Voyage he had been 9 months on the Coast & winterd at Cloiquot a district a little to the Eastward of Nootka where he built a small sloop which was at this time employd in collecting Furs to the Northward about Queen Charlotte's Isles—That in the winter the Natives of Cloiquat calling to their aid 3 or 4 other Tribes collected in the number of upwards of three thousand to attack his Vessel, but their premeditated schemes being discovered to him by a Native of the Sandwich Islands he had on board whom the Chiefs had attempted to sway over to their diabolic plots in soliciting him to wet the locks & priming of the Musquets & Guns before they boarded. By this means he was fortunately enabled by timely precautions to frustrate their horrid stratagems at the very moment they had assembled to execute them.[139]

An echo of this is to be found in Vancouver's published narrative. It is clear that Gray intended that Vancouver should be warned of the warlike propensities of the Nuu-chah-nulth.

Menzies' recounting of the meeting with Captain Gray just after the event is as close as we will get to confirming this matter. Gray's view was that his vessel was going to be attacked by a large number of Natives gathered from various locations. A sailor's first instinct is to save his ship, and thus Gray sent Boit to put the matter out of all contention. Gray did not mention the Opitsat matter directly. Or if he did, Menzies and Puget did not take note of it. But what Gray did say seems like an epitome of his feelings about the whole matter. It is close to being the corroborative evidence we have been seeking. If he ordered the village's destruction, it was part of a general reprisal against the gathering of warriors intent on attacking the American ships. In Gray's thinking, the second

Fort Defiance and the Destruction of Opitsat

(the Native attack) would be more important than the first (his own attack on the village).

Thus, in conclusion, I would not, as Dr. Lane did, say that Boit's written appreciation of the episode lacked credibility; only that it stands nakedly alone. It is true that Gray did not tell Menzies and Puget that Opitsat had been destroyed, but what he did tell them could explain why he destroyed the village, if he did.

One last and illuminating point from an outside source. In the journal of Charles Bishop, captain of the British trading vessel *Ruby*, we have an insightful explanation of Wickaninnish's possible motivation for approaching the Americans at Adventure Cove so boldly and so often. This occurred three years after that violent year of 1792. When Bishop met Wickaninnish, the chief gave the captain two otter skins, and in return received a beautiful greatcoat and a hat. The preliminaries had been accomplished. Bishop then purchased a good many furs from that chief. Now came a twist in the story, unique in trading annals of this coast. Wickaninnish, to the captain's surprise, demanded to buy the *Ruby*, for which he would procure the necessary furs. He even suggested that Bishop and his crew could sail to China with an American snow—that is, the *Columbia*, which had gone into the cove to clean her bottom before clearing the coast for the voyage to China. Sale of the *Ruby* was impossible, naturally, for Captain Bishop did not own the vessel. Discussions continued, involving two brothers of the chief. Bishop took down these details of what Wickaninnish was hoping for: a schooner-rigged vessel, 54 feet in length and 16 feet in beam, mounting six carriage guns and complete with gig or whaleboat.[140] Such a vessel was never forthcoming, it is true. But the point is this: Wickaninnish wanted to keep his ascendancy, and possessing his own sailing vessel—his own instrument of sea power—would be advantageous to his wealth, power and position. Here is exhibited Wickaninnish's acumen at business and his foresight. Having a schooner would also bring the Clayoquot people greater power and prestige, plus commercial benefits.

This is a possible, and I think likely, explanation for the attempted seizure of the *Columbia*.

In any event, the Opitsat episode did not halt the trade: in later years American ships arrived and departed—for example, the *Hope* in the summer of 1792; the *Jefferson*, which wintered 1793–1794; and the *Union* in 1795. "Thereafter," writes Mary Malloy, "the decline in sea otters led to a decreasing trade."[141]

6
Tales the *Tonquin* Tells

We will find no makúk in this next chapter of Clayoquot history, no meeting of minds and aspirations. Communication across cultural lines is one of humanity's most stubborn problems. Gestures and verbal signs might express intentions and meanings, but they are commonly misinterpreted and misunderstood. Uncertainty can easily exist in these circumstances.[142] Patterns of doing business on this coast were not known to the visitors, who knew the sea otter trade only by hearsay. In the event, trade broke down, a great ship was blown up, and nearly all aboard perished or were badly wounded. The story of the *Tonquin* has all the dimensions of a fateful encounter caused by cultural assumptions and misunderstandings, and it will continue to live on as a subject of fascination and mystery, a story of how badly matters can go wrong when communications break down and aspirations and expectations are not met, echoing down through the years.

Historians are itinerants. We wander through time and space, trying to make sense of how problems of the past arose in the first place, how they developed over time, and how they were resolved—if they were. These are long arcs of history. If there is spice to the story, some romance or even attention-getting tragedy, the work moves along a little more quickly and with some hoped-for intensity. Or we might run into a dead end. Many historians abandon the pursuit in despair, never manage to take up a second project.[143] On occasion, surprises present themselves. More often than not we historians soldier on alone, in quest of our particular version of the holy grail, but the world of the working historian is always enlivened when he or she meets an unusual and well-informed person in the history line. Here is an example, bearing directly on the *Tonquin* affair.

In late July 1968 I came in contact with Edmund Hayes of Portland, whose office was in the US National Bank Building. In those days, historians sent letters by mail to one another and expected something in return. We might even exchange offprints of articles. I was then an aspiring young lecturer at Western Washington State College (now Western Washington University) in Bellingham. I knew of Hayes as a persistent historical sleuth. I had written requesting a copy of the recently published issue of *Oregon Historical Quarterly* that contained his article about Fort Defiance and Adventure Cove, Clayoquot Sound. Hayes happily obliged me with a copy of the issue in question. In consequence, I had to hand much information about this early chapter in Clayoquot Sound and sea otter history when I came to write my own account of this incursion by Captains Gray and Kendrick into Vancouver Island's waters, the building of the little schooner *Adventure*, and the destruction of Opitsat, Meares Island. Copies of maps, charts and photos, printed therein, also gave immediacy to my inquiries about the unsolved mystery of the *Tonquin*.

In his letter (July 30, 1968), Hayes proceeded to give an update and summary of his proceedings: "I returned the end of last week from an extended cruise up Vancouver Island's West Coast, which I believe, is the 8th trip I have made to that interesting area. The main purpose of this cruise was to obtain information concerning the ship *Tonquin* which was sunk, presumably, in Clayoquot in 1811. The exact location of this vessel, as you undoubtedly know, has been very uncertain and sought by many others. I believe we obtained some fundamental information concerning the possible

Paintings of *Columbia Rediviva* by George Davidson, illustrator for Robert Gray's second voyage on the ship: (top) canoes greet the ship, which fires a salute; (right) the ship braves a squall under full sail.
Oregon Historical Society Research Library

J.J. Astor's *Tonquin* before meeting its fiery doom, an epic made famous by Washington Irving's book *Astoria*.
Edmund Fanning, 1838, Wikimedia Commons

A panoramic view of houses and canoes at Ahousat (circa 1914).
Alberni Valley Museum Photograph Collection PN01913

In ceremonial welcome to a potlatch, a large canoe filled with twelve honoured guests is carried by men using poles under the canoe, on the shore at Opitsat on Meares Island. A Union Jack flies from a pole at the canoe's stern (circa 1916).
Alberni Valley Museum Photograph Collection PN02077

View of Clayoquot village (Opitsat) showing two carved poles, one probably a grave marker. The canoe in the foreground may also contain a burial, and carved houseposts can be seen on the left side of the picture (circa 1900).
Alberni Valley Museum Photograph Collection PN03205

Left: Maquinna, famed chief Tsaxawasip of the Mowachaht of Nootka.
Fernando Selma, 1802, Harbour Publishing Archive
Right: John Meares, ardent merchant adventurer, master and commander, and wizard of geographical spaces. Meares Island commemorates his name.
W. Beechey, 1790, Harbour Publishing Archive

First regular trading vessel to west coast Vancouver Island ports, the lovely *Tees*, seen here approaching the dock at Alberni (circa 1910).
Robert D. Turner Collection

Famed CPR passenger and cargo carrier *Princess Maquinna*, "Old Faithful," linked Victoria with all major west coast Vancouver Island communities. Built in Esquimalt in 1913, and shown here in the 1920s, she was a lifeline to the wider world for decades.
Cyril Littlebury photo, Robert D. Turner Collection

Indigenous men and women, many of them cannery workers, depended on the *Princess Maquinna* for transport to and from places of work. Here are some of them, with their belongings, crowding the foredeck.
Harbour Publishing Archive

Top: Declaration of Meares Island as a Tribal Park, April 21, 1984.
Wilderness Committee Archive

Right: "Save Meares" protest of 1,200 people gathered on the steps and lawn of the British Columbia Legislature in Victoria on October 21, 1984.
Wilderness Committee Archive

Left: Meares Island crisis led to others, seared deep in memory. Here is the 1993 Clayoquot "War in the Woods" protest on the Legislature grounds, Victoria. Meanwhile, on forest access roads, protesters put up blockades. These led to arrests, charges, and many criminal sentences.
Wilderness Committee Archive

January 1985 report of events of November 21, 1984:
(top right) Moses Martin, chief councillor of the Tla-o-qui-aht, tells loggers that the island is his people's garden and they are not to cut the trees;
(top left) tree protectors greet the loggers' boat as it lands at C'is-a-quis (Heelboom Bay); (middle left) RCMP officials observe the confrontation; (bottom left) a small flotilla of fishing boats meets MacMillan Bloedel's crew boat, *Kennedy Queen*, and explains their resolve to protect Meares from logging.
Wilderness Committee Archive

Aerial view of Meares Island.
Adrian Dorst photo, Wilderness Committee Archive

A spectacular cedar tree found along the Big Tree Trail on Meares Island, where some old-growth is estimated to be more than 1,000 years old.
christopher, Adobe Stock

spot but as we only had one scuba diver, it was impossible to find any of her wreckage."[144]

As Rick said to the police chief Captain Renault, "Louis, I think this is the beginning of a beautiful friendship." And indeed it was. A diversion is called for here. American philanthropy in regard to museums and galleries differs from the Canadian experience; tax law fully favours American benefactors in their pursuit of cultural excellence. Hence, nowadays, the United States has the Public Broadcasting System, sustained by big foundations and individuals; Canada has the CBC, backed by no foundations except the taxpayers of Canada. More significantly, Hayes was the powerhouse chair of the Oregon Historical Society board, and he and his business friends, without qualification, backed the energetic executive director, Thomas Vaughan, in making that organization into arguably the finest state museum, gallery and archives in the western United States. In contrast, it saddened me then, as it does now, how little support our wee Maritime Museum of British Columbia receives, suffering the death of a thousand cuts.

In 1978, ten years after my friendship with Hayes began, it brought me once more to the City of Roses, Portland, this time to speak at a conference on Oregon and the bicentenary of the United States. Two centuries before, in 1778, just at the time James Cook was visiting Nootka, the American patriots were in full revolt against King George III. What a contrast between affairs on the Atlantic seaboard and those of our distant, foggy coast. My task was to explain what British navigators were doing on the Northwest Coast and why they resisted so strongly Imperial Spain's "pretensions" to full rights of trade and sovereignty. In this, my first publication about Nootka Sound, I filled in the basics of what British explorers and fur traders had experienced on this coast from 1778 to 1840.[145]

Later I returned to Portland to speak on other themes and to work in the archives there, where, thanks to a munificent grant, many documents on John Meares, other fur traders and George Vancouver's imperial mission had been copied from London archives. Americans do things in big ways, and they love heroes and heroines.

PART I The Empire of Fortune

At the Oregon Historical Society they knew all about my sea otter ships and their captains, all about trade to celestial China: *Soft Gold* they entitled the exhibition they mounted some years later—all about the sea otter business and vital cultural exchanges between Northwest Coast Natives and early European traders and explorers.[146]

But to return to benefactor Hayes—and indeed to a related story—he was then so attracted to the story of the *Tonquin* in Meares Island waters that he arranged to have the acknowledged dean of maritime artists of the Northwest Coast, Hewitt Jackson, prepare plans and make a model of the *Tonquin* for the Oregon Historical Society. You will find it there on display to this day. Hayes opened his wallet, wrote all the cheques. And what a fabulous model it is, based on the most thorough research and demanding the most exquisite construction. I attended the opening of that exhibition. Later I wangled an invitation to visit the reclusive and fearful Jackson to see his plans, drawings and models and discuss marine history with the living legend. I say "fearful" because he worried, perhaps with due reason, that his work was being pirated, used without credit or recompense. And here's the next part of the story.

In 1981, by appointment, I climbed the stairs of Hewitt Jackson's white clad house in Kirkland, Washington, to meet the great artist. I was welcomed by a cautious person in his late sixties bearing a happy countenance of fair and freckled skin, long white hair tied up behind and hanging below his shoulders; his snowy moustache and beard gave the impression of a seadog who had at last come to shore after long voyages. He was ex-Air Corps. As a lad he had sailed on a schooner carrying lumber from the Columbia River to Australia. He had formal training as a draftsman and worked for oceanographers at the University of Washington. He led me through to his studio at the back of his darkened house, where books were stacked; here instruments of measurement and magnifying glasses were tools of his trade. Paintings and drawings stood arranged in vertical files, and rolls of draft plans piled in assorted clumps. Here was order on a grand scale. We sat down to talk over coffee. He knew my work, had my books to hand. At his request I happily signed his copies.

Tales the *Tonquin* Tells

Jackson wanted to know all about those insightful Admiralty in-letters that had been my bread and butter as a historian when re-creating a world we had lost—that of the nineteenth-century Royal Navy on our coast. He wanted to know, too, about the pleasures of working in the Public Record Office. He knew the ships I was talking about; I knew their background stories—their tonnages, drafts, steam fittings, rigs and more. One of them was the British sloop-of-war *Racoon*, a near contemporary of the *Tonquin*, that had run up the Union Jack at Astoria during the 1812 war. He yearned to hear how I came to know all this. I told him of London student days, and of train journeys from central London out to Maze Hill Station (closest to the National Maritime Museum) and the Park Row walk leading to the museum. I described the statue of General Wolfe standing high on the hill, and nearby the Royal Observatory with its white pole holding the big red ball in anticipation of the daily drop at 1 p.m., indicating Greenwich Mean Time by which clocks around the world could be set. This was, I recounted, the purposeful walk in expectation of more treasures to be found, "history's gold." And then it was past museum security and upstairs to the vast oak tables where the dusty documents awaited long hours of examination, each hour yielding some golden nugget or, sadly, none at all. I told him of ventures to Scott Polar Research Institute, Cambridge, examining papers about John Franklin's futile attempt to rendezvous with the British sloop-of-war *Blossom*, Captain Beechey's ship—which during a happier part of the ship's cruise found Pitcairn Island, where Beechey interviewed the last of the *Bounty* mutineers and learned the sordid story of the end of that experiment in mutiny.

The afternoon lengthened, and with it came on the gathering gloom. A glass of sherry appeared. I told my host how I would shift places of research depending on the weather: if London was excessively cold that particular day, I would head for the well-heated Hudson's Bay Archives in the City of London (where researchers were given tea from the trolley), but if the weather were scorching, that would be the day to go to the cold and ominous Public Record Office, Chancery Lane, where "central heating" existed but all radiators

PART I The Empire of Fortune

were stone cold. The City of London of the 1960s was still experiencing the aftermath of the Blitz. There were huge craters near Hudson's Bay House, I told him, and many an open wall shored up by big timbers to prevent collapse. I remember it to this day.

As to Hewitt Jackson and his experiences, I did not ask him about his private life. If he had wanted to tell me, he would have. Nor did I quiz him on his technique. I was only there to soak up the ambience, to take in the essence of what a true marine artist is like. Here I was at the pinnacle of the marine artist's line of work. His deserved reputation as a maritime scholar and an assiduous researcher began with his work on the *Discovery*. He had found there were no trustworthy visual reproductions of George Vancouver's ship. He patiently recreated all the details, and he showed me the full-sized ship's plan, a copy retrieved from the National Maritime Museum, Greenwich.

Captain Vancouver's friendly rival Bodega y Quadra provides words that became Hewitt's mantra: "I pressed on, taking fresh trouble for granted." It is like that for any working marine artist, or a maritime historian, for that matter, if serious about the craft and the project. I agree with what Thomas Vaughan and Bruce T. Hamilton wrote of Hewitt's recreation of the pageant of Northwest maritime exploration: "Jackson's rich mixed-media technique, combined with now prodigious research-skills and dazzling draftsmanship, have yielded a treasure of magnificent studies and finished drawings, acclaimed by a growing body of connoisseurs in North America and Great Britain."[147] They are brilliant representations born of intense study and mastery of materials brought together in a lifetime at sea under sail and steam, to say nothing of countless hours at his drawing table.

In any event, that long afternoon we had a most pleasant time and a good chat, facilitated by the fact that my first book, with the necessarily long-winded title *The Royal Navy and the Northwest Coast of North America, 1810–1914: A Study in British Maritime Ascendancy*, had been published a few years before, in 1971. We did our own form of potlatching.

As I was taking my leave, and carrying with me his gracious

well wishes for more prosperous voyages in the writing of history, he turned and said, "Just a minute, I have something for you." He returned with a copy of the January/February 1980 issue of *The American West* with, on the front and back covers, Captain Vancouver's *Discovery* and *Chatham* making discoveries in Puget Sound. He signed the front cover. And inside he inked this inscription: AFTER A GREAT VISIT, BEST OF LUCK, GOOD VOYAGE, . . . ETC followed by his signature. Memories of that day live with me even now. In my mind's eye, out from the gloom of the house in the northern woods, I see shining the bright light of excellence, of supreme dedication to task, and of the ardent pursuit of perfection. His was, and is, the true art. There is no substitute in our line of work for authenticity.

The wandering scholar, enriched by such an encounter, continues his more prosaic travel. But, on reflection, I have never forgotten how one search leads to another. My correspondence with Hayes had led to Vaughan and then to Jackson. Then, all of a sudden, the whole started to loop back upon itself.

I was then, I believe, the only scholar doing naval history of the West Coast. That may seem strange at this date, but it is true. Peace was the thing in those post–Vietnam War days, and even discussing weapons of naval warfare was seen as a dangerous pursuit. Military history was frowned on save in military academies. "Study war no more" was on everyone's lips. But ships of yesteryear, particularly those of what we call "the age of fighting sail," have staying power in our imaginations. And so it was with James Cook's *Resolution* and *Discovery*, George Vancouver's *Discovery* and *Chatham*, John Meares' *Felice Adventurer*, John Jacob Astor's *Tonquin* and many other ships of our past—each with enticing stories and legendary careers.

Edmund Hayes made clear in his letter that he wanted to pick my brain on a certain matter. I expect he had learned about it from reading George Nicholson's *Vancouver Island's West Coast*. In his letter of inquiry, Hayes wrote, "Another vessel which we sought was the trading sloop *Kingfisher* which was overcome by the Ahousaht in August 1864 and her captain, Stephens and Mate, Wilson were murdered. In

PART I The Empire of Fortune

October HMS *Sutlej* and HMS *Devastation* shelled the village at Ahousat and later destroyed nine villages and 64 canoes." This incident occurred near Hesquiat, at the north end of Clayoquot Sound.

Hayes understood, and rightly, that the naval report of this retaliation by gunboats would survive among the vast Admiralty Papers in London's Public Record Office (PRO). He wrote: "I am not sure whether I have the initials correct but it is the large records office not far from the British Museum which I visited one time in the past." The PRO was then in Chancery Lane; it now is in Kew, Surrey, under a new name, the National Archives. And, I might add, it is the most fabulous archive in the world, for the British were not only meticulous record keepers but also global citizens. Hayes knew that I had been researching coastal naval history and that I was interested in the history of the sea otter trade. He not only asked me for details as to how he could get that report (I supplied him with a study copy), but said that if ever I were in Portland, he hoped I would look him up and we might discuss these matters of mutual interest.[148] Over the years, at conferences or research visits to Portland, the association was maintained. Hayes visited Burnaby for the Captain Cook and His Times conference in 1978, and was in Vancouver for the Captain George Vancouver history gathering. It is these sorts of personal connections, with collateral benefits, that keep historians going in their line of work. Incidentally, and not to be forgotten, I told Hayes that I would be writing a companion book on gunboat activities on the British Columbia coast, and that the *Kingfisher* story would play a special part. He was pleased at the prospect. And when *Gunboat Frontier: British Maritime Authority and Northwest Coast Indians, 1846–1890*, was published by UBC Press in 1984, I gladly sent a copy his way. I think it my most original book, and even today it is still in print. The story has staying power. A chapter is devoted to the *Kingfisher* episode and the navy's reprisal. It is not a happy recounting of the past, as it gives an example of the Royal Navy "teaching Indians a lesson." Such was the pacification of the frontier.

Edmund Hayes never flagged in his quest for finding the sunken wreck or remains of Astor's ill-fated *Tonquin*, so we now return to this story of one of the most famous ships of the American sea saga. After arriving on the stormy Northwest Coast after a six-month voyage from New York port, the *Tonquin* shuddered to safety through the tortuous channel past the roiling Columbia River bar. Earlier, two boat parties, one after another, had been swamped at a cost of eight lives in an effort to find a safe channel. The *Tonquin* brought Astor employees to establish a fur-trading post on the south shore of the Columbia River estuary—an emporium in the wilderness, some thought. This ship's subsequent voyage to northern waters ended in disaster. Her shockingly destructive disappearance, the loss of her crew and the mystery of where their bones lie all add terrible details to a chapter in the larger epic of men against the sea. Not least is the death by explosion of between 80 and 200 Clayoquot; the estimates vary wildly, but none are small.

The particulars speak out from the documents and accounts in compelling fashion, moving slowly and surely, this historian thinks, to sure and inescapable destruction. We retrace our steps, begin at the beginning, although a slight detour is called for first. Our sorrowful story begins in the early nineteenth century, almost two decades after Gray's wintering at Adventure Cove. Just as the maritime fur traders had made the Northwest Coast (with main rendezvous location Nootka) a hot place of economic activity, hardy and often hungry overlanders from eastern North America were advancing across the vast yawning spaces of the greater northwest to create a similar hotbed farther south. These commercial agents of empire by sea and by land were drawing that far shore and its peoples into global commerce, meeting local needs.

Canadians led the quest, in keeping with what they had done since the days of Champlain and Nicolet. The Hudson's Bay Company, founded 1670, had come south and west from Arctic waters to dominate a trade that stretched nearly to the Continental Divide. But it was the North West Company, the Montreal-based trade forerunner of a transcontinental Canada, that was moving overland to the Pacific coast. In 1793, one of the boldest and most highly motivated rivals of the HBC, the forward-thinking Nor'wester Alexander

PART I The Empire of Fortune

Mackenzie, set out from Peace River, his advance base upriver from Fort Chipewyan on Great Slave Lake, and crossed the "sea of mountains," as he called the Pacific mountain cordillera. It was a trek of unimagined hazards. Against all odds he reached Pacific tidewater. "Alexander Mackenzie, from Canada, by Land, 22nd July, 1793" is the famous inscription he left on Mackenzie Rock, Dean Channel. Thus was laid down what I like to think of as the charter of a Canadian dominion from sea to sea. Mackenzie traced a northwest passage by land, one that would be followed in due time by telegraph, railroads and road. His book, published in 1801, presciently warned the British government to act on his vision and design of great commercial promise before the Americans could seize the day. He proposed the formation of a "Fishery and Fur Trade Company" to open a communication through the North American continent. This, he said, would be of incalculable commercial advantage to Britain: Canada's destiny lay with Pacific commerce.[149]

No one read this volume—this compelling geopolitical treatise on the concept of the empire of the St. Lawrence linking London with Montreal, and Montreal with Nootka and other trade posts on the far Pacific shore—more eagerly or more closely than Thomas Jefferson, then US Secretary of State. He took action, convincing Congress to fund a western reconnaissance to the Pacific. Thus, in 1805, US Army captains Meriwether Lewis and William Clark arrived at the estuary of the Columbia River. "Ocian in view! O! the joy!" the much-relieved Clark scribbled in his notebook when he saw the wide Pacific on November 7. The party built a wintering shelter in a wooded, damp place they called Fort Clatsop. They departed near winter's close and reached St. Louis in late September, sending reports to Jefferson on the prospects of a western empire that might be added to the Union. Captain Clark's map included reference to Point St. Raphael (Raphael Point), Clayoquot, Nootka Sound and the Strait of Juan de Fuca, all gathered from Captain Vancouver's engraved chart.[150] In other words, American cartographers began to possess the west coast of Vancouver Island.

Jefferson, though no fur trade businessman, demonstrated

geopolitical vision and grasping tendencies: he had arranged the purchase of Louisiana from Napoleon in 1803, giving the United States title to lands west of the Mississippi and north of Spain's Mexico. The northern limit was ill-defined save to say that the watersheds draining to the Mississippi were included. At the time it seemed that Spain's ancient claims to the far Northwest Coast could not be sustained. Therein lay Jefferson's opportunity: he could ally in informal ways with Spain against Britain, and bring in Russia, too. A contest sprang up between the Nor'westers and the Pacific Fur Company, an American firm headed up by John Jacob Astor of New York. Here was a naked American quest for empire in internationally contested lands. As described by historian Bernard De Voto, "Astoria followed from the expedition of Lewis and Clark as the flight of an arrow follows the release of the bowstring."[151]

All these larger movements of history were to have an influence on the history of the west coast of Vancouver Island and Meares Island, particularly the troubled future of the Pacific Fur Company and the trading expedition of Astor's *Tonquin*, which ended in one gigantic explosion in Clayoquot Sound.

In New York in 1810, Astor founded his commercial trust, with the aim of exploiting the trade to China, supplying the Russians in Sitka, Kodiak and elsewhere, and planting the first seeds of American monopolistic empire at the mouth of the Columbia River—thus beating Mackenzie and the Canadians at their own game. Russian authorities, also keen to check the vision of Mackenzie, encouraged the plan. Thus Astor determined that two expeditions would go to the Columbia country—one by sea, the other by land. By March 1811 the one party had arrived by sea in the *Tonquin* and began building the fort called Astoria; the land party arrived in 1812.

Meanwhile, methodical Nor'wester David Thompson had instructions to map the Columbia country and determine the nature of its main stream and tributaries, all with the intention of exploiting the fur trade of the far west. His task was gigantic! So much rested on his energies and zeal. So many obstacles lay in his way. Given the resources at his disposal and the complicated nature of cordilleran

PART I The Empire of Fortune

geography, he was, not surprisingly, late (not tardy) in reaching the Columbia estuary. His task—that of years—began in 1807–1808 when he wintered at Kootenai House, north of Lake Windermere. There Natives from near and far came to trade. Some, seeking allies against their dreaded enemies the Blackfoot, described the country he wished to explore. He wrote, "After drawing a chart of their Country . . . from thence to the Sea, a[nd] describing the Nations along the River, they assured me that from this House to the sea a[nd] back again was only the Voyage of a Summer Moon." Other duties took Thompson away for a while. Company directors, meeting in Fort William on Lake Superior in the summer of 1810, decided they must claim and occupy the Columbia watershed before the Americans took hold there. On July 3, 1811, at Kettle Falls, Thompson set out in a canoe, "by the Grace of God . . . on a voyage down the Columbia River to explore this river, in order to open out a passage for the interior trade with the Pacific Ocean."[152] At the mouth of the Snake River, he claimed the country for Britain as part of its territories and stated that the North West Company intended to erect a factory at this place. The next day Natives told him the disheartening news that Lewis and Clark had passed this way years before and that more recently a ship had arrived at the mouth of the river. This was the *Tonquin*, and the matter is discussed below. The fact of the matter was that the river was now known, a great mystery disclosed. All that Lewis and Clark had found in 1805 and 1806 was about to be turned into a commercial empire of the Columbia.

On July 15, 1811, Thompson came down the river to Astoria in a canoe that sported a North West Company–marked Red Ensign on its stern. Thompson's arrival surprised the Astorians.[153] Thompson took it all in stride, thanked God for the safe arrival of his party and their canoe, and was politely received by the rival traders and managers. He told them that a coalition of the two companies was then being undertaken, and he produced as evidence an official letter to the effect that Astor had accepted the Nor'westers' offer. In fact, the negotiation had failed, but on the spot, at and near the mouth of the great river, warm within the confines of Astoria's walls, it seemed as if the rivalry had come to a happy ending—and a truce. Our admiration, or more correctly speaking my admiration, for Thompson grows. He was a cool hand in difficult circumstances, a brilliant wilderness traveller, and a self-contained individual, God-fearing and stolid. He was a trader, of course, but we like to see him best as a surveyor, geographer and mapmaker. Admiring Indigenous people referred to him as "He who shoots the stars." He had already set up a post at Lake Windermere, upper Columbia River, and had built a number of other posts besides, thus establishing footholds of trade in the interior west of the Continental Divide. But the Astorians had beaten him to the mouth of the Columbia, thus forestalling the imaginative scheme, loaded with possibilities, that Mackenzie had advanced for a Pacific network of commerce with bases at Nootka and at the mouth of the Columbia. It is not surprising then that Thompson has been attacked by historians for his dalliance, for he could have been there first had he not been so methodical in his surveying and setting up of establishments—but that's a story for another time and place.

So we turn our attention to those rivals of the Nor'westers, the Astorians. It is clear that Astor and the Russians intended to forge a commercial alliance. For a moment this was stalled by disagreements over the respective boundaries claimed by the Americans and the Russians in northwest America. But finally, in 1812, the two companies agreed not to trade in each other's lands, the boundaries of which were left undefined. Astor got an American monopoly of trade at Sitka, under promise not to trade arms and ammunition to the Aleuts (who were held in slavery by the Russians), and the freedom to carry the Russian firm's goods to Canton. By the time Astor signed this agreement, in December 1812, Britain and the United States were at war. The War of 1812, not least in Pacific waters, ruined Astor's chances of success at Astoria. Many misfortunes beset his ships, and the *Tonquin* disaster, to which we now turn, ranked highest in destroying Astor's dream of empire. Washington Irving, the famous diplomat and author, related the story in telling fashion in his 1834 book *Astoria*. Consequently, well-informed US citizens came

PART I The Empire of Fortune

to know what had transpired at Clayoquot Sound. It is a melancholy tale, told on a large scale.

No fort erected on the Northwest Coast could be self-sustaining in foodstuffs and trading goods. The raising of crops and the arts of animal husbandry were not then exercised there, or, for that matter, elsewhere north of San Francisco. Salmon and deer flesh were not enough for the newcomers. Such a start-up establishment necessarily depended on regular imports by sea. So the *Tonquin*, a three-master of 269 tons, was a settlement and supply vessel besides being an intended coastal trader.

The *Tonquin*'s commander was Captain Jonathan Thorn, a stern, irascible and still relatively young naval officer who had served with conspicuous bravery in US naval actions against the Barbary pirates of Algiers. On leave from the navy, he accepted command of the *Tonquin*. The voyage round Cape Horn was filled with bickering and feuding between the captain, his crew and his passengers. Ignominy has been rained on his head for his high-handed actions. Yet looked at differently, we realize that he had been given a mixed crew that was probably unprepared for the rigours of North Pacific sailing and coastal navigation. He was in a hurry. Trading was not his line but offered financial gain. In mentality, his passengers differed wildly from him. Perhaps his mission was doomed from the time he cleared port at Sandy Hook, New York, on September 8, 1810. The reader is asked to keep all these factors in mind when judging what led to the tragedy and led to such loss of life and such misfortune and misery.

The Canadian fur traders who sailed with Thorn from New York exhibited a different character than he was used to. Most were Scots, strong individualists, disliking any master. Many had been enticed by Astor from employment with the North West Company. From the outset, differences of opinion bordered on acrimony. Alexander McKay, main trader and a partner in the firm, was a master of wilderness travel and bush diplomacy. He had been Alex Mackenzie's right-hand man in that epic 1793 westward passage, and he knew what was described at the time as "Indian character." He also knew of Mackenzie's hope to trade with the Russians in Alaska. He comprehended the politics of barter. Experienced in frontier matters, we can see McKay as the opposite of Thorn.

Astor had warned Thorn in regards to the Northwest Coast: "All accidents which have as yet happened there arose in too much confidence in the Indians."[154] What expectations did Astor lay on Thorn? Astor, like Jefferson, believed in exclusive possession; thus did they combine to imagine, if a little wildly, an independent republic formed on Spanish-claimed lands that would keep out other traders. A complicated arrangement. In order to achieve this, they would profit by trading with the Russians in Alaska, open up trade to China via Hawaii, outmanoeuvre the Nor'westers in the Columbia country and even push the Bostonians out of the sea otter trade. This was a New York scheme, one promoted by the leader who had come from Waldorf, Germany, selling clarinets, mouth harps and other instruments. Astor's problem, and his mistake, was that he worked from the top down rather than building up from the bottom, as did the Bostonians and the British traders, who selected their commercially minded mariners from experienced mates and midshipmen.

The *Tonquin* reached the mouth of the Columbia on March 22, 1811, eight months from home port. Thorn did not have an up-to-date chart of this hazardous river entrance, with its constantly shifting sands and roiling winds and seas. Whatever channel existed, none was marked. Thorn sent a boat to find and mark a channel. The first mate and four sailors perished in the attempt. He sent a second boat: three more men drowned. Undaunted, Thorn took the *Tonquin* through and, finding a place to anchor, began to send men and supplies ashore to build a post. Trader Duncan McDougall chose a spot just within the tip of Point George on the south bank for the site of a fort they called Astoria. The work proceeded dispiritedly: misery prevailed on that damp and dark shoreline. An establishment 75 by 80 feet was laid out, with a dwelling house and a trading house, all within a stockade. Such was Astor's infant seat of empire on Pacific shores.

What, you might ask, has this to do with Clayoquot and Meares Island? A good deal, for harmony on board a working ship, where discipline is essential and procedure in trade must be conspicuously followed to meet Native demand, was fundamental for success in the sea otter trade. And it must be remembered that the Indigenous Peoples of Clayoquot Sound were masters of trade. They expected gifts to facilitate friendship in advance of trade. They expected outsiders would respect their protocols. They were heavily armed and they were militant. They also had old scores to settle, Gray's destruction of Opitsat being one. There was another incident, on August 8, 1792, when a clash occurred between Wickaninnish and Captain Brown of the British ship *Butterworth*. Brown had sent a party to raid one of Wickaninnish's villages of furs, killing some Natives who resisted. Captain Magee of the Boston ship *Margaret* had intervened and stopped the conflict.[155]

Seasoned mariners knew the value of good relations and protocols. But for newcomers, Clayoquot Sound could be a sea of difficulties; all outsiders who came to trade had to be on their guard. Elsewhere, too, warning signs had been put up. In 1803, Maquinna killed the crew of the *Boston* in Nootka Sound; the argument is that he was responding to insults from other traders in former years. One crew member, John Jewitt, survived to tell the tale. Can there be any doubt that this was a dangerous coast for navigation and trade?

We cannot expect Thorn or McKay to have known about these earlier incidents at Clayoquot or elsewhere. Neither had been on sea trading voyages. Nor can we expect them to have known, as did Captain Bishop of the *Ruby*, that Wickaninnish had adopted a "take it or leave it" attitude to how trade would be carried out. Bishop, there in October 1795, recorded in his journal the Wickaninnish rule of exchange: "He Prides himself in having but one Word in a Barter: he Throws the Skins before you, these are the Furs, I want such an Article: if you object, they are taken back into the Canoe and not offered again. A Stranger not knowing this Whim of his, would loose [sic] many skins."[156] By this Bishop meant that if the preliminaries were not observed punctiliously according to the sea otter chief's rule, no further trade could be discussed and carried on. The captain, used to customary bickering and position taking, thought the chief of Clayoquot one of the easiest people to deal with in all the considerable coastal trading that he had done, from the Columbia River north to the Queen Charlotte Islands, and on the continental shore north to Portland Canal. Here, surely, is a factor in what went wrong when the *Tonquin* entered the Sound.

On June 5, Thorn steered the *Tonquin* safely outbound across the Columbia River's troublesome bar. He wanted to make the best of the summer's trading. Time was of the essence. His intention was to sail north along the coast, head for Vancouver Island's celebrated localities, trade with the Russians in southeast Alaska, then return to Astoria before clearing for China and carrying on round the world to home port in New York. No confirmation exists that the Queen Charlottes were considered a place to barter for furs, but he intended to go north to find the Russians and talk to the head man, Alexander Baranov. The distances were vast for the time available before crossing to Hawaii and China, and it does not appear that Thorn had a navigating officer on board with experience on this coast. In short, he was an innocent in matters of trade and not equipped with local knowledge of the coast. The surviving mate, John Mumford, was sent ashore just before departure. "You see how fortunate we are," said the despairing Alexander McKay to a clerk at Astoria. "The Captain, in one of his frantic fits, has now discharged the only officer on board. If you ever see us safe back, it will be a miracle."[157] They made sail for northern waters.

From the nautical observations of Cook and Vancouver, Thorn knew the latitude and longitude of the entrance to Nootka Sound—all mariners did; and from Meares' voyage account he would have known about Clayoquot Sound as well. We do not possess a copy of his instructions, which he likely kept in his head in any case. Whereas Cook, Vancouver and Meares were excellent at communications with the Natives and knew how to makúk, Thorn had no knowledge of this. He had, like Wickaninnish, a take it or leave it attitude. McKay, who sailed with him, would have been the guiding force in trade logistics but, again, his papers do not survive. Besides, he was no mariner. And so *Tonquin* set sail for the west coast of Vancouver Island.

PART I The Empire of Fortune

At Astoria weeks, then months, passed anxiously with no news of the *Tonquin*. Her return was overdue. She was the vessel upon which so much depended, for certain supplies in her hold had been destined for Astoria but had not been unloaded, so hurriedly had Thorn sailed forth on his trading venture. Cannon for the fort were in the hold of the ship. And pelts gathered from the upriver Columbia needed to be shipped to China upon *Tonquin*'s return from northern waters, and letters sent home and communications maintained with the outside world. It is hard for us nowadays, connected as we are instantaneously with every part of the world by satellite or landline, to imagine the isolation of Astoria. Traders lived with uncertainty and loneliness, overcome by rain and wind and the psychological effects of a forested, water-drenched and stormy shore. It is not paranoia; it is a fear of solitary abandonment. The operators and workers of the Pacific Fur Company's Astoria post felt the same. Young clerk Alfred Seton longed for hearth, home and family.[158] Would the *Tonquin* return?

Tonquin would have sailed into oblivion had it not been for the survival of one man, Joseachal, a Quinault guide or trade facilitator, who happened to be married to a relative of Maquinna. He was brought to Astoria to be quizzed by the managers and clerks about the tragic events. The clerks took close notes, then wrote up their various account. Some appeared in books.

It is estimated that the *Tonquin* cast anchor in Clayoquot five days after departing the Columbia—likely June 10, 1811. Recent scholarship contends, with good reason, that the vessel entered Clayoquot Sound by the customary southeast entrance shown in Meares' chart. The vessel came to anchor off E-cha-chist, a village on a small island south of Wickaninnish Island. The ensuing saga spanned four days.

We will never have all the details—I wish to make that clear at the outset. Many of the accounts overlap with reinforcing details; others provide contradictory evidence. All was hearsay. Memories fade all too soon. The event was theatrical and cataclysmic. The officers, traders and crew all died, and the number of Native casualties is of catastrophic proportions. The best I can do is reconstruct the essence of the story, though I cannot claim any authenticity as to main details. We would like closure on this, but that is impossible. So here's my representation of the historical details.

When barter began, Thorn became angry at the complaint of the chief, Nookamis, about the low prices being paid for sea otter. (For Nookamis we can substitute Wickaninnish, for he set the style of trade.) Apparently Thorn threw a sea otter pelt in the chief's face, an incendiary act of stupidity and bad manners. With Wickaninnish, friendship and strict order had always been the necessary preliminary to trade, as stated by Captain Bishop of the *Ruby*.[159] And Wickaninnish disliked any visitor to his realm exhibiting a high-handed and abrupt manner. There were other matters that led to the destruction of the ship: boarding nets—the rope nets used to prevent boarding by attackers—were inadequate or not rigged, and Natives were allowed freely on board the vessel. Disregard of precautions led to disastrous consequences.

Days later, with night falling, Nookamis (and subordinate chiefs) arrived in two heavily manned canoes. Here was dire warning. The captain, alarmed, ordered the ship to make sail. Sailors scurried aloft, unloosening sails. Seven sailors in the rigging above attempted to come down to where guns and ammunition were available. It was too late. The Natives came on board, the crew took shelter and huddled below decks, and then one of the officers, taking charge—deliberately planning to take revenge—put a torch to the powder magazine. There was a vast explosion blowing everyone sky-high, arms, legs, heads and bodies flying in every direction. There was a vast volume of smoke. Not all perished; three men escaped out a stern opening and found a boat, eventually to die.

"The ship had disappeared, but the bay was covered with fragments of the vessel, with shattered canoes and Indians swimming for their lives or struggling with the agonies of death." So wrote Captain John Walbran, the specialist in place names, who had inquired into the event. "The blowing up of the *Tonquin* was long remembered in and around Clayoquot sound, the place tradition assigns to the tragedy being in Templar channel, near the old village of Echatchet."[160]

Father A.J. Brabant, featured elsewhere in these pages, provided Walbran with critically important particulars. It is said that after the explosion, blankets, scarce in those days, were found floating on the water. Father Brabant stated in 1896 that the Natives called them "Cla-o-kwat-skene," that is "belonging to Clayoquot," and that they held them in great esteem and passed them on to their children. This is proof that Clayoquot and not some other locale, such as Nahwitti, was the scene of the tragedy.[161]

Evidence supplied by Joe Martin confirms that it was his great-great-grandfather Nookamis who did the trading with Thorn and suffered the latter's abuse. Nookamis, a powerful war chief at the time, survived the blast and lived to pass down the story, but Father Brabant recounted in 1896 that very few Clayoquot men were left after the explosion. A recent view comes from Eli Enns, a Tla-o-qui-aht who works on land development for the community. He concluded that it was "a grim event in our history. Some of the community took it as a sign, that they shouldn't participate in international trade."[162] That is probably true, at least in the near term. But the Clayoquot showed great resilience in the long run, and recovered their strength and authority. Had they not, they would not have been able to engage in the warfare that occurred forty years after the *Tonquin* event.

The affront to Nookamis, Thorn's rage, McKay's failed attempts at mediation, the ill preparations made to defend the ship from boarders, the hasty readying to set to sea to escape the perils, the blowing up of the ship—these details and more survive, though only from one primary source: Joseachal, also known as Jack Ramsay or Lamesee, and we are not sure that we can place full veracity on his evidence. He had been in the mizzen chains, trembling for his life, and when the blast occurred he jumped into the water and swam ashore. He said that the whole number of Indigenous people killed on the occasion amounted to near two hundred.[163]

There are variants of the story, many coming from bits and pieces of oral evidence gathered from various Native sources or informants who were either on the spot, or wished they had been or were recounting the story third-hand. This was such a calamitous event in Northwest Coast history that it is not surprising so many—one is tempted to say "everyone who survived"—wanted to take a part, to be a witness to history, as it were. ("Where were you when President Kennedy died?" suggests itself as a parallel.) One of these attestations seems to have great merit because of the details it gives about McKay's last fight. I quote here, in full, the entry of August 11 in the Astoria headquarters' log, given to Pacific Fur Company trader Duncan McDougall by "one of our Chinook friends." This was about four weeks after the event. Some Natives had lately arrived at Astoria from a place called Neweetie with a report that the *Tonquin* had been cut off at Nootka. The geographical terms are not accurate and are suggestive, giving no reason to think the locale was not Clayoquot. Here's McDougall's recounting:

> On her arrival there, the Natives went on board to trade, but Capt. Thorn giving them only two Blankets for a Sea Otter displeased them so much that one of their chiefs gave him some insolent language, which he resented by rubbing the Otter across his face, this so enraged him that he ordered all his tribe immediately ashore. Next day the ship proceeded to Nootka, and they accompanied by a considerable number of the Neweetians (say 50 or 60 canoes in all) followed her. On their arrival they requested the Nootka Chief to join them, to which he at length assented, and next day they all repaired on board with their furs, which they traded at the rate of two Blankets & two knives for each Sea Otter, appeared very well pleased and carried on a brisk trade, until they had a sufficient number (on board) with knives to answer their diabolical purpose: when the signal was given, and four of them laid hold on Capt. Thorn whilst a fifth stabbed him in the Neck. A number got round Mr. McKay, but he made his way to the forecastle, where he killed three of them with his Dirk. However, they at length got hold of him and one gave him a mortal blow over the eye with an Iron Bludgeon. Whilst this was going on, two had sprung on each of the ship's crew, and after a short conflict killed every man on board excepting four, who got into the Magazine and there heroically terminated their fate by blowing up the Ship, with about 100 of the Indians who were on board.[164]

I do not believe the event happened at Nootka, but I think that term was used by the Neweetie as a general description of the Nuu-chah-nulth nations in that area. I have no reason to think it was not Clayoquot. All details point to it, and the event certainly was not at Neweetie.

I always pondered the possibility that there might have been other witnesses to this historical act. As I said, surprises present themselves to the working historian, and here is a case in point. When reading *Tales of Conflict*, written by B.A. McKelvie, an inspired interpreter of British Columbia's past who wrote for the Vancouver *Daily Province*, I discovered that some years after the *Tonquin* event another witness came forward with collaborative evidence—an unusual fellow indeed. He was Tent-a-coose, a slave, who had been ransomed by the Hudson's Bay Company and lived at Fort Langley. "He saw the blowing up of the *Tonquin*," writes McKelvie. "It was his favorite story, and with delight he told how more than 200 Clayoquots perished in that blast, while others were mutilated. He saw the white men slide down out of the rigging, and the next morning he watched as Lewis, standing on the deck, lured the Indians on to their doom."[165]

In this version, also described in Walbran's *British Columbia Coast Names*, the Tla-o-qui-aht people attacked the ship and killed all but five crew men, who "cleared the ship of the Indians, and after nightfall attempted, with the exception of one who was badly wounded, to make their escape in a boat. The next day the Indians crowded on board the apparently deserted ship, and when the decks were filled with them she blew up with a tremendous explosion." The wounded man was "Mr. Lewis, the clerk," and in this telling, he was the one who set the magazine alight to kill himself and the Tla-o-qui-aht. "The men who escaped in the boat were ultimately captured and killed."[166]

Where did the destruction of the *Tonquin* take place? Father Brabant obtained Native evidence that the *Tonquin* lay at anchor "near the tree- and brushwood-covered Lennard Island, called *Eitsape* by the Natives, and near the long barren rocky Village Island in Templar Channel."[167] Where did the *Tonquin* sink? John Hosie, provincial archivist of British Columbia, studied the mystery of the wreck.

He drew his conclusions in 1929. He suspected that the ship was lost just beyond Echatchets (E-cha-chist) Island. If this is correct, an anchor might be found near that location. In any case, whatever remains of the hull survives beyond the extremity of the low peninsula west of Tofino. The reason for this is that the *Tonquin* drifted from off E-cha-chist to the location proposed by Hosie's findings.[168]

Others pressed their inquiries besides Hosie. Given the importance of the ship in the founding of Astoria, it was natural that the State of Oregon would take a keen interest in finding the wreck and the anchor. The Oregon Historical Society, and particularly Edmund Hayes, led various on-site investigations, explored all the historical records collected at its Portland headquarters, and compared documentary findings with the geographic features of Clayoquot Sound. The advent of scuba apparatus made possible an extended search beginning in the 1950s, and groups from Oregon, Washington and British Columbia joined the quest. Rod Palm of Strawberry Isle Marine Research Society and David W. Griffiths, commercial diver and documentary and television producer, with a passionate interest in the ship's history, championed the search for what had come to be called the holy grail of BC shipwrecks.[169] An anchor found with trading beads encrusted on it seemed a promising sign but the beads found were not of the type traded at the time; they were of a later vintage. The hunters might wish to widen their search. I have learned that the vessel's half dozen brass cannon could lie somewhere deep in the shifting sands of that treacherous entrance. If the wreck is found by the "sea hunters" and identified as Astor's ship, the discovery may finally supply some of the missing pieces of the mystery of the ghost ship of Clayoquot Sound. The search continues; the dreams lead on.

It is time to draw the history of the sea otter trade at Clayoquot Sound to a conclusion, and to make some observations. We will never know how many sea otter pelts were "drained" from Clayoquot Sound, or collected, during the fur rush period. No one was keeping score. We have no idea what the population of sea otter was in those waters

PART I The Empire of Fortune

when the first traders arrived in 1784, but it was bountiful. We know that the mammal was hunted to near extinction here, as elsewhere in the North Pacific, and was only saved from total extinction when family clusters were discovered in Alaska and relocated to the BC coast in the mid-twentieth century. In the late eighteenth and early nineteenth century, the suppliers thought nothing of conservation, or of setting quotas in their hunt. The maritime traders took all they could in exchange for arms and ammunition, cloths and clothing, fishing gear, implements and tools, iron and copper, in bulk or fashioned—and much else. The Natives hunted at will. They richly fed the international economy, particularly the transoceanic link to China, and they entered the global economy without objection and with some enthusiasm, thus aiding and abetting globalization. They were not victims; they were participants.

Let's take four years, for which we have statistics of sea otter pelts collected by trading ships. These were big years for the export of sea otter pelts for the Canton market, and it bears remembering that these figures come from the entire Northwest Coast, from Cape Flattery to Haida Gwaii. Seven ships took a total of 11,000 sea otter skins in 1799. The next year, 1800, six ships took a total of 9,800 skins. In 1801, ten ships took 13,000 skins. And in 1802, ten ships took 14,000 skins. That's 47,800 sea otter skins in four years. These are the tabulations of William Sturgis of Boston.[170]

One of the last references to Wickaninnish and the Clayoquot comes from the September 1818 visit of the *Bordelais*, a French merchant vessel commanded by Lieutenant Camille de Roquefeuil.[171] This three-masted vessel of 200 tons was well-armed, and Roquefeuil's obligation was to seek out new markets for French manufacturers in the years of French imperial resurgence. He spent about two weeks in Barkley Sound. Very few furs could be gathered, the trade was paltry and the vessel made for San Francisco, then returned to France.[172] By this time, then, the sea otter trade was in decline, though it is said that it continued to 1830. By then the resources of the maritime fur trade had been exhausted to the unprofitable level. The Clayoquot could offer nothing to entice trading ships to come

Tales the *Tonquin* Tells

to their waters. As far as internal Native trade is concerned, haiqua—that is, shells from Clayoquot—were exchanged at the Columbia River, where they were in great demand. Haiqua was the Native currency of the country, and rated as the jewels of it too.[173]

Sea otter did not disappear completely from British Columbia waters. They were seen, or known, in Clayoquot in the 1830s and again in the 1860s.[174] But it was generally known by natural scientists that they had been hunted to near extinction. Waters of Haida Gwaii, formerly a prolific habitat, seemed a sterile sea to the sea otter. Still, hope persisted that they might one day return. In the 1970s came the turnaround. In 1976 I was on a biological and anthropological trip to the southern islands of Haida Gwaii, conducted by the University of British Columbia's Centre for Continuing Education. On the morning of August 30, Professor Roy L. Taylor, our lead scientist, and I were happy to obtain a new sighting of sea otter in Flamingo Inlet, Moresby Island. Professor Taylor and I published our findings in the Royal British Columbia Museum's *Syesis* for 1977.[175] We stated our opinion that the animal was a remnant of the original population of sea otters of the Queen Charlotte Islands. This was an exciting find, corroborating another find four years previously at Cape St. James. The revival of the sea otter was underway. Quickly thereafter the sea otter came to reclaim its old littoral habitats.

What role did the Clayoquot nations play in the ending of the trade, the making it unprofitable? These are uncomfortable questions, worth asking but seldom answered, for First Nations are invariably said to be guardians of resources. In reading the admirable *Sea Otters of Haida Gwaii: Icons in Human-Ocean Relations*, by N.A. Sloan and Lyle Dick, I was struck powerfully by their statement, hidden deeply in a telling footnote, that very little discussion exists in the published literature in regards to Indigenous Peoples' sea otter overhunting during the age of the maritime fur trade. They quote John Vaillant, acclaimed author of *The Golden Spruce*: "And yet, despite its practical importance [providing fine fur for elites' clothing], and despite a necessarily keen sensitivity to the rhythms of the natural world, the West Coast Natives pursued this creature to the brink of extinction. In doing so, they demonstrated the same kind of profit-driven short-sightedness that has wiped out dozens of other species."[176] Here is bold testimony frankly stated: we need more of it. In short, furs from the Northwest Coast were the first export item, and when sold or bartered in China via agents and local compradors, they yielded Oriental goods destined for European and American markets—teas, silks, porcelains and other. Clayoquot and Meares Island had been brought, by the early 1790s, into a new global economy.

Before closing what I could call the sea otter trade phase of our tales of possession, and the land deal arrangements and destruction of Opitsat sections of this book—I fear they make for an untidy and complicated combination, but such is history—we can take a look from the perspective of our times and see that the Bostonians' presence at Clayoquot Sound was transient.

The ships came as long as the quickly dwindling sea mammal resources lasted, as long as a fickle market in China remained profitable and, further, as long as Native demands for goods, notably metals, muskets and powder, remained strong. Market conditions ruled all. There were so many variables in this luxury business. By 1830 the trade had ended in these latitudes; the quest was pressed elsewhere, south to California and north to Alaska. The ships came no more to Nootka, Clayoquot and Barkley Sound. In later years a petty coasting trade was carried on by vessels of the Hudson's Bay Company but mainly by itinerant traders. Kendrick's scheme of trade, settlement and dominion came to naught.

In the circumstances, as late as the mid-nineteenth century, Wickaninnish and his kin remained in peaceful possession of Clayoquot Sound. One phase of empire-making had passed; another was on the verge of beginning. The Nuu-chah-nulth peoples had not died off. They had showed resilience in the face of the industrial revolution brought to them in the holds of ships. "The actual lives of the Nootka changed remarkably little," wrote George Woodcock of this time. "They had acquired considerable quantities of European goods, including many muskets and much cloth and metals, but a great deal of this material they appear to have used merely as gifts in the round of potlatches, and except for an increasing use of iron in tools and weapons, their daily life remained surprisingly unchanged . . . As for social and ceremonial patterns within the community, these appear to have been entirely unaffected."[177]

Meanwhile, as the next chapter explains, the long arm of international law was being extended to the Northwest Coast, that distant dominion whose geographical isolation made it the last of the world's northern temperate forested zones to come under control of modern states. The Kendrick visit, like those of Barkley, Gray and Meares, was unauthorized by government, though the ships sailed under their respective flags, some of convenience. While these expeditions of commerce and discovery were proceeding, a different sort of rivalry, one underpinned by concepts of sovereignty and recognized in international law, was bringing the Northwest Coast into world diplomacy and statecraft.

7

The In-between Time

The old coastal order was changing quickly when the British warships *Sulphur* and *Starling*, on reconnaissance to see if the Russians had arrived at Nootka Sound, came to anchor in Friendly Cove on October 3, 1837—"the very interesting point of Cook and Vancouver's operations," noted Captain Edward Belcher, in command of the *Sulphur*. The weather was cloudy, unpropitious for astronomical observations to check positions and chronometers. There was no sign of the Russians. The Indigenous people gathered around the ships in their canoes, as was customary, and Belcher took note of a quiet fellow, dignified in behaviour, who turned out to be none other than Maquinna—or Maquilla, as Belcher spelled it.

This couldn't be the legendary Maquinna, but what was the genealogy here? Age about fifty, five feet eight inches in height, his shoulders square in proportion, and limbs muscular, this Maquinna was light skinned. Belcher wrote: "His superiority consists of a dignified, unobtrusive mildness of manner and deportment." This was altogether impressive. He was husband of the descendant of the Maquinna of Vancouver's time and recounting. Belcher reasoned that Captain Vancouver's Maquinna had left his daughter his successor, and this man had probably assumed the name with his wife. After this preliminary explanation, Belcher was told directly by Maquinna—and of significance for us—that Wickaninnish now stood first in repute on the West Coast, and that he, Maquinna, was next, and Nookamis third. The physical features of the chiefly family may be followed in Belcher's voyage and in a related account.[178]

The mariners made observations of Nootka, noting its decay, the remnants of Spanish occupation, and various posts perhaps used for shipbuilding or repair. History had passed the place by. A clear sky allowed for an observation, and next day, October 9, the vessels sailed for San Francisco. No visit was made to Clayoquot, but Wickaninnish's premier position had been acclaimed by a fellow high-ranking chief.

Suffice it to say that in the years when Cook met the celebrated Maquinna and Meares met the equally celebrated and rising Wickaninnish, the estimated population of the Nuu-chah-nulth was ten thousand, and the total number of villages on Vancouver Island's west coast was twenty-five, of various sizes.[179] Within a century this had changed dramatically. The 1850s and 1860s mark turbulent and uncertain decades in the annals of Clayoquot Sound. They are characterized by changing economic circumstances, internecine wars, Indigenous population dispersals and declines at least partly owing to Native wars (but also to spirituous liquors and disease), and the coming of an entirely new force and influence—the intervention of British concepts about "Aboriginal affairs," or what was called "the future of the Indian" or "the Indian problem." Clayoquot Sound was no place for colonial settlement, for there was little land for crop cultivation or animal husbandry. Even so, British authority and law were beginning to extend their influence here, by peace if possible, by force if necessary.

Clayoquot Sound remained a backwater to business enterprise; all the same, its coastal waters and interior coastal passages needed to be surveyed as an encouragement to coastal shipping and a measure to prevent ships running aground. This was Admiralty policy for the world. In this connection the surveying of these waters by

PART I The Empire of Fortune

ships and men of the Royal Navy forms a central chapter in the Sound's history. We will look more closely at this in the following pages, and we will be introduced to the first general comments by colonial authorities and naval officers about the decline of Native numbers and the social disruptions faced. There were minor episodes of piracy, murder and retributive justice. The story of these decades is not a pleasant one, marked as it is by some rather frank truths of that age, and it is salutary to remind ourselves that some of the most militant persons of the nineteenth century—officers of the Royal Navy—were among the most humanitarian in their thoughts about the "future of the Indian race." Our central figure is Captain George Henry Richards, RN. We examine in this chapter, as well, the rapid political and constitutional changes that enveloped the British territories of the Pacific cordillera, its inlets and islands—and the changes that came over the controls of the Hudson's Bay Company (HBC), that remarkable empire within an empire.[180] The HBC, it may be said at the outset, had no interest in Clayoquot Sound except to keep rival traders out. There is, in all, a crowded background here: the study of history reveals many entanglements.

As can be appreciated, at mid-century the economy of Clayoquot Sound stood in decline. In contrast to earlier days, when Clayoquot Sound had been a locus of a vast Native trade system, the disappearance of the sea otter had brought many consequences to the area, disrupting old shipping patterns and the customary exchange of commodities. No longer did mariners in search of sea otter pelts seek out the Native suppliers. Those ships of olden days that had been trading in muskets and ammunition came no more. Even so, in transitional years a petty trade in pelts may have had incidental interest in Clayoquot Sound and Meares Island.[181] It seems likely that trails would have been used to freight furs across to the east coast of Vancouver Island, to Fort Rupert and Fort Nanaimo; there furs could be bartered for goods and supplies needed out on the coast. Fort Rupert had connections near and far that made that post (and later Alert Bay) significant in commercial activity. Casual visits by steamers from Victoria also kept up an occasional commerce on

The In-between Time

the west coast of Vancouver Island. The channels of commerce ran much more strongly on the island's east coast, notably where ship construction and supply, provisioning, and coal mining were the engines of a growing economy, one with tentacles to Alaskan ports and the canneries, missions and trade stations near the mouths of inlets or rivers.

In these depressed circumstances, sea otter chiefs such as Wickaninnish and his subordinates no longer enjoyed the buoyant income that their exports of fur skins had given them in the days of Meares, Kendrick and Gray. Nor did the trade goods arrive as before in the holds of the ships that called there; this, too, affected the middleman roles of the chiefs. The armaments import trade dried up just as the sea otter trade neared extinction. Wealth was now differently acquired and differently distributed. An occasional schooner might arrive in search of whale, seal and, especially, dogfish oil (used as a lubricant in the logging industry). It is recorded that in the late 1850s the master of one such vessel, working villages of the West Coast, set up a store or depot beside a village in Clayoquot Sound. He was a useful interpreter for visitors, knowledgeable as he was in the language of the Nuu-chah-nulth.[182] What was sold and what was bought is not known; perhaps liquor was part of the exchange for furs and oil. We can only speculate.[183]

All indications point to the conclusion that this was, as this chapter is entitled, an "in-between time." It was also perhaps a period of "salutary neglect" for the Indigenous Peoples of Clayoquot Sound, as it was for others at Nootka Sound, Kyuquot Sound and elsewhere along the western flank of Vancouver Island. These locales were left well enough alone, for a time of cultural enrichment perhaps, and one of inter-tribal competition and social strengthening. No ethnological expeditions were mounted here by such organizations as the American Museum of Natural History, which went to the Queen Charlotte Islands. The channels of anthropological inquiry ran elsewhere on the coast. Old paradigms of settler dominance and Native victimization, so commonly expressed these days, have no standing here. There was no agricultural land to grab, no gold yet found and

PART I The Empire of Fortune

no port of strategic value to take possession of and hold on a permanent basis.

By contrast, Barkley Sound was a hive of activity. The industrial age arrived here early. In April 1860, Gilbert Malcolm Sproat and Edward Stamp, representing shipowners Anderson & Co., who founded the Orient Line, purchased land at the present Port Alberni, at the head of the deep inlet penetrating almost to the eastern side of the island. The intention was to export spars and masts for ocean-going ships, to erect a sawmill and to establish a fishing settlement. (First boards were cut and shipments made to Callao, Peru. By 1863, when the business was momentarily halted by the Civil War in the United States, 1,000,000 board feet had been shipped.) When in August 1860 Sproat and Stamp had arrived in the armed vessels *Woodpecker* and *Meg Merrilies* with a force of about fifty men, they told the local chief that they had purchased the surrounding land from Queen Victoria. The chief replied that this could not be, for it belonged to him and his people, but they would sell it for £20 worth of goods. Sproat consented on condition that the people and possessions be moved the next day. This did not eventuate. The Tseshaht (or as Sproat spells it, Sheshat) donned their war paint and gathered their arms. The intruders fired cannon, and the frightened inhabitants dispersed.

Then followed a sharp exchange of opinion, the sort of thing that is at the raw edge of imperial processes. I repeat it here, as imagined by a local writer over 100 years later:

> Sproat came ashore: "Chiefs of the Sheshats," said he, "Are you well; are your women in health; are your children hearty; do your people get plenty of fish and fruits?"
>
> "Yes," replied an elder, "our families are well, our people have plenty of food; but how long will this last we know not. We see your ships and hear things that make our hearts grow faint. They say that more King-George-men will soon be here and will take our land, our firewood, our fishing grounds, and that we shall be placed on a little spot and shall have to do everything according to the fancies of the King-George-men."

The In-between Time

"Do you believe all this?" asked Sproat.

"We want your information," said an old man.

"Then," he answered, "It is true that more King-George-men are coming: they will soon be here: but your land will be bought at a fair price."

"We do not wish to sell our land or our water; let your friends stay in their own country."

Sproat rejoined, "My great chief, the high chief of the King-George-men, seeing that you do not work your land, orders that you shall sell it. It is of no use to you. The trees you do not need; you will fish and hunt as you do now, and collect firewood, planks for your houses, and cedar for your canoes. The white man will give you work and buy your fish and oil."

"Ah, but we don't care to do as the white men wish."

"Whether or not," said Sproat, "the white men will come. All your people know that they are your superiors; they make the things which you value. You cannot make muskets, blankets, or flour. The white men will teach you printing and [to] be like themselves."

"We do not want the white man. He steals what we have. We wish to live as we are."[184]

Sproat was trained in the civil service and was a gifted and versatile businessman, also a scholar and explorer. On the west coast of Vancouver Island, he was magistrate, translator, anthropologist and government agent. His *Scenes and Studies of Savage Life*, published in London by the distinguished house Smith Elder, is our first narrative and ethnology of the west coast of Vancouver Island. Sproat, like many of his age, was interested in marketing the frontier and wrote *British Columbia: Information for Emigrants* (1873). He studied England's rural poor. British India's opium trade to China also attracted his attention, as did Sir Walter Scott's poetry. This polymath wrote many books, but none of such staying power as his book on the Nuu-chah-nulth. And we look back on it with fascination

PART I The Empire of Fortune

and curiosity, recognizing as we do that it is a form of cross-cultural analysis. Sproat knew the new world that was about to beset the Nuu-chah-nulth, and he was not shy in stating his views about what he saw as inevitable.

I was struck in reading, or rereading, his book by how he describes a certain defeatist attitude that developed among the Indigenous people. This showed itself to him a couple of years after the settlers had arrived at Barkley Sound. The Indigenous peoples' curiosity had ceased to exist. There was also a morbid acceptance. "They had ample sustenance and shelter for the support of life, yet the people decayed."[185] He notes the discouragement of the Natives. He does not talk about suicides among those displaced or removed from their sites of occupation and labour, but that can be imagined. It is a sad and moving tale, and unique in that most anthropologists do not discuss matters they cannot measure or take down in their notes.

Although in the 1850s the Clayoquot and Ahousaht remained largely undisturbed by the outside world, inter-tribal rivalry persisted in Clayoquot Sound, and on the west coast more generally, and raiding and internecine warfare continued, reaching a climax in 1855. Wars, mercilessly waged in northern Nootka territory in the mid-1850s, were fought chiefly for spoils, prestige or revenge. The desire for retaliation and the hope of gain worked together.[186] Anthropological authority attests that here on the Northwest Coast, where kinship was of great importance, competition for productive places of marine resources—salmon streams particularly—was keen. Competition in accumulating wealth and prestige was accordingly strong, and disputes were common between kin groups. Feuds were long-standing. Surprise attacks taken on moonless nights, just before dawn, were led by war chiefs chosen as most adept at organizing such. "Among the Nootka, however, these economy-motivated raids of extermination took place between speakers of the same language," wrote anthropologist Harold E. Driver. "Here, there was true political organization, at least in the historic period, so that the larger encounters of this nature involving its people may be labeled 'war.'"[187] In fact, 1855 marks the last "Indian war" on the West Coast.

On this subject we can turn with profit to the admirable work by Eugene Arima and Alan Hoover, *The Whaling People of the West Coast of Vancouver Island and Cape Flattery*.[188] In contrast, Vincent Koppert, anthropologist and author of *Contributions to Clayoquot Ethnology*, published 1930, missed a glorious chance to record oral evidence about this seminal event in West Coast history. He was content to say, in a mere two pages, that these were hand-to-hand encounters using stones, clubs of stone or bone, and daggers, as well as spears and war knives ("never left out of sight," he says). Elk-hide armour gave protection. Warriors readied themselves for war at any time, and acts of bravery were part of the preparation, also songs and prayers taught by a warrior's father.[189]

The subject of war in Indigenous societies has been extensively studied. Battles rage among anthropologists as to various phenomena such as warfare, feuding, armed conflict or armed combat. "Warfare exists if the conflict is organized and socially sanctioned, and the killing is not regarded as murder," wrote Margaret Mead. She posits that war must be organized, for there must be willingness and intent to kill and readiness to die, and so the process is not murder.[190] In regards to the matter of oral testimony: we wish we had more. Edward Sapir and Morris Swadesh provide indicative evidence in *Native Accounts of Nootka Ethnography*, printing testimony of episodes in Native orthography and English translation.[191] We learn a great deal from these. It was the possession of resources and the defence of these resources against encroachment by rival nations that was the key, as far as I am able to determine from evidence dating from 1916, entitled "War Among Ahouset Bands." This accords completely with established views of the Mowachaht and Muchalaht, at and near Nootka Sound, that it was not rank and station that was sought but places for resource extraction and life-giving sustenance.[192] Revenge was an undoubted factor, too, but possession of property the essential requirement. The war described extensively by Arima and Hoover virtually annihilated the Otsosat, and placed the Ahousaht in the ascendant.[193]

PART I The Empire of Fortune

The reader is best served by Ahousaht Elder Peter S. Webster's extensive commentary on this important martial episode. He says the war lasted fifteen years. Both sides fought each other using guns and ammunition. He says those who murdered the crew of a lost sailing ship supplied these weapons. The war began with provocation. The Ahousaht decided to go to war against the Oo-tsus-aht (Webster's spelling), who owned eighteen fish-producing rivers in Clayoquot Sound. The Ahousaht demanded little girls be given to each member of their war party. To this there was agreement but not fully. There were further provocations, killings and mutilations. In the end the Oo-tsus-aht lost the war and lost lands, including Flores Island, where the Ahousaht and Kelsemaht lived in the time of which Webster tells. The Oo-tsus-aht moved from Clayoquot to take up residence on the coast of Washington and Oregon. "Following this event," wrote Webster, "peace returned at last to Clayoquot Sound."[194]

In nearby Barkley Sound, too, Indigenous warfare was a component of life in the 1850s, for there was fought what is called the Long War in Barkley Sound, lasting several years (about 1850–1860).[195] Then it stopped completely. No rival nations came to possess Meares Island or to take away the resources of the Ahousaht, Kelsemaht and Clayoquot.

The Clayoquot were involved in this last war, but only indirectly. It brought to the fore their powerful war chief Sitakanim (or Seta Kanim). Stirring contemporary accounts by two visitors to Clayoquot Sound pay him splendid tribute.[196] In the early 1860s he remained, without question, the supreme warrior chief, having benefited from the late wars against the Ahousaht and their allies. He was grand in outdoor settings, his natural arena, and as Gilbert Malcolm Sproat put it, as if by comparison, "We Englishmen converse well indoors across green tables, but out of doors the savage beats us in public speaking beyond compare."[197] Sitakanim differed from Wickaninnish in that he appeared to outsiders as both villainous and treacherous. One of the testimonials in his possession, which (not knowing its damning contents) he produced for yachtsman Barrett-Lennard,

The In-between Time

stated that if necessary he "would murder his own father for a groat [a small coin of little value]."[198] That may be the case or it may be a fabrication. Sitakanim wanted to peruse the yachtsman's credentials, and he was much impressed by a Masonic jewelled emblem brought up from below in the vessel.

The end to the blood feuds and the internecine wars is conspicuous by its suddenness and does not seem to have been accompanied by Indigenous regrets, save for guarded suspicions about inveterate enemies. All the same, the old order was changing, and the power of Wickaninnish's successors was changing with the times. A web of administrative legalese was possessing Meares Island and, indeed, all of Vancouver Island. In fact, the old order had changed very quietly and quite unexpectedly, even before a boundary was agreed to separate British from US lands west of the Rocky Mountains along the forty-ninth parallel, leaving Vancouver Island in British sovereign possession. The boundary treaty of 1846 is the watershed date for Meares Island: it announced British sovereignty, foreshadowed colonial administration from Victoria and hinted at a distant future in which Canada would control "Indian affairs" under the *Indian Act*.

Since 1821, the Hudson's Bay Company had held the exclusive privilege of trading with the Indigenous peoples of the territories west of the Rocky Mountains. These territories were not annexed to Rupert's Land, though the Company would have liked that. No, the Colonial Office, which oversaw this empire within an empire, wanted the colonizing power of the firm to be limited to Vancouver Island and its dependencies. A licence from government was required to trade in HBC territories, and that kept rivals away.[199] This great monopoly was backed by the power of the British parliament.

In 1846, the possession of Meares Island and Clayoquot Sound (and all of Vancouver Island and its dependencies) passed to the management of the Hudson's Bay Company. The Colony of Vancouver Island was established by royal charter of grant under direction of the British Colonial Office in 1849,[200] and on March 11, 1850 the governor, Richard Blanshard, fresh from London and unconnected with the HBC, proclaimed the colonial government at Fort Victoria.

PART I The Empire of Fortune

The Crown retained title to the Island and its dependencies; the Company held the charter of development, for seven shillings a year. A fair bargain! The British government had no intention of spending a penny on the Island's development, save for naval protection, so the Hudson's Bay Company remained all-powerful in its commercial, legal and political activities. The HBC's monopoly gave it exclusive rights of trade with Indigenous peoples on the Island and its dependencies, as well as in New Caledonia—that is, the mainland British sovereign territory, as acknowledged by the Oregon Treaty of 1846. Lands and forests came under Company control, and such Indian reserves as were established by treaty or other arrangement were taken out of the domain, Native places of occupation being left largely undisturbed. Notably, the Colonial Office made sure that Indigenous peoples were not denied their traditional economies of fishing (including whaling) and hunting. Peace for the purpose of profit was the intention, and we will return to this later. The Company established posts at Forts Victoria, Langley, Nanaimo, Rupert (Beaver Harbour) and Simpson, but there was no need for a post on the west coast of Vancouver Island, a backwater.

All the same, this octopus-like monopoly worked itself out in specific ways, shaping the character of the imperial frontier in these parts. For instance, Governor James Douglas, Blanshard's successor and a powerful Company man, controlled the registry of colonial shipping at Victoria and was capable of intervening in any colonial trade. Thus, when one Robert Swanston proposed to sail his trading vessel *William Allen* to Clayoquot and other harbours of the Island "for the purpose of collecting native produce," Douglas refused to grant the necessary permit. Douglas's explanation was that there was no settlement at Clayoquot or the other places.[201] (Swanston may have intended to peddle booze.) Truth is, Douglas wanted to keep American and other foreign traders out of British waters.

The Company held firm on its monopoly of trading with the Indigenous peoples of the Island. Governor Douglas wanted no foreign poachers. The monopoly had been licensed by London in order to save Indigenous peoples from the dreadful coerciveness of the

The In-between Time

American western frontier. This was a powerful factor in the making of imperial policy for Vancouver Island.[202] At the same time, it was an anachronism in current British political economic thinking. The coming of free trade theory and practice in British imperial management had its influence even at far-distant Vancouver Island: the Hudson's Bay Company monopoly disappeared by London's intervention, effective 1859. Meantime, the gold rush on the Fraser River brought a new mainland colony into existence in 1858. The two colonies were merged in 1864 as the united colony of British Columbia. It, too, went through a transition, and the Province of British Columbia emerged in 1871, with representative government and as a part of the Dominion of Canada. These changes hardly influenced the course of Meares Island history, save for the fact that "Indian Affairs" became the purview of the Dominion of Canada. We will refer to this later, and it is essential to understand the transitions we are identifying.

Governor Blanshard's role in the shaping of this frontier must not be ignored. His first action as governor was designed to control the importation and sale of spirituous liquors. To him the reason was clear, as his proclamation says: "The free and unrestricted traffic in spirituous liquors has caused and does still cause great damage and inconvenience to the Inhabitants of Her Majesty's Colony of Vancouver's Island, by debauching and corrupting the population, both native and Immigrant."[203] Various penalties were imposed. Smuggling had to be checked. Public health needed to be improved. But in later years the Colony took no substantial measures to check the illicit liquor trade, a trade in spirits many of which had poisonous characteristics. In Blanshard's day there was no high density of Indigenous population near Fort Victoria. However, as the 1850s wore on, Native numbers increased in and near Victoria. Numerous local press organs, some hysterical, made much of this, giving rise to "settler anxiety."[204] Governor Douglas was advised to take action, but it was not until the 1862 smallpox epidemic that various groups were escorted home to their native villages to prevent an even greater public health catastrophe in the colonial capital. How many Clayoquot people were involved is not known. Some authorities believe the 1830s to have been a more devastating time for Native depopulation from smallpox, and 1855 may have been more significant at Clayoquot than 1862.[205] Syphilis was extensive in Victoria, an additional contribution to the decline in Native numbers through sterility. Factors related to spirituous liquor, venereal diseases and the outflow of persons from Native communities must have taken a terrible toll on population numbers in their villages, to say nothing of dark and depressing psychological impacts. It is impossible to calculate the number of homicides, the cases of family violence, the maiming and the injuries suffered in consequence of these causes.

The number of Indigenous peoples in Clayoquot Sound and British Columbia in the mid-1800s is devilishly hard to pin down, though many estimates were made in the mid- to late-nineteenth century. Some estimates are wild. We recall that some of the maritime fur traders and Spanish explorers of the late 1700s had estimated in the thousands in regards to some of the Clayoquot villages. No such figures can be found for the mid-nineteenth century. In fact, the 1849 estimates sent to the Colonial Office in London do not mention any west coast Native numbers, though this may have been because the coast, to repeat, was a backwater to commerce, settlement and colonial administration. But make no mistake, population numbers here had declined: the last internecine war, that of 1855, accounts for some of this; so did diseases. Smallpox affected many and must have influenced the Ahousaht and Clayoquot, though Kwakwaka'wakw, Tsimshian and Haida suffered more in the 1862 pandemic. In addition, Indigenous people moved to places where wages could be earned—Nanaimo, Alert Bay, Alberni and Victoria—and some headed for American territory. In 1864 the west coast of Vancouver Island was described by the Admiralty surveyors as thinly populated, with the highest estimate of Indigenous peoples not exceeding 4,000, divided into a number of very small nations.[206] There is a danger in overestimating the numbers of "Indians of Canada," and the Dominion of Canada statistics for 1911 report a total of 25,149 in

The In-between Time

British Columbia. This was a larger number than that determined by the province's official estimate of 21,591, compiled in 1911 by Dr. C.F. Newcombe, of the British Columbia Museum. Newcombe's figure for the Nootkan (that is, the Nuu-chah-nulth) peoples is 2,055. As to the decline in the population of the First Nations of British Columbia, R.E. Gosnell reports in the 1911 edition of his *Year Book of British Columbia* that when British Columbia entered the Canadian federation in 1871, there were approximately 35,000. When he compared this historical information to that of the 1911 estimation, as given above, the decrease over those forty years was indeed large.[207]

We recall that census figures are, at best, wild guesses. The European population of Vancouver Island and mainland British Columbia was a transient one. Population figures for colonial Vancouver Island, found in its colonial records, state there were, in 1855, 774 whites. By 1871 there were 36,247 whites.[208] Our best estimate for the late nineteenth century comes from observer Vincent Koppert, the anthropologist, who learned from reliable sources that in 1881 there were 324 Clayoquot and 140 Kelsemaht, and that in 1929 there were 177 Clayoquot and 66 Kelsemaht.[209] Indeed, the numbers had gone down, but the important point (not least in regards to *Meares Island*, where continuity of occupancy had to be demonstrated) was they had not disappeared. What is equally significant, they had not abandoned their place of occupancy at the time the British colonial government was established. This is a critical point: Meares Island had not been abandoned by Indigenous peoples.

We can imagine that the 1850s and 1860s were unusual times for the Clayoquot Sound peoples, for commercial connections with the outside world were uncertain, and internecine rivalries prevailed. All was in flux. Merchant ships in quest of sea otter pelts came no longer. A few vessels arrived in search of seals or whales. There must have been petty traders, too—small-tonnage coasters, most of them from home port Victoria, the colonial capital, looking for furs, oil or Native curiosities. It was not until 1860 that a strong outsider presence was felt, and this was not specifically at Clayoquot but at the head of the Alberni Canal, where, as explained above, a stout party

PART I The Empire of Fortune

of timber fellers arrived. They set up the first commercial timber operation on the west coast of Vancouver Island. The vessels therefore came and went there rather than Clayoquot Sound.

The long arm of colonial justice stretched out to embrace Clayoquot Sound. As the fatal *Tonquin* case had testified, this was a treacherous coast for shipping, and as in the days of Wickaninnish, mariners needed to be on their guard. Once the Indigenous peoples began to rob and kill persons travelling to the coast, the officials in Victoria, backed by the power of London, made sure they felt the influence of British law and authority.[210] British gunboats made their appearance on this shore after 1858, when the maritime frontier was "sealed" and the Pax Britannica established and enforced.[211] The process was gradual.

In 1852 the HBC ship *Eagle* was lost and plundered at Clayoquot. Governor Douglas, regretting the "bad conduct" of the Indigenous people on this occasion, and having no force at his disposal to respond or to prevent such acts in the future, could only report the event to the Colonial Office with the hope it would bring some imperial intervention. There were other such cases, and captains of trading vessels raised a general alarm.[212] As one skipper declared, the coast from Clayoquot Sound to the Island's northwestern tip appeared absolutely unsafe for traders. He warned that the Natives arrogantly boasted that they cared nothing for British gunboats, for Governor Douglas or, for that matter, anyone else.[213]

The American brig *Swiss Boy*, carrying lumber from Puget Sound with destination San Francisco, was beached for repairs in Barkley Sound in 1859, and was plundered by the Huu-ay-aht and Tseshaht. Captain J.C. Prevost of HMS *Satellite*, a steam sloop, answered the governor's urgent appeal to investigate and used soft diplomacy to convince the local Indigenous people that their acts must not be repeated; to this, they agreed. The Huu-ay-aht, he wrote, seemed well disposed to British influence. Persons Prevost identified as responsible for the plundering of the *Swiss Boy* were taken to Victoria for trial, but for lack of evidence were not convicted. They were released, much to the fury of the traders. Prevost was told that the

The In-between Time

Huu-ay-aht believed that any property that came to their shores—including a disabled ship—was their property and a rightful subject for plunder. That may have been the case. But an attack against British or other European persons was another matter, and the governor would not stand aside in such cases. Nor could the governor countenance any piracy. It was Captain Prevost's view that the colonial government should appoint an Indian agent for the Island's west coast from Port San Juan to Cape Scott, where in his estimation, five thousand "souls" lived under "no control or restraint."[214] Taking up this recommendation, William Banfield was appointed magistrate and Indian agent. He was there until October 20, 1862, when a Huu-ay-aht chief, Klatsmick, murdered him.[215]

The colony had no money for marine policing, and no gunboat. The work fell on the Royal Navy. Admiral Joseph Denman, commander of the Pacific station from 1864 to 1866, recommended regular policing by steam-powered vessels; he also recommended that, for this particular service, officers familiar with local tribal ways and language would be advantageous. "The aggressions on the coast of Vancouver Island and British Columbia against British traders by the Indians has by degrees increased to a formidable account by long continued impunity," he advised the Admiralty, "and though the severe examples I have felt myself to make in Clayoquot Sound will probably for a long time prevent their recurrence, yet it is most desirable that such cases of murder and piracy should be prosecuted, and the painful necessity of such examples avoided." Gunboats and even more powerful gun vessels were deployed from the base at Esquimalt, near Victoria, to patrol the west coast. These were challenging waters even for a steam vessel—the gunboats proved to be under-powered where the heavy seas were so common.

Prevost's initial belief that the local peoples would accept British influence gave way to stronger views and demands for protection from traders and from the governor. The navy came under pressure to exact justice at the cannon's mouth. Such was the case in 1864 when the sloop *Kingfisher*, trading in seal oil, was pillaged and burned, and the crew members murdered, at Matilda Creek

PART I The Empire of Fortune

in Clayoquot Sound (the northern end). The lamentable story of the navy's hunt for the pirates and murderers and the destruction of their property and their trial has been told in detail in my *Gunboat Frontier*.[216] The navy carried out reprisals with dedication and determination, but those hunted down put up a serious resistance. Nine villages and sixty-four canoes were destroyed, and at least fifteen Indigenous peoples killed. "The success of this attack," Rear Admiral Joseph Denman reported to the Admiralty in London, "conducted after the fashion of their own tactics, has produced profound discouragement, Chapchah [regarded as the Indigenous leader] being in hiding and pursued by his own people, who had abandoned all ideas of resistance and look on him as responsible for all the evils." Governor Arthur Kennedy, Douglas's successor, was satisfied. He thanked the navy for its work and confidently maintained that the measure would promote the colony's security and check the "piratical and bloodthirsty attitudes of the Coast Indians, which have been left too long unpunished." The Ahousaht, implicated in the *Kingfisher* matter, did not accept their guilt; rather, they held the belief that they had survived the ordeal. That was their point of view, and is justified in their logic.

But the problems continued: at Estevan Point, north of Clayoquot Sound, the barque *John Bright*, laden with lumber, went aground in a southwest gale in February 1869. Of the twenty-two people on board the vessel, none survived. A report reached Victoria, via a passing trading schooner, that the Hesquiaht had plundered the ship and ten survivors of the wreck had reached shore and been shot, their bodies hacked to pieces and mutilated. The gun vessel *Sparrowhawk* was sent from Esquimalt to investigate, a magistrate on board. Two arrests were made, a trial held in Victoria, and the accused, found guilty, were hanged on a scaffold erected at Hesquiat, despite a coroner's report that the mutilations could not definitively be attributed to human intervention but could well have been caused by the bodies being battered on the rocks by rough seas.[217] The morality of this episode caused a stir at the time, mainly in London, where humanitarian views were

The In-between Time

strong at the Admiralty and in the Cabinet of W.E. Gladstone, the prime minister.

To make navigation safer on the west coast of Vancouver Island and elsewhere, the Royal Navy commenced a systematic survey of these complicated, rock-strewn waters. The task was daunting. This heroic but little-known work began in the mid-1840s, when Lieutenant James Wood had surveyed the Strait of Juan de Fuca, resulting in the first authorized Admiralty charts and, later, advice to mariners known as sailing directions. The entrance to and anchorages in Esquimalt were laid down on the charts. The Fraser River gold rush of 1858 induced the Admiralty in London to undertake a systematic hydrographic survey of British Columbia waters, especially the lower Fraser River. Survey results encouraged commerce. This was the reason that Clayoquot Sound was surveyed over the course of a few years in the early 1860s, and it forms part of this chapter's story, not only because of advantages given to safe navigation, but also because the surveyors sometimes gave new names to islands, water passages and dominant mountains, changing names that had been given by the Indigenous peoples.

On July 21, 1861, the throbbing pulsations of the big paddlewheel steamer *Hecate*, commanded by Captain George Henry Richards, could be heard near the southeast entrance to Clayoquot Sound.[218] This man-of-war had been sent from England to carry on surveys in locations where tidal flows and currents proved her predecessor, *Plumper*, inadequate. Richards, rather small in stature, was an energetic fellow with a reputation noted for bravery in battle. He was a careful observer and zealous in carrying out his responsibilities. A man of humanitarian views, he was blessed with a lively sense of humour that endeared him to all under his command. Desertions were non-existent from his ship, though in other ships "on station" they were substantial, the lure of the gold fields being irresistible. Richards was a proven man of science and an Arctic explorer.[219]

When approaching the passage to Port Cox, the expected place of moorage, a whaleboat previously detached on the survey was seen coming out to the ship, its mission to warn Richards not to enter

PART I The Empire of Fortune

by that way, for at low water there was only fifteen feet. This was a significant detail gratefully received, for earlier a Native canoe had come off from the shore to advise that there was certainly a passage for the ship, "and if I had taken their word I should have run on shore," Richards noted ruefully in his private journal.[220] The *Hecate* drew thirteen feet (four metres); thus, no chances could be taken in shallow waters. Master John Gowlland, in the whaleboat, transferred to the steamer and piloted the *Hecate* north via the outer coast to the entrance the Spanish in Quimper's day had called Point Raphael, but which was by this time known by the Indigenous name Manhousat. Gowlland remarked that the Ahousaht were "very civil and bring great quantities of Salmon to trade: there are three or four kinds at present being traded."[221]

The work of the surveyors was arduous and fundamental. Part of their business was to make exact scientific observations of latitudes, longitudes, heights and distances on which every chart had to be founded; they had to determine the channels and the passages, and note the hazards to navigation. The weather was overcast and sometimes rainy, so astronomical observations were delayed awaiting clear weather. Even so, once at anchor within the Sound, the officers directed that parties be detached from the vessel to run base lines for purposes of triangulation. The survey was carried out largely by Masters Gowlland and George Browning, the latter an excellent draftsman. Boat crews took soundings, noting reefs and shoals, sand banks and kelp beds, and channels and shallows, and all the time the midshipmen and clerks entered data in Admiralty notebooks. It was a demanding business, especially during heavy rains. The boat work was tedious and tiring. On July 25, Richards went to the northwest entrance to Clayoquot Sound, measured a base and thus got the means of putting on paper the considerable work already done by the detached parties.

It now being time to shift to the southernmost entrance, Richards, accompanied by the ship's surgeon, Dr. Charles Wood, in the pinnace, headed for Port Cox. He wryly notes that he sailed right through the land shown in the "old chart"—that is, George Vancouver's chart (Vancouver had never been there). He arrived at his destination at noon on July 29, 1861. They set up camp on the west side of Tofino Arm, where they found the mosquitoes very troublesome.

Soon the First Nations made their appearance. "The tribe about a mile below us are shifting their village close to us," wrote Richards in his journal, "I suppose for their own convenience. Instead of going to and fro twice a day the[y] spend the greater part of their time lying alongside the ship—trading berries for biscuit and whatever they caught—and as our men are fools enough to pay higher prices than the things are worth, it is worth their while to stick to us. In shifting a village, they place the large cedar boards which form the sides of their huts across 2 canoes, forming a platform of them. On these boards they stow all their boxes and household goods and so shift very easily."[222] Once again the utility of local timber was displayed by Native use.

Already, on June 27, Gowlland had sent a surveying crew to mark out and measure a base line of 2,600 feet on the beach at Opitsat. From thence a triangulation was commenced toward the east. He estimated that the Natives of Opitsat numbered 700, which may be taken as a good guess, and he was impressed by the Natives' close ties of kinship. The Opitsat, he noted, were "very civil and obliging but cautious," fearing that the British intended to spread disease among them as, they stated, had once been done by the Americans at Cape Flattery. They also feared that the survey markers that were put up contained evil spirits. Young Wickaninnish, about age nineteen, interceded and aided in reducing the Opitsats' fears that the British were trespassing or intending harm. The survey was completed in August, by which time the British had got to know the summer village, E-cha-chist, and other locales.[223]

Clayoquot Sound, Richards concluded, differed from the other embayments on Vancouver Island in that all the lower or outer parts of it were shoal and sandy instead of deep and muddy, as found elsewhere; this constituted an important observation in regards to matters of safe anchorage, shoal and sandy being far less reliable for holding an anchor. Richards' summary of navigational challenges of

PART I The Empire of Fortune

Clayoquot Sound appeared in the first edition of *The Vancouver Island Pilot*, published in 1864. In future, mariners using this *Pilot* could reliably be guided to a safe approach and entrance to Clayoquot Sound and its inner reaches. It is not that the Indigenous peoples did not know all the reefs and shoals; it is that larger vessels, or those with such draft as the entrances would allow, could now come into such places as Port Cox or Hesquiat, farther to the north. Empirical observation and scientific reckoning had now come to possess the Sound. And, as noted above, Richards gave the name of Meares to Meares Island. Gowlland and Browning were honoured in other locales. One more detail: the information Richards and the ship's company gathered was shared with Dr. Charles Forbes, a naval surgeon and a person knowledgeable in engineering matters. He won the £50 prize for his essay, published by the colonial government, *Vancouver Island: Its Resources and Capabilities as a Colony* (Victoria, 1861) in which he gave this notice of the mineral potential he saw there: "The narrow arms more resemble the neighbouring sounds except in geological feature. A gneisso-granite rock (metamorphic) forms the axis of elevation, associated with which are hornblende and coarse grained quartzose rocks, intruded traps and quartz veins, indicating a region, most probably rich in mineral wealth."[224]

All the possessions for science that were required had been secured. The *Hecate*'s officers and men concluded their survey on August 15. That morning the veteran paddlewheeler passed out of Clayoquot Sound and shaped a course for Barkley Sound. The vessel reached Esquimalt before taking in coal and provisions for the voyage to San Francisco for repairs at Mare Island.

Richards and the officers and men of the *Hecate* left a rich legacy: for the first time a reliable description of Clayoquot Sound would be available from the Admiralty's Hydrographic Office in an engraved chart and also a published pilot. A new dawn had arrived. Possession of these aids to navigation to mariners, especially newcomers to these treacherous waters, reduced chances of disasters to shipping but by no means eliminated them: this coast was and continues to be a graveyard of ships. But the fruits of the survey reduced risk. The

The In-between Time

Richards legacy is therefore of incalculable value: when he wound up his efforts, 357 charts were published showing locations big and small on the Northwest Coast, especially British Columbia waters, and his Pilot, or *Sailing Directions*, became the guide to limiting tragedies at sea. All the gleanings from hydrographical science were of vital importance in demonstrating the continuance of Indigenous occupations at Clayoquot Sound. Empire had not swept these peoples aside or removed or crushed them.

By the 1860s, independent sailors, unconnected with government or commerce, began to make their appearance at Clayoquot. Such persons are vagabonds of the sea, seeking adventure—and even today they can be found venturing in remote waters. As for the west coast of Vancouver Island, perhaps the most unusual adventurer was yachtsman Lieutenant Charles Edward Barrett-Lennard, late of the British 5th Dragoon Guards, and a veteran of the Crimean War, who shipped his cutter yacht *Templar* on the settlement vessel *Athelstan* to the Vancouver Island colony.[225] At Esquimalt naval base he had the assistance of naval personnel, in their spare time, to refit the *Templar* in readiness for cruising local waters and, later, a circumnavigation of Vancouver Island.[226] Barrett-Lennard's *Travels in British Columbia, with the Narrative of a Yacht Voyage round Vancouver Island*, published in London in 1862, tells much of the story, and a fascinating one it is. We can see him now at the wheel, dressed in the brass-buttoned jacket of the Royal Thames Yacht Club and an old cavalry cap with its gold band, the blue ensign of the Royal Thames at the peak, coasting south from Resolution Cove, Nootka, his most recent port of call. "I always passed in this nondescript costume for a man-of-war Tyee, or officer," he says cheerily.[227]

In all likelihood, Barrett-Lennard had been at Clayoquot at least once before—that is, before his circumnavigation. He told a correspondent that he thought a good trade could be entered into at Clayoquot Sound.[228] In any event, Barrett-Lennard did not meet Richards, but he knew Gowlland and others; indeed, he and his crew enjoyed many an agreeable encounter with the British navy at Clayoquot. We retrace our steps to early 1861, when the decked cutter

PART I The Empire of Fortune

Shark arrived at Clayoquot from nearby surveying duties. The main surveying vessel, the *Hecate*, was then in Barkley Sound. On coming into what is now Templar Channel, the naval men spied the *Templar* riding at anchor. Nearby they found its crew encamped on the sandy spit of what is now called Stubbs Island. Barrett-Lennard was not present at the time, but his associate Captain Napoleon Fitz Stubbs, late of the North Gloucestershire Regiment and also a Crimean War veteran, was there in charge.[229] One can only imagine the convivial exchanges between the vessel crews out there on what Europeans regarded as the margins of the known world.

"Clayoquot is a very extensive Sound, having several arms or inlets communicating with the interior," wrote Barrett-Lennard. "The anchorage is generally good, but the water is much shallower and the shores lower than at Nootka. The growth of timber is less dense, and there is some good open land in its vicinity." Thus did he point to the commercial prospects of the place. He continued: "The summer village of the Clayoquots is situated near the sea, the entrance to the cove on which it stands being surrounded with rocks and exposed to the most dangerous winds from the sea; in fact, offering no shelter to any vessel seeking refuge there." He knew this from a previous coasting passage when storm surge made such an entry impossible; indeed, it is a tight entrance in difficult weather. But, he remarked, farther up the Sound "plenty of places may be found in which a vessel can lie safely at anchor. We were much struck with the immense size of some of the beams of timber used in the construction of several of the huts in this village, those of the chiefs being here, as elsewhere, the largest." He marvelled at how the Indigenous peoples managed to raise a beam perhaps one hundred feet in length to a height of ten or twelve feet from the ground. "The sight of these buildings produced much the same effect of wonder on my mind as did the first visit to Stonehenge. I may mention that many of these erections are evidently of great antiquity."[230] After the cruise, Barrett-Lennard sold the *Templar* to a Victoria concern. Some years later she dragged anchor in Foul Bay, Victoria, and became a total wreck.

The In-between Time

Had Clayoquot in the 1850s been a promising centre of economic enterprise, an active port or a place for coal mining, Governor Douglas, who was also head of operations for the HBC on Vancouver Island, would have had a treaty signed with the local chiefs, as he did at Victoria, Sooke, Nanaimo and Fort Rupert. But it was not to be. In fact, no planned colonial settlement was imagined in this densely forested place. Furthermore, navigation for deep-water shipping was better elsewhere—at Alberni Canal, for example. No developments by the Company or the government were planned. Accordingly, Clayoquot remained outside of treaty arrangements. Any of the humanitarian intentions that had been inserted into the charter of the colony, to be carried out by the HBC, were now a dead letter. When former governor Richard Blanshard testified before the Select Committee of the House of Commons on the Affairs of the Hudson's Bay Company in 1857, he was asked if the Company's policy was to improve the Natives off the face of the land, as in the United States. "Exactly so," he replied. By virtue of the fact that colonization of Vancouver Island was slow and ineffectual, the Committee wanted to know if Blanshard thought "the Indians are no obstacle to the colonization?" They were no obstacle, he replied, adding that those Natives living around Fort Victoria were very useful. At and near Fort Rupert, he said, they were "a very fierce and warlike set."[231] The Company, as a matter of policy, intervened little in Indigenous culture, apart from economic matters. I agree with authority Philip Drucker when he writes, "It offered them the trade goods they steadily demanded in return for their furs, and made little attempt to modify their culture in other respects."[232]

Although the tendency of this chapter has been to describe Clayoquot Sound, as of the mid-1860s, as a backwater to commercial development, and a location in which the Indigenous population was perhaps in an unsettled state, we have to remember a central fact of British Columbia history: this was the last part of the temperate zone of the world that was essentially unoccupied for European settlement and industrial development. It awaited the steamship and the steam engine, the gas engine and outboard motor, the float

PART I The Empire of Fortune

plane and the age of coal as a heating and transportation influence. Clayoquot Sound could not remain isolated from global changes, and it had already been influenced by outside forces in so many ways. Herman Merivale, a former principal undersecretary at the Colonial Office, made this clear when he wrote in 1860 of British Columbia:

> Its climate has proved much better, and in particular much drier, than hitherto supposed; its soil not generally attractive, but very various. Whatever use Britain may ultimately make of her portion of North-Western America, it is a region of no small interest to observers of our times, as affording the last open field for European emigration. The remainder of the extra-tropical world is now filled up. No other site is left for the foundation of future empires. Its occupiers will be the latest adventurers in that vast work of European colonization which began scarcely four centuries ago. The duty left for future time will be only to fill up the outlines already traced in days of more romantic adventure.[233]

Merivale was, by this time, an Oxford professor of political economy, and he knew all about the British Empire, including India. It is fascinating to think of those various British persons who were to come to Clayoquot Sound in later days—and many a curious individual did so—to establish outposts of the British Empire on their own individual terms, some of them reclusive and many of them human oddities who could not stand, or could not survive, ordinary life in town or country. Vancouver Island seems, from early settlement days, to have been a place of unusual characters, like the kind that enliven the pages of Jack Hodgins' latter-day book *Spit Delaney's Island*. Professor Merivale understood that some of the most adventurous and romantic human agents of empire would set up their bastions on Vancouver Island.

This book does not trace the history of these people, but I can mention a few by name, with a brief outline of their lives. For example, the Dane Frederick Christian Thornberg, a merchant sailor, took charge of Clayoquot Station in 1874, buying furs, seals and dogfish oil, the main trade. His recollections, fortunately, survive, an important literary possession. He thought the Nootka Indians, as he called them, very suspicious: "The Nootka and Hesquiat Indians had said that we white men (only 3) had put small pox in bottles with water and pouret [sic] some water in to theire [sic] rivers and drinking water so that all the Indians would die and then we the white men would have all the Land on the West Coast."[234]

Far different from raw-boned Thornberg, who settled into married life, was Frederick Gerald Tibbs. This well-moneyed fellow—perhaps a remittance man from London, "sent to the colonies" to find his way—was a loner not by choice but because of a terrible affliction. He had big holes on the left side of his face caused by a riding accident or other misadventure, the details of which no one has been able to track down. Disfigured as well as short of stature, he was understandably self-conscious. A poet with a public-school education, and the complete gentleman in every way, though lonely because of his affliction, Tibbs arrived at Long Beach in 1910 or 1911; he may have worked at the new fish hatchery. He removed to his self-styled "Dream Isle"—now Arnet Island—where he built a three-storey wooden castle with rose trellises in the clearing made by his own hands. Here was a man-made possession of solitude. Atop the only remaining 100-foot spruce he built a viewing platform, where he could play gramophone records to his heart's content. When war came in 1914, this son of Empire made plans to enlist, and he went overseas and joined a regiment. Returning to Dream Isle he was never able to marry. He died a cruel death entangled in the weeds off a beach at Clayoquot, having gone in his skiff *Agnes* to tend a coal light buoy put there as a navigational aid. Somehow he lost, or became separated from, the skiff in the tide and breeze. Eventually he reached shore, exhausted, and there he died, aged 35. The date was July 5, 1921. Tibbs has been portrayed as a freak and a wild man, a loner; in fact, he is a figure who invites our compassion and understanding, a man doing his civic duty and paying the price. As to his death, one informant of the time, Winnie Dixson, says that he called to get some Native women to bring a rescuing canoe, but they did not know his language (or he theirs). Dixson's view is that they should have gone and told the policeman, who would have effected a res-

PART I The Empire of Fortune

cue.[235] He is buried in the old Morpheus Island cemetery.

Others arrived from England. Dorothy Abraham accepted the invitation of her future husband Ted Abraham to live on Vargas Island, where he had 160 acres. She tells her tale in *Lone Cone*, a classic of life in Clayoquot Sound. Another unique settler, "Cougar Annie," Ada Annie Rae-Arthur, arrived in 1915 with her family at Boat Basin, in Hesquiat Harbour. These and other lives make for engaging reading, for they were strong persons living frontier lives. Bob Bossin tells their tales in *Settling Clayoquot*, one of those extraordinarily significant issues of *Sound Heritage*, published by the Aural History Division of the BC Provincial Archives in the 1970s and 1980s.

Prominent in the commercial affairs of Clayoquot at the end of the nineteenth century was the arrival of Walter Dawley and Thomas Stockham. They set up a store on Stockham Island, near Opitsat on Meares Island. This store was the centre of their business empire and a regular port of call for supply steamers. They also had stores at Nootka and Ahousat, where Frederick Christian Thornberg was storekeeper. Taken all together, the three stores were a tidy and profitable network. Stockham Island boasted a hotel, the first in Clayoquot Sound, built 1898. As to the population of Clayoquot Sound, it has been estimated that at the turn of the century about 800 Indigenous persons and probably fewer than a hundred white people lived there, largely in scattered locations. Beaches, inlets and islets were new places of domicile. The largest Native villages were Opitsat, Kelsemat, Ahousat and Hesquiat.[236] All were drawn together by water—by canoes, outboard motorboats, rowboats and coastal steamers. It was a floating world. And it was a place of rain.

The epoch covered by this chapter witnessed the arrival of the camera. Several noted pioneer photographers, including Charles Gentile (in Clayoquot around 1864), Frederick Dally (1866) and Hannah and Richard Maynard (1874, 1879), captured early scenes and persons, as well as rapidly changing styles of clothing—blankets, cottons and hats are new items, indications of an evolving mate-

The In-between Time

rial culture. Many other photographers came later, including C.F. Newcombe, Leonard Frank and Edward Curtis; they found much of interest on the west coast. Photos of great canoes are featured, and whales on beaches. Not all photographs can be credited to an individual photographer. For instance, in John Sendey's 1977 book *The Nootkan Indian*, published by Alberni Valley Museum, we find a marvellous photo of a crowd coming ashore at Opitsat in 1915. In this remarkable image, guests for a feast or potlatch are being carried ashore in their canoe. Two men with tambourine drums accompany the group ashore.[237] Another photo in the book, of Ahousat circa 1910, shows how modern housing had replaced traditional structures. Glass windows have been introduced. Carved house posts, and there are several, were photographed before subsequent sale or removal to private collections or distant museums. A third photo, from 1910, shows Opitsat village, with three carved house posts, and also a great canoe. One pole depicts two human figures holding wooden coppers, above which is a mask with rays; another shows an encircling snake with its head projecting sideways from the pole. From these and other photographs and etchings connected by Sendey, we can see that the traditional arts and crafts, and the traditional ways of hunting and celebrating, were emblematic of a way of life still vigorously being lived in the first two decades of the twentieth century. Those photographers captured a rich culture in their lenses, not a dying society but one going through progressive adaptations for the future. The fascinating point is how quickly this society changed, how quickly it made accommodations for survival, a subject of celebration for all humanity.

Before closing this chapter, and this segment of the book, the historian needs to draw some conclusions and make some observations. These represent his views and are not to be found elsewhere. Government had asserted its presence at Clayoquot Sound only in a general way. In a more specific way, however, change was in the wind. The navy's survey of Clayoquot Sound stands at the gate of history: the ancient giving way to the modern, the Aboriginal world view to that of Western science. There may be other demarcations,

PART I The Empire of Fortune

but the above demonstrate the tendency of the age. Statistics came to possess the lands and seas. Nautical surveys were harbingers of commerce. And those same charts allowed the navy to police the coast at the behest of colonial and later Canadian government. A new age of law and authority had arrived.

Forces of the external world were pressing in on Clayoquot Sound and other embayments of Vancouver Island. Steam navigation and marine engineering of the age produced the kind of powerful, seaworthy vessels required to service the remote communities and businesses of the west coast and other remote shores of northern British Columbia and Alaska. Steam-driven vessels brought an age of reliability of performance that was hitherto only in the world of fantasy. Thus, we find in our annals of coastal affairs a gradual increase in the size and power of steamships. First in the coastal work was the lovely *Maude*, a 175-ton iron passenger and freight steamer, built at San Juan Island in 1872. Then came more powerful, larger carriers. Of signal importance is the 165-foot, Stockton-built *Tees*. Propeller-driven and capable of 10½ knots, with cabin accommodation for 75 persons, she was state of the art for the year of her arrival, 1893. Her ear-shattering steam siren, the first ever heard in remote British Columbia locations, proclaimed a new age—and caused a great deal of consternation until the locals got used to it. For a time the Klondike gold rush took her away to northern waters for that fortune-seeking trade. In 1911 the railway reached Alberni from Wellington via McBride's Junction, an extension of the Esquimalt & Nanaimo Railway.[238] Alberni prospered as a seaport, shipping masts and spars, as well as cut lumber. Another form of western civilization—the Canadian variant—reached Pacific tidewater as tourism by ship arrived, and also new potential for agricultural, mining and fishing interests.

Other vessels served the west coast, among them, and taking pride of place in succession, were the well-built *Princess Maquinna*, which replaced the *Tees* in 1913 and steamed thirty-nine years on the demanding west coast run for which she had been designed, and the handy *Princess Norah* on summertime duties beginning in 1929.[239]

The In-between Time

This was the golden age of west coast Vancouver Island shipping, reducing the isolation of coastal communities and providing essential services and links to the outside world. Richard Atleo, Chief Umeek of the Ahousaht, recalls his people going out in small boats from the village to meet and then board the *Princess Maquinna* to sail to the cannery at Nootka where they worked. They didn't have cultural eyes for such things as English bone china, he said: "We were more aware of spiritual connotations—a different way of looking at the world."[240] All this was to end. The *Princess of Alberni* was the last, and was not a paying proposition, for freight and passenger traffic sagged terribly. When she was withdrawn and sold in July 1958, the historic west coast service came to an end.

However, it was the *Princess Maquinna* that looms largest in memory, and when she was withdrawn from operation, partly because of boiler problems, the locals considered the imagined end of service to be a betrayal of a trust. "But the truth was that trucks and aeroplanes had made such inroads on traffic that the *Princess* had long since ceased to pay her way," according to Norman R. Hacking and W. Kaye Lamb, historians of the west coast service.[241] The history of transportation is the moulding factor in the history of our province. The coastal steamers were the link with the rest of the world: "The boat was the only way you found out about the outside world," recalled Chief Earl Maquinna George, hereditary chief of the Ahousaht.[242]

No account of west coast Vancouver Island history can be written without some reference to this storm-tossed and dangerous shore's reputation as the graveyard of ships. "The southwest coast of Vancouver Island," writes Clayton Evans, former superintendent of maritime search and rescue for the Canadian Coast Guard in Victoria, "was a notorious lee shore lying on the northern side of the entrance to the Strait of Juan de Fuca, gateway to the Pacific Northwest."[243] Evans notes that the area was a sailing master's worst nightmare on account of prevailing storms and currents that combine to bring ships ashore. The late nineteenth century, which witnessed a rapid increase in shipping, also saw many wrecks on this

PART I The Empire of Fortune

coast. The federal government in Ottawa was slow to act, even though the Canadian Lifesaving Service was an integral part of the Department of Marine and Fisheries. Although lifesaving stations were set up at various Canadian sites, the west coast was ill served until another great shipping disaster occurred.

In 1906 the American passenger steamer *Valencia*, northbound from San Francisco for Seattle and Victoria, ran aground in thick fog off Pachena Point, breaking up and taking 126 persons to their deaths. "Aside from two lighthouses in the area and the rickety telegraph wire that connected them," Evans writes with dismay, "there were no lifesaving facilities on the outer Pacific coast to assist the *Valencia*." Boards of inquiry recommendations led to establishing lifeboat stations at Bamfield, Clayoquot, Clo-oose and Ucluelet. The old telegraph trail was enhanced to become the Dominion Lifesaving Trail, completed in 1912. Now a popular but challenging hiking trail, it was chopped through dense forests, crossing ravines and circumventing other obstacles. A lifeboat station was built at Bamfield, where there was an existing establishment to serve the trans-Pacific submarine telegraph, "the All-Red Route," which linked the British Empire. Based at the Bamfield station was a powerful "lifesaving steamer," a 36-foot Electric Launch Company (ELCO) motor lifeboat.[244] A lighthouse was erected at Pachena Point, and opposite, on the American shore, a new lifeboat station was established at Neah Bay, thus providing some coverage to the entrance of the Strait of Juan de Fuca. The Canadian government had been shocked into action.

In 1950–1951 the Canadian government purchased another lifeboat for Bamfield, one for Tofino and a third for Clarks Harbour, Nova Scotia. Other vessels were supplied in later years, and it is clear from the historical record that Canada and the United States had common ideas regarding the types of lifeboats and surfboats best suited for rescue work along respective Pacific and Atlantic coastlines. History, too, demonstrated the common need for rugged, serviceable, and mechanically reliable craft that can go out, perform a rescue and return to safety.

The In-between Time

A little-known factor in the sweep of change for all of Clayoquot Sound was air power, and once again external forces made an impact on its isolated communities and villages. In the run-up to the Second World War, military strategists planning for a war against Imperial Japan saw in the area between Tofino and Ucluelet great possibilities for a base of operations. These would embrace reconnaissance—the finding of enemy submarines and surface ships—and "seek and strike." In 1936 Ucluelet was selected as a place for "flying boats"; soon after hostilities began, a bomber squadron was deployed there. RCAF Station Tofino came into existence, and at one time a thousand personnel were based there. Details of construction cannot detain us here save to say that this was the biggest infusion of capital and manpower to that point in time, with remarkable influence on the landscape and the local population. One other impact of the war was the removal of several hundred Japanese residents, who had started arriving in the area in the 1920s. After Japan's attack on Pearl Harbor, their fishboats were impounded and moved to Steveston. In January 1942, all Japanese in Canada were declared to be "enemy aliens"; those on Vancouver Island's west coast were rounded up, taken to Victoria on the *Princess Maquinna* and relocated to distant, interior parts of Canada.[245]

PART II

War for the Woods

8
Possessions and Dispossessions

The original human inhabitants of Clayoquot Sound, like those of Nootka, formed a culture dominated by two concepts: hereditary rank and kinship. Rank was based on possession of rights to inherited property of the land and the sea and the ability to exercise these rights. Ownership of nontangible items—names, legends, dances, histories—was also a matter of bright pride and possession. Much may have changed over the years since John Meares' visit, but the legacies of culture cannot be swept away.

And so it was that when the linguist Dr. Barbara Efrat went to interview the Hesquiaht for an oral history project of the Provincial Archives of British Columbia in the 1970s, she found that information supplied to her was dominated by matters relating to possession, or possessory rights that had been encroached upon, or trespassed, by non-Natives, governments and corporations. Much attention was given over within the culture to property rights both on land and in the water, but there was also a focus on property rights in their language and dialects. She learned of Native resentment. She found that not long before a Cultural Committee had been established to protect Hesquiaht culture and how it was to be interpreted by outsiders. "The culture has not died out," she wrote, "despite severe

PART II War for the Woods

provocation from white institutions, but has changed and adapted to the new conditions introduced by the Europeans."[246]

Here, then, is the basis of the persistent claim of rights and privileges to the forest and to the sea that emerged in dramatic fashion and gained prominent public attention in 1984, when Moses Martin declared Meares Island "a garden." It was the Nuu-chah-nulth version of "They shall not pass."

Indigenous nations of Clayoquot Sound had been actively protesting for years, but in 1984 their cause became a matter of intense interest, gaining public attention at last, and with it the attention of the media. Logging company MacMillan Bloedel (MacBlo) had made clear its intentions to clear-cut sections of Meares Island, as was the company's legal right under rules of forestry management regulated by the Province of British Columbia, and the Tla-o-qui-aht were determined to prevent this happening.

On April 21, 1984, at the Meares Island Easter Festival in Tofino's Wickaninnish School gymnasium, 600 people, including local residents, musicians and members of the media, gathered for an urgent meeting arranged by the Friends of Clayoquot Sound. Vancouver Island artist Godfrey Stevens had carved *Weeping Woman Cedar* for the event, and the carving became an enduring symbol for conservation. An air of seriousness filled the room. Momentous announcements were about to be made.[247]

At this meeting Moses Martin, Chief Councillor of the Tla-o-qui-aht, and already introduced as the leading voice championing the *Meares Island* case for recognition of Aboriginal title and rights, declared Meares Island a Tribal Park. Perhaps a little unusually in the circumstances, this, "Tribal Park," was the term he used to declare Tla-o-qui-aht territorial rights on Meares.

The formal Declaration, dated that same April 21, 1984, had been signed by two hereditary chiefs, George Frank and Alex Frank Sr., and carried the name of the Clayoquot Band Council. "We would permit access to the island for Recreational purposes," says the Declaration. It also included the demand that outsiders "Recognize our Land Claims and that there be no resources removed from Meares

Island excluding watershed [by which was meant water to supply Tofino and its worried inhabitants]."

The Western Canada Wilderness Committee, headquartered in Vancouver, circulated the Declaration widely, accompanying it with a request for donations to the Committee, tax deductible. In consequence, wider audiences were now being informed of the process, and special interest groups defending landscapes, birdlife, natural wildlife, watersheds, hunting rights and much more came forward in support.

The partnership of Friends of Clayoquot Sound and the Tla-o-qui-aht (formerly Clayoquot) now took action on Meares Island. They laid out a trail from Heelboom (C'is-a-quis) Bay (on the far side of Mount Colnett as seen from Tofino) to "the forest giant," one of the oldest and biggest trees (measuring a nearly unimaginable nineteen metres in diameter). Others took initiatives of a different sort. Joe and Carl Martin revived tradition and started carving canoes at C'is-a-quis Bay. A nastier turn of events came when eco-warrior militants took independent and unauthorized action. They began driving big metal spikes into trees on Meares—an act of protest with results sure to impede loggers, damage equipment, destroy chainsaws and injure operators.[248] Tensions continued to rise.

On September 11 of that year, the Tla-o-qui-aht and Ahousaht, backed by other representatives of the recently established Nuu-Chah-Nulth Tribal Council (NTC), staged a protest at the Legislative Buildings in Victoria. A month later, on October 21, a "Save Meares" protest of 1,200 people gathered on the lawn of the Legislative Buildings. Events were moving toward an encounter of forces at Heelboom Bay, where MacBlo had a landing stage, or timber berth.

Sentiment against the company had risen to fever pitch. Here was a case of traditional Native rights and claims to resources advanced against the claims of a corporation. Because the Province held the legal and administrative machinery to grant tree-cutting licences (and this was all above board, so to speak), the Government of British Columbia also became a target of the Indigenous nations. And because the Government of Canada, which had

PART II War for the Woods

legislative powers over Indian Affairs, owned property on Meares Island, in the form of the two Indian reserves, it, too, was targeted by the Indigenous peoples as a future defendant in a legal case the NTC intended to launch. The only thing missing was an event that would galvanize Native forces and bring in allies to the cause.

Exactly a month after the "Save Meares" protest in Victoria, on November 21, 1984, the loggers, with their chainsaws, plus MacBlo officials, approached Heelboom Bay in the company workboat *Kennedy Queen*. A flotilla of small boats greeted them, an unarmed Native force of resistance.

A violent encounter was expected, and the RCMP were there in what was regarded as sufficient force, but there was no armed resistance, no worry or intention of violence on the Native side: only a declaration of positions based on rights proclaimed in the Declaration of the Tribal Park. The Ahousaht and Tla-o-qui-aht had no quarrel with the loggers, but they did want to preserve the forests. Moses Martin told the loggers that this was his people's garden and that they were not to cut trees.

The result of this encounter was a decision by MacBlo not to proceed with a forceful occupation. The NTC had made it known that it would request an injunction against timber cutting on Meares Island, and was prepared to go to the Supreme Court of Canada. Two days after the standoff, on November 23, MacBlo brought forth its own case, an action against Michael Mullin (local head of the Friends of Clayoquot Sound), Moses Martin, eight others and "anyone else" seeking to block access to the timber reserves within the licence. Shortly thereafter, Moses Martin et al. brought forward their claim to seek an injunction against clear-cutting, arguing that Meares Island was Aboriginal territory where their Aboriginal rights existed.

The Tla-o-qui-aht and Ahousaht bands on their own could not wage such a fight against the powerful controllers of the public patrimony in trees. But the NTC's fast organization and the political will of many of its member nations brought muscle and zeal to the cause; indeed, the NTC had anticipated these events. Rosenberg, Rosenberg

Possessions and Dispossessions

and Woodward were handed the file to commence, when ready, the legal proceedings on behalf of the NTC against MacBlo, the Crown in right of British Columbia and the Crown in right of Canada. It was a bold move, with uncertain results. And it was as a consequence of these events that I was brought in as one of the subject experts to prepare the historical report for the NTC.

It is hard to imagine an Elysium less conducive to considering weighty matters than rustic Yellow Point Lodge, near Nanaimo, on the east coast Vancouver Island. Here, perched on a sandstone abutment facing out to Georgia Strait, gazing across to the snow-clad mountains that flank the mainland of the continent, we gathered to make sure we understood "the rules of the game." Truth to tell, the scenery was distracting at times. Perhaps, I amused myself at a later date, that is why serious seminars at the university are held in what might be best described as windowless cellblocks!

The legal team of Rosenberg, Rosenberg and Woodward had convened our meeting: Jack Woodward, David Rosenberg and Paul Rosenberg had all the facts to hand. All the "specialist subject experts" were in attendance. I was meeting most of them for the first time: John Dewhirst, the famed archaeologist of Yuquot; Barbara and Robert Lane, anthropologists with bullish credits in that line of scholarly work; and Arnoud Stryd, expert in prehistoric archaeology, soils and geology. As said, I had been admitted to this learned circle because of my knowledge of coastal communities during the colonial period of British Columbia's history. All present knew about my book *Gunboat Frontier*. We set aside disciplinary rivalries and all points of scholarly disputation. The historian's epistemology, for example, veers radically away from that of anthropologist. As we sat and talked, getting acquainted for the first time, I realized that this was a top team, each and every one at or near the peak of their game. We were inspired, I recall, by the expansive venue, but we were equally taken and inspired by the professionalism of our legal leaders.

"The question of the effectiveness of the pre-Confederation enactments to extinguish title has risen again in the aboriginal title cases presently before the courts in British Columbia," Woodward later wrote in *Native Law*. This was so, he explained, "especially in the *Meares Island* case, which, as pleaded, places this as a central legal issue before the court."[249]

At the time we were meeting in 1984, the *Calder* case (1973) had produced inconclusive results on whether Aboriginal title had been extinguished—half the justices in that case had argued there appeared to have been no "clear and plain" intention to extinguish title, which suggested it still existed. By 1980 a test to determine the existence of Aboriginal title in Canada was developed in *Baker Lake v. Minister of Indian Affairs and Northern Development*, a case involving an Inuit band. According to Justice Mahoney:

> The elements which the Plaintiffs must prove to establish an Aboriginal title cognizable at common law are:
>
> 1. That they and their ancestors were members of an organized society.
>
> 2. That the organized society occupied the specific territory over which they assert the aboriginal title.
>
> 3. That the occupation was to the exclusion of other organized societies.
>
> 4. That the occupation was an established fact at the time sovereignty was asserted by England.

In short, proof of Aboriginal title required an organized society, specific territory, exclusive occupancy and occupancy from date of British sovereignty.[250]

We who were preparing for the Meares case were instructed by counsel to present irrefutable evidence of the highest scholarly standards of verification. We did not want to be pilloried on the witness stand, so we all worked extremely hard to defend the highest goals of accuracy, rigid analysis, thorough research and sober judgments. If nothing else, *Meares Island* demonstrated the need to have irrefutable reporting of the subject evidence. I had to learn the basics of all the relevant modern litigation. The landscape was shifting quickly, and the results were progressive, beneficial to Native causes and rights. Canada was not entering new territory: this was a well-seasoned business for Ottawa, and before that the Colonial Office and Board of Trade of the United Kingdom. But in Canada, at that time, there were very few cases in which First Nations or Inuit had advanced Aboriginal title through the courts to the point of resolution.

The more I thought about it, the more I saw that British Columbia was an empire by default. The British acquired sovereignty to this great expanse of land out of necessity, not desire. They wanted to keep other nations out. They had laid down a marker against the Russians in Alaska in 1825, establishing a southern boundary to the Czar's pretentions. They did the same in 1846 to keep the American settlers out of Vancouver Island and the continental mainland north of the forty-ninth parallel. They did all this before gold was found in tributaries of the Fraser and Thompson rivers. Vancouver Island may be seen as a reluctant empire. On reflection, it is a phenomenal development—and its legacy was Canada's window on the Pacific.

The supreme agent of empire was the Hudson's Bay Company. The Gentlemen Adventurers of England Trading into Hudson's Bay had no desire for settlers; they wanted exclusive trade with the Native peoples, which they had by authorization dating to the reign of King Charles II. Here was empire within an empire. The Company flag was a red duster with HBC in the field. Some thought their imperium so strong that they believed HBC stood for "Here Before Christ." The Company rooted out free traders and kept the Russians and American traders at a distance. They controlled prices and looked after their interests with true corporate zeal. From Fort Vancouver on the Columbia River they had extended their coastal trade, bringing stability and order to the entire region. "Through its rocklike policies of fairness for the natives, discipline for the whites, an end to cut-throat competition in the fur trade, the prohibition of liquor, and the conservation of fur resources, the company became an institutional force for law and order and church and state."[251] This is the view of the American commentator Professor Norman H. Clark, and

PART II War for the Woods

it stands the test of time. He points out that the HBC men worked with the Natives, mingled freely with them, gained their confidence by learning how to appeal to their sense of private property and by teaching them to be of service to themselves and to the Company. He concludes in ringing tones, "Gentlemen and men of the marching brigades took Indian wives and raised families. As a bridge between two very different cultures, the Hudson's Bay Company was perhaps the most humane and effective ever conceived by Europeans for North America. It was far superior to either slavery or war." HBC men gave British Columbia and Canada a remarkable inheritance, not least of which was the "Indian Policy" that emerged in Canada and was well rooted in Company practices. We return to this presently.

The HBC came to Camosack and built Fort Victoria for commercial reasons, to have an agricultural base to supply the northern coastal trade to Alaska. The harbour at Esquimalt took on imperial qualifications as a naval station for the Royal Navy, which, we saw in Part I, also helped with local policing. Otherwise, this area—Vancouver Island and its dependencies, as well as the mainland of New Caledonia—was, comparatively speaking, a wasteland for future development when so many other better places existed, notably in Australia, New Zealand and southern Africa, to say nothing of the Canadas, East and West, and the Maritime colonies. None of these were acquired in a fit of absentmindedness. External pressures invariably existed requiring a British response, a pre-emptive impulse.

The British at home needed places to export the surplus population. But they did not want Vancouver Island to be an open frontier. The colony, and the province that succeeded it, demonstrated similar measures of control—"keep the Yankees out." If it had been otherwise, and the British had wanted to throw the whole country and its huge resources open, a very different scenario would have followed, with the American pursuit of land and resources possibly overwhelming the British and annexing the colony to the United States. In that case, the Indigenous peoples would not be protected under law by what is known as the fiduciary obligation that Canada, by court ruling, is bound to observe. All Indigenous claims to land would have been fully and irrevocably extinguished. Reserves would be "reservations." Treaties of extinguishment would have been activated, with the forced removal of Natives from their home territories, and there would have been "Indian wars" as in Puget Sound, Yakima, Oregon and Northern California (and elsewhere).[252]

British—that is, HBC—pressures on the Indigenous peoples were benign in comparison to what was happening in adjacent American western frontiers. There, frontier justice, vigilantes, miner's meetings and courts, whisky traders, horse thieves and other desperadoes formed the commonality. Settlers were encroaching on tribal lands. The reader will find all the troublesome details in classic surveys of Pacific Northwest history by George Fuller and Dorothy Johansen.[253]

Compare all this to the British Columbia experience. Governor James Douglas always said that the Natives of Vancouver Island should have what they needed in terms of their reserves. On behalf of the Hudson's Bay Company, which directed his actions, he arranged the various deeds and sales agreements. They were not treaties but somehow acquired that name, becoming known as "the Douglas Treaties." These arrangements were only implemented when economic requirements existed—that is, when there was a need to clear away any impediment to local colonial and economic growth, whether for agriculture, mining or forestry. Otherwise the Indigenous peoples were left well enough alone and did not face the harsh removals to lands considered of little value to white men that were common in the adjacent Washington Territory.

But the Natives on Vancouver Island did not prosper. By and large the resource-extractive industries did not favour them, and the newcomers often had better training and tools to do the jobs required for coal mining (at Fort Rupert and Nanaimo) and in the "boom" economy of Vancouver Island in the 1850s and afterwards. The imported industrial economy, too, which was driven by technology and fuelled by capitalism and trained labour, swept into the harbours of Vancouver Island and British Columbia, dramatically changing local economies. This was only the beginning. The coming of the telegraph, railways and steamships, the donkey engines and

PART II War for the Woods

steam water pumps, tramlines, canals, bridges, roads and enabling rights-of-way was a rapid process. Pre-industrial peoples were disadvantaged in this process. They were further disqualified from entering any colonial executive or legislative assembly that might be instituted. Then again, the "male only" nature of these institutions was a further complication for matrilineal societies.

But the First Nations were not swept away; they were not removed far away from their original places of occupation and activity. They diminished in number, mainly because of disease, particularly on the North Coast and on Haida Gwaii. But they did not have to face the US Army or vigilante justice. The influence of the Crown and its agents was not benign—indeed, it could be forceful in the establishing of Indian reserves—but there was no "war against the Indians" in British Columbia. Police actions certainly, but not war. The HBC exhibited a benign policy in regards to criminal law cases, for they could not otherwise police the frontier. James Douglas, I once read, had an "Indian policy" which he described as "giving them a little bread and treacle." The Company, pure and simple, was in the imperial business of looking after its stockholders. Peace for the purpose of profit was its goal. And from this devolves much Canadian and British Columbia policy-making in the nineteenth century. When Dominion law came, circumstances and practices changed.

Another digression is called for here. As students of history we have always to differentiate between the intentions of policy and the implementation of policy. The former invariably has high and august intentions, and statements to this effect are written by literate people. Sometimes these statements reflect cold realities. Here is an example: reviewing with satisfaction his policies as colonial governor, James Douglas spoke in the Legislative Council of the Colony of British Columbia in 1864: "The Native Tribes are quiet and well-disposed. The plan of forming Reserves on land embracing the village sites, cultivated fields, and favourite places of resort of the several tribes, and thus securing them against the encroachments of the settlers, and forever removing the fertile cause of agrarian disturbance, has been productive of the happiest effects on the minds of the Natives." Natives could not pre-empt Crown land as other British subjects could. But the plan was that every "Indian family" was to have ten acres of land, and the land was to be communal. Thus, said Douglas: "The areas thus partially defined and set apart in no case exceed the proportion of ten acres for each family concerned, and are to be held as the joint and common property of the several tribes, being intended for their exclusive use and benefit, and especially as a provision for the aged, the helpless, and the infirm."[254]

Douglas wanted peace on the frontiers of influence; his natural mindset and long experience favoured just such a policy. I do not think it strikes as benevolent or despotic; it was realistic to the times. As time passed, however, it became clear that these families and tribes had holdings in land that were small indeed in comparison to the lands that settlers and corporations were acquiring and occupying. The decline of coastal Aboriginal populations from various forces—disease, alcohol abuse, inter-tribal warfare, accidents and other factors—weakened or diminished their resistance to the taking away of the lands of occupation. The important matter that needs to be remembered is that the common lands remained accessible to Indigenous peoples, and it is in this regard the various legal fights and court rulings have upheld the interests of the Indigenous peoples (for example, in *White and Bob*).

British sovereignty, acquired in 1846, meant that the control of lands was vested in the Crown. "Crown lands" are public lands that belong to the Crown in right of Canada or the Crown in right of British Columbia.[255] Today, Crown lands make up over 90 percent of the province.

In 1867 the Dominion of Canada came into existence, and in 1871 the Colony of British Columbia agreed to terms of union with the Dominion, becoming Canada's sixth province. Canadian authority now reached to the Pacific on certain matters pertaining to the "peace, order and good government" of Canada, including under sub-section 24, section 91 of the *British North America Act* (1867), "Indians, and Lands reserved for the Indians." In British Columbia, it was specified, Indian Affairs were to be administered in terms as "liberal" as existed during the colonial era. By these measures, Ottawa came to possess various means of control over Clayoquot Sound (and elsewhere in the province), while Victoria continued its control of civil law and the administration of lands, mines and forests, and justice, law and order. In short, two levels of government possessed jurisdiction over Clayoquot Sound.

Let's turn to Canadian "Indian policy," with particular reference to land questions. In many matters, Canadian policy differed from British Columbia colonial policy. The Canadian policy was an inheritance from British practice and political theory in regards to Aboriginal peoples in the British Empire. Colonial wars and administrative experience had led to the appreciation of "Indians" as His Majesty's Allies. Right through to the War of 1812, the Crown and its representatives had courted and secured the alliance of the Native peoples. One of the reasons Canada was able to defend its borders in that war was that the Indians and the Métis backed the British cause. The fur trade, too, relied on Native allies. In Britain, meanwhile, the Aborigines Protection Society worked diligently to pressure the government, and particularly the Colonial Office, to look after Aboriginal interests in Canada, Australia, New Zealand, South Africa and other colonies. We see this as late as July 1870, with the imperial declaration transferring Rupert's Land—the HBC chartered territory—to the Dominion of Canada. Canada was thereby charged with looking after the interests of the Natives. This was a legacy of the British Empire duly inherited by Canada.

Another legacy of empire is the paperwork of administration, and British Columbia's *Land Act*, I have learned on close study, is perhaps the most tightly configured piece of rules and regulations known to mankind. When you run an empire, you establish the rules—rules about resource development, rules about transportation rights-of-way, rules about settlement, rules about who then could pre-empt land (British subjects, naturally), and rules about keeping Indian reserves to what were regarded by outsiders as suitable areas or size. I always thought that land policy in the Colony of Vancouver Island was run on tight lines; now I realize this was only

Possessions and Dispossessions

preliminary to what comes down to us today. Meares Island entered the land title deeds files in the third quarter of the nineteenth century. There were three, and only three, distinct developments regarding Meares since then. We will discuss two, Indian reserves and an Indian residential school, in the balance of this chapter. The third, a timber lease, is the subject of Chapter 8.

The first development established Indian reserves. As of 1877, when the dispute between the Province of British Columbia and the Dominion Government was at last resolved so that lands could be designated for such reserves, it was agreed that "where land cannot be had in the immediate vicinity of Indian Settlements, the Reserve Commissioner shall be at liberty to select lands for the Indians elsewhere and in as close proximity to their settlement as possible."[256] The Indian Reserve Commissioner at the time was Peter O'Reilly, king of all he surveyed in this line of work.

O'Reilly arrived in Clayoquot Sound in 1889 to determine the reserves for the Clayoquot, Ahousaht and other Nuu-chah-nulth peoples. On April 26, 1890, he sent the respective minutes of decision for Reserves of the Clayoquot Sound Indians—there were twenty-nine reserves in all—to the British Columbia Chief Commissioner of Lands. It fell to the latter official to record the deeds for these separations of lands from the Crown in right of British Columbia's ownership. Indian reserves constituted less than 0.5 percent of the total territory of Clayoquot Sound.[257] The Crown continued to hold title (as it still does), but the reserve lands now fell firmly under the control of the Crown in right of Canada according to the terms of the *British North America Act*. By 1894, after the field surveyors had done their measurements and put down their pins and markers, the survey for two Indian reserves on Meares Island was completed, and they were designated Indian Reserve 1, Opitsat, and Indian Reserve 2, Cloolthpich.[258] I.R. 1, Opitsat, measured 73 hectares.

The second distinct development was the issue of a Certificate of Pre-emption, dated April 1899, to Father A.J. Brabant, OMI, to 175 acres of land on Meares Island, fronting on Deception Channel. This was subsequently surveyed and designated Lot 642,

PART II War for the Woods

Clayoquot District. On February 25, 1905, a Certificate of Purchase to the same was issued to Father Brabant. This records the only case of purchased land on Meares Island, and the only "private" purchase or fee simple property there. The property was bought on behalf of the diocese of the Roman Catholic Church, headquartered in Victoria, for the clearing of land and the building of what was known as Christie Indian Industrial School, opened in 1900. The Province also issued a water use record for domestic and agricultural uses at the Christie Industrial School.[259]

We now retrace the history of this portion of Meares Island, a remarkable chapter in the history of Aboriginal lands, and the paperwork that is the web of legal authority in regards to lands and resources in the province.

The nineteenth-century history of the Roman Catholic Church and its missions on Vancouver Island's west coast is told elsewhere, notably in Brabant's memoir and in biographies.[260] But the essentials need to be summarized here. In those far-off days, commerce and Christianity marched hand in hand. In remote quarters of the world, Christian religious organizations established missionary stations, put up churches and rectories, established schools, founded brass bands and set about the business of possessing souls regarded as heathen. They came "at heaven's command," and so it was at Clayoquot Sound and notably Opitsat, Meares Island. Governor Douglas had discouraged the formation of missionary stations among the Indigenous peoples, except within limits of the colonial settlements, and had discouraged missionaries from venturing into locations away from settlements without adequate means of personal protection. His reasoning was clear: experience had shown that when difficulties arose away from the settlements, rescue efforts had to be mounted.[261] For example, in May 1852 the zealous Father Lempfrit found himself in danger in Cowichan. Depredations had been committed on his property by some parties of the Cowichan tribe. Douglas sent a canoe that brought the priest back safely to Victoria.[262]

It is noteworthy that the Roman Catholics, persistent and disregarding advice, were first in the field as missionaries to the

Indigenous peoples of Vancouver Island. Their stated intent was to bring salvation to Indigenous peoples, a process that involved building churches at various places where future converts could be found, including Hesquiat.

Winter was hardly over in April 1874 when Bishop Seghers and Father Brabant cleared Victoria harbour in the hired schooner *Surprise*, 28 tons, bound for the west coast. The captain was addicted to drink, but the mate, a Swede named Peterson, and the crew were stout sailors. One of the sailors was Nomukos, a Kyuquot, who was cook, sailor and boatswain. Another of the sailors was Chegchiepe, a Mowachaht. Steady progress was made but only after the initial setback of contrary winds, tides and currents obliged the vessel to return to Victoria before making a second attempt. On April 21 they reached Clayoquot Sound, and Sitakanim of Ahousat came out in a canoe with the customary welcome to visitors. Here the strangers were entertained. The ecclesiastical reconnaissance continued as far north as Kyuquot, the largest village. Hesquiat appeared to be the best location for the missionary station.

Father Brabant received instructions to establish the mission the following year, in March 1875. He came to evangelize among the Nuu-chah-nulth and made clear that he wanted to isolate the local population from deleterious circumstances and influences (including white man's drunkenness and depravity). He saw himself as a guardian. And he was fearful of British intervention and retaliatory measures carried out by British gunboats.[263] All the same, he was dependent on the same naval force for his personal protection. Taking "the wings of the morning," he arrived in the uttermost parts of the sea in an attempt to possess the souls of the Indigenous peoples, bringing them salvation under the symbol of the lamb and the cross.

He tells how Nuu-chah-nulth shamans resisted, declaring him *Chinga*, the devil. The older persons put up the greatest resistance. They blamed him for the absence of food. They laughed at the doctrine he taught. A chief, believing Brabant responsible for smallpox he had contracted, shot him twice with a shotgun, wounding him in the back and damaging one of his hands. Undaunted, Brabant

PART II War for the Woods

continued in his calling. Incidentally, he worked hard to make sure that his charges did not come under the damaging influences of "the sects"—that is, the Protestant churches, notably Presbyterian (at Ahousat) and Methodist (at Tofino and, alarmingly for the priest, at Opitsat, where they established a day school). There was much ill feeling. Reading the account of religious rivalries at Clayoquot Sound, as examined by Horsfield and Kennedy, we can see how these "turf wars" reverberated through the nations and villages, accentuating internecine rivalries and causing distrust.[264]

As the cash economy had replaced barter, Brabant encouraged adult males to sign up to work on the sealing schooners that called at Clayoquot Sound in search of mariners for the summer's hunting in the breeding rookeries of the Pribilov Islands, Bering Sea. The pelagic seal hunt lasted until 1911, when it was shut down by an international treaty signed by Britain (for Canada), Russia, Japan and the United States. When the hunt closed, the Nuu-chah-nulth were deprived of an important source of income. They also lost the right to hunt seals for food except when using traditional methods, in other words abandoning the gun and returning to the spear.[265]

In 1895, Brabant, a modernist and a believer in the European education that had given him his own foundation of knowledge and worldview, began to advocate building a residential school in Clayoquot Sound, bringing Native children in from scattered villages as far away as Squamish. He was supported in this by Harry Guillod, Indian agent for the West Coast Agency, who opened Ottawa's doors on the project. The education of children had not become a general principle of governments until the 1840s, and in some cases later. But public school acts had passed in British Columbia for primary and elementary schooling, and later for high schools, if an entry examination were passed.

Brabant selected a location called Kakawis at the foot of Lone Cone on Meares Island. Here, at low tide, a beach of hard sand would afford a place for football, baseball, races and other games. A level site on land was needed for the school building and its facilities.

Supply barges could land at low tide and the students would form a line and pass the goods up to the school. As always, legal records document the school's progress. Under the British Columbia *Land Act*, 175 acres (Lot 642, Clayoquot District) were registered in the name of Augustin Joseph Brabant.[266] The Dominion of Canada provided the essential student per-capita sum, and Bishop Alexander Christie of Victoria, Brabant's superior, guided the project through critical hours. But the work was Brabant's and those, including the Rev. Charles Moser, who followed him.

Christie Indian Industrial School took in its first students in 1900, and by December 1925 the 167th boy and the 154th girl had enrolled. "It was hard to get children," writes Father Moser. "The parents did not like to part with them. It needed a lot of coaxing and persuading."[267]

When in 1922 the federal *Indian School Act* made school attendance mandatory, what is now sometimes stated as the genocide of the Indigenous peoples had been sanctioned.[268] After becoming mandatory, the residential school was often overcrowded and six children died of tubercular meningitis between 1939 and 1941. In total, twenty-three students are confirmed to have died at the school.[269]

Christie School had a chapel, the usual classrooms and dormitories, a bell marking the progress of the school day, and a new brass band, typical of Indian schools in British Columbia. Father Moser gives this account, as of 1926: "In this school they get a thorough instruction in their religion, they are taught also the secular branches of reading, writing, arithmetic, etc., as thoroughly as in other schools. They are, moreover, taught to work. [Manual and sewing arts were taught.] Each child goes to school daily half a day—the other half is for work, recreation excepted. The girls in the kitchen, sewing room and laundry; the boys in the barns, gardens and carpenter and shoe shops."[270]

The school functioned until 1971, when residential schools were closing all over Canada and local day schools being developed, and the pupils were integrated into public schools. A detailed photographic archive of Christie School survives and can be viewed online.[271] In the mid-1980s a fire consumed the main building, leaving only some outbuildings.

In 1991 the Missionary Oblates of Mary Immaculate issued a formal apology to the First Nations of Canada, including a specific apology "for the existence of the schools themselves, recognizing that the biggest abuse was not what happened in the schools but that the schools themselves happened . . . that the primal bond inherent within families was violated as a matter of policy."[272]

The more recent history of Kakawis (or Ka Ka Wis) speaks to regeneration and rebirth. From 1974 to 1994, Indigenous people claimed it back, imagining it as a place of rebirth and renewal. They camped and walked on property owned by others, though they claimed it as their own. For a time Kakawis was an addiction treatment (or healing) centre until those services were moved to Port Alberni. In 2012 the Ahousaht First Nation acquired the property. Commerce was in the air, and in 2015 the location became a campground under the management of Maaqutusiis Hahoulthee Stewardship Society (MHSS) and the Ahous Business Corporation (ABC), with the Nuu-chah-nulth Economic Development Corporation holding a mortgage as of 2013. Today the project is advertised as the Lone Cone Hostel and Campground, and its brand connects the site with Sasquatch or Bigfoot sightings. In retrospect, the acquisition of Kakawis was "an incredible milestone," as was said at the time of purchase, and the Ahousaht First Nation has worked to cleanse the place of its dark past.[273] At another level the development was an example of a form of decolonization, an opportunity for Indigenous commercial enterprise as well as extended stewardship of this corner of Meares Island's extensive real estate. Lying beneath the brow of Lone Cone, it is a symbol of a return to Native control of a small portion of eminent domain.

9
Maximum Yield in the Balance

In the case of Meares Island, the focus wasn't always the land, strictly speaking, but the trees on the land. The Crown in right of the Province of British Columbia owns timber designated and reserved for forestry development. That is the long and the short of it.

With respect to the third distinct matter disclosed in land title deeds, we find that on March 15, 1905, the Province of British Columbia issued Timber Lease 4 to Sutton Lumber & Trading Company, doing so under the *Land Act, 1905*. By chance I found a copy of the transaction in Walter Guppy's Clayoquot Sound history, and I note with interest that it is called an Indenture.[274] It's for the lease of timber on 18,614 acres (7,532 hectares) with most of the lots on Meares Island and the adjacent mainland. This covered the following lots within the Clayoquot Land District (please bear with me here): Lots 627 to 641 inclusive, 645, 646 and 647, also 649, 925 and 926; of these, 632 to 638 inclusive, as well as 649, 925 and 926 are located on Meares Island. This lease to Sutton Lumber & Trading Company, renewed March 1, 1912, gave the company authority to cut trees and carry away the spars, timber or lumber of the same, and to put up such mills and establishments as were required. The lease included an important provision, perhaps unnoticed by interested parties at the time, that contained a strict reference to Indian rights

PART II War for the Woods

in lands and reserves, and here I use the language of that day. The Company could do its business wherever necessary within its lots, "EXCEPT and always reserved thereout all Indian grounds, plots, gardens, Crown and other Reserves."[275] Here we see clear recognition by lessor and lessees that Indian rights, both in the leased territory and outside the leased territory, were to be observed. This lease was to lapse on March 15, 1930, but no matter, for in January 1980, the same block of land was acquired by the powerful and energetic timber giant MacMillan Bloedel as part of Timber Lease T0140. This included a portion, indeed much of, Meares Island.

In the years since European discoveries and trade began on the west coast of Vancouver Island, the pristine locales had become few and far between. Most of Vancouver Island had been, or was in process of being, transformed from a wilderness into a varied complex of humanized landscapes.[276]

Make no mistake, forests constituted the single most valuable indigenous resource in the province. At mid-century in British Columbia, the net value of production was $170,000,000, and some 15,000 persons were employed in forestry operations. Many communities had come into existence owing to forestry development. International and interior trade and commerce, transportation by sea and shore, manufacturing and services all reflected the profitable exploitation of the basic forest resource. "Recognition of these facts has resulted in government dedication to a policy and program of sustained yield." That is the view of the *British Columbia Atlas of Resources* (1956).[277]

Here it seemed was a limitless bounty, and foresters argued that the major tree species—Douglas fir, western red cedar, western hemlock, spruce, balsam, lodgepole pine, yellow cedar, cottonwood and other deciduous—were sustainable for forestry regeneration on 90,500,000 acres, or 150,000 square miles suited for tree growing. Looked at differently, this was about three times the size of England or a little less than the states of Oregon and Washington combined.[278] No wonder the forestry companies thought in big terms, the forestry department encouraged production under certain rules and regulations, and unions and non-union workers, including so many who were helping to harvest the trees and bring them to mill or boom ground, could think in rather prodigal terms, with not so much as a side glance at the rape of the timber stands, the scalping of mountains and hills, the despoiling of creeks and streams, the diverting of water channels, and the building of hydroelectric turbine installations to bring "juice" to the frontier.

As scholar Michael Edgell of the University of Victoria's Department of Geography put it, on the eve of the Meares Island fight, "The landscapes and economy of Vancouver Island are dominated by forests and the forest industry."[279] In the early twentieth century, timber companies began laying the foundations of the industry in the Georgia Strait region, and they started to make inroads, mostly in the accessible valleys and slopes of coastal eastern Vancouver Island. The industry overall held a firm grip on the British Columbia economy as a source of wealth, investment and employment.

As always, getting access to forests and prime timber depended on transportation—of supplies, manpower and equipment coming in and hauling, shipping or trucking out. The big industrial diesel motor engines made this possible. In 1959 the winding road to Ucluelet and Tofino was opened, used mainly by logging trucks—car traffic preferred Sunday, the logger's day off, for a safer passage. Adventurous tourists were delighted, and those who catered to them similarly. But the shadows were now gathering around Meares Island and its forests: this was what I will call "the crossing of the Rubicon" in regards to Tofino's history, and Meares Island's too. The iron fist was closer to arriving in the heart of the wilderness.

On a parallel note, John Steinbeck noted that the Gulf of California and the Gulf ports had always been unfriendly to colonization, but once good roads and high-tension wires make their appearance, the invasion begins. "Localness" is destroyed by the concrete highway, and political forms come once the radio is hooked up. So it was at La Paz, and so at Tofino. "Once the Gulf people are available to contact, they too will come to consider clean feet more important than clean minds." Roads and high-voltage operating day and night

PART II War for the Woods

"will draw the people into the civilizing web, whether it be in Asiatic Russia, in rural England, or in Mexico. That zeitgeist operates everywhere, and there is no escape from it."[280]

As the logging frontier shifted to Vancouver Island's west coast and to the northern portions of the Island, "the move from accessible, high quality stands into less accessible, low quality stands . . . imposed strains on extractive, transportation and processing techniques, and raised the cost of obtaining a less valuable raw product."[281] The old-growth forests now lay nakedly open before the lumber barons, MacBlo and BC Forest Products (BCFP). Clearcutting was the intent. These two firms, and smaller ones that often worked in conjunction with, or on contract for, MacBlo and BCFP, now had a chance to get at the untouched old-growth trees. These were usually found in valleys or in defiles. Others existed in otherwise inaccessible places where helicopters might be used. The bulldozer made possible the ingress of the logging truck long after the railway lines and small locomotives and flatbed had arrived. Coastwise shipping presented unique problems, seasonally overcome. Aerial surveying and photography made it possible to seek out the last remaining timber treasure troves.

Small companies made inroads in select places, a couple of them on Meares. In the 1950s, "a logging outfit based in Tofino, Knott Brothers Logging, with the agreement of the Tla-o-qui-aht . . . logged the southern face of Lone Cone, directly opposite Tofino." One local resident observed, "It was a terrible scar, they just shaved the side of that mountain, you could see it from everywhere . . . But it's all grown over now."[282] Another small outfit logged Windy Bay, on the east side of Meares, in Fortune Channel. From a distance offshore, untouched timber seemed to cover the coast in the 1960s, but that was passing quickly with the years and decades.

Already by the 1940s, some were beginning to ask how the yield could be maintained. A Royal Commission in the 1940s led to politicians, bureaucrats and the forest industry working up schemes of sustained-yield units and how to regulate them; this was when the calculation and allocation of allowable cut was introduced. Tree farm licences (TFLs), that is cooperative management ventures between the industry and the BC Forest Service, were introduced to expand and control areas of timber supply on public lands. MacBlo's tree farm licences were particularly in the Alberni-Great Central and Sproat Lake areas. That company had previously acquired some of the lands granted to the E & N Railway (later held by Canadian Pacific), and also controlled private holdings and temporary tenures on the Island.[283] According to authority Dr. Edgell, portions of these private holdings were combined with Crown land into two of the Company's TFLs, Alberni and Tofino, which were composed of a number of separated blocks. By the mid-1970s, MacBlo accounted for about forty-five percent of productive land and harvest on Vancouver Island.[284] The regional supply-processing for pulp, paper, plywood and lumber was at MacMillan Bloedel's complex at Port Alberni, which rejuvenated that town as a forest industrial centre, no longer dependent only on ailing lumber and cedar shingle mills. Road networks and marine services aided the process.

Through the 1950s and 1960s, all species of timber were still being sought out for voracious extraction. Optimism was replaced in the 1970s by guarded pessimism. "The industry," Edgell remarked in 1979, on the eve of the Meares Island crisis, "[had] grown from a boisterous teenager to a worried and harassed adult."[285]

In preparing this book I looked long and hard for testimonials from loggers and logging families about Meares Island's future. I found little if anything of significance. I should not have been surprised. Even any Indigenous persons who were in the industry at the time would have been members of the International Woodworkers of America, the powerful union whose main mission was to maintain pressure on the corporate sector and the BC government for best practices and maximum yields. The corporate sector, in turn, fights its battles for possession behind the scenes.

What I did find, and it is something of generic interest, is a memoir by Ian S. Mahood entitled *The Land of Maquinna*, privately printed in 1971. Mahood was in the forestry business (a forester first and a logger second, he proclaims), and he writes that, except for fisheries, the West Coast made little contribution to the economy of British Columbia until the 1950s, when farming trees as a crop began in earnest. Then the area emerged from an isolated frontier to become a contributor to BC's well-being "and thereby serve not fifty thousand [the local population] but more than two million people. There are villages again, where loggers, fishermen, miners and factory workers have homes and school their children." Mahood exhibits deep concern for stewardship, and I must quote his telling, hard-hitting lines: "Do [visitors] understand that the society of Maquinna was simple, although violent; primitive, but still splendid? Does the visitor realize that modern society is incredibly more complex, much less violent, vastly more comfortable and, in its own way, more splendid? The Nootkas lived off the sea, keeping as far away from the resources of the land environment as possible. We use the resources of the total environment, and we have a responsibility to maintain it to the full."[286] Here, unmasked, is the forester's and the logger's best credo: Mahood is surely a representative, and an articulate one at that, of the progressive commercial view, one that, at the date of writing, has become rather muted, if voiced at all, in the discourse about the future. Certainly no television or radio network is going to give it any time. Mahood's operative word for the forests is "harvesting," surely indicative of the cutting and replanting mentality so common in forestry practices these days.

At Clayoquot, a clash of ecological interpretations was about to occur. The industrial logging described by Mahood was foreign to Indigenous protocols of respect for the forests or use of the same. For First Nation caretakers of the old Aboriginal world, the turbulence created by logging trucks and high-pitched screaming chainsaws signalled the breaking of a new and terrible dawn. Indigenous peoples naturally objected to such a prospect, and this was an underlying cause of the emerging alliance that led to the founding of the Nuu-Chah-Nulth Tribal Council.

Residents of Tofino were equally alarmed, for they knew that a scar-faced mountain would rob the town and the island of its magic. Besides, clear-cutting would affect Tofino's water source. Tofino residents were also conflicted, because many (Indigenous and non-Indigenous) worked in forestry.

Out of these local storms came informal global alliances of certain Indigenous peoples and some members of environmental groups. If I comprehend Andrew Struthers' *The Green Shadow* correctly, and take that book as a memoir of experience, Tofino as a community found itself in an existentialist flap over the future of Clayoquot Sound, the matter of Meares Island being a preliminary to the main event, so to speak.[287] It could only be imagined at this time what might happen if MacBlo was not stopped. In response, protests by environmental entities, some old and seasoned, others new and recently established, against the near and present danger, became part of the political scene in British Columbia.

Similarly, MacBlo's interest in Meares Island quickly took on an importance much larger than the actual size of the island. The outcome of this case might have a serious impact on other areas—and on other companies.

In the matter of Meares, MacBlo and the BC Ministry of Forests were powerful agencies with history and experience on their side. The government, culpable in the circumstances, ignored the protests, and in November 1983 gave the company permission to log 90 percent of its lease on Meares. The remaining 10 percent was deferred for twenty years.[288] So began the intended assault on the forests of Meares Island.

Meares Island became the focus of a political and economic (or commercial) firestorm pitting residents, environmentalists and the tourist industry against loggers. Both sides depended on the woods for a livelihood and had families and communities to support. In their 2014 history of Tofino and Clayoquot Sound, Margaret Horsfield and Ian Kennedy tell the story of these conflicting interests,[289] both of which were claiming possession of Meares Island. The days of Wickaninnish were long gone—or were they? The Indigenous

PART II War for the Woods

voice was to play the critical part in what transpired, and we return to it presently. For the moment, we turn briefly to the other factors that drew people to join in the chorus for the common cause.

In Tofino it was well known that sooner or later Meares would be logged, for already at nearby Ucluelet the clear-cutting had been extensive—and a visual eyesore to residents and visitors. However, Pacific Rim National Park was now seeing tens of thousands of visitors annually, so protecting tourism was a consideration, as was protecting the local water supply. Another consideration was fighting big business, and still another was combating government indifference.

I personally remember a visit to Long Beach in ever so long ago 1977, when regulations were just being put in place to prohibit vehicular traffic on the beach. Parks Canada was seeking new measures to protect an important part of the biosphere of the west coast of Canada. This was one example of the environmental concerns that became a major aspect of the *Meares Island* case. The Sierra Club, founded 1892, and Greenpeace, founded 1972, joined the fight against the logging companies. The Friends of Clayoquot Sound, which grew out of discussions in Tofino in the late 1970s, became the local and indeed provincial organization of resistance.

The Meares Island Planning Committee, established by the government in 1980, was the first entity that began to look at the future of the island. Possession of the present for the preservation of the future was its remit. As Horsfield and Kennedy write, "Consultations began among concerned citizens, local environmentalists, First Nations, forestry union representatives, the provincial government, and MacBlo to see what could be done... Over the next three years, the committee tried to reach consensus, suggesting a number of options to preserve Meares Island."[290] The process was protracted. MacBlo finally walked from the table, frustrated by the slowness of procedures, and suggested that it log 53 percent of the land over thirty-five years.

As Jack Woodward and I travelled by float plane from Vancouver to Ahousat to report to the NTC and the Chiefs and Elders on our findings, below me I could see the heartbreaking vistas of a clear-

Maximum Yield in the Balance

cut Vancouver Island—vast bald brown spaces, some with sharp-line boundaries that defied topography and geographical logic. Down at sea level there had been many encroachments on the forests of Clayoquot Sound and nearby. Below me, too, lay the small communities, among them Grice Bay, Calm Bay, Ahousat, Ucluelet. A sadness overwhelmed me.

10
Contested Ground

Our concern is Meares Island and its history. All the same it is necessary to remind ourselves that Indian blockades were being put up in these same critical years in such places as Gustafsen Lake in the BC interior, Oka in Quebec, and also at Lyell Island, in the South Moresby wilderness area of Haida Gwaii. The latter was another forestry matter, bearing on a timber licence in the possession of Rayonier Canada. Lyell Island was where the Haida Nation came forward in 1985 to block logging and make a strong statement about the importance of the forests to Haida life as sacred spaces and for plant use.[291] Details of this may be found elsewhere, but my point here is that the 1980s signalled the beginning of an epoch in British Columbia and Canadian history about Indigenous rights and uses of forest resources.

It's also important to remember that other court cases were then proceeding in Canada and British Columbia, backing Native claims for Aboriginal title and Aboriginal use of resources. In Haida Gwaii, the blockade at Lyell Island was upholding Haida law and was coupled with a declaration of Indigenous self-determination.[292] At this same time, a matter on the Fraser River was receiving widespread attention as it worked its way through various courts. Those of us working on the *Meares Island* case watched the proceedings closely. Ultimately, in May 1990, the Supreme Court of Canada rendered a decision in this case—known as *Sparrow*—recognizing that the Musqueam Indian Band had unextinguished Aboriginal rights to fish for food for ceremonial and societal purposes. This decision modified the relationship of First Nations to the Crown in right of British Columbia, and the provincial Minister of the Environment, Lands and Parks subsequently issued guidelines on Aboriginal use of fish and wildlife. *Sparrow* built on other cases whose decisions had enlarged the scope of permitted hunting and fishing in tribal areas in and out of season.

All these court cases had a bearing on how our researchers, including me, were tutored in the law by Rosenberg, Rosenberg and Woodward as we proceeded with our inquiries. Guidance was welcome through these minefields of "Indian Law." In short, the use, possession, harvesting, management and conservation of resources were all rights that the Nuu-chah-nuth peoples were claiming with respect to the forests of Meares Island. The NTC also wanted recognition of Aboriginal title. The Crown had never extinguished the Indian or Aboriginal title to Meares Island, and that was true elsewhere in British Columbia except in Treaty 8 area (northeastern BC) and in the "Douglas Treaties" locations on Vancouver Island.

In the Supreme Court of British Columbia, at Vancouver, on September 30, 1991, in a courtroom with standing room only, David Rosenberg, counsel for Moses Martin and others, opened the arguments. The key points he made were that not only did his clients claim the right to use the living forest with its 1,500-year-old cedar trees; they also claimed that the intricate biodiversity was necessary to sustain their living culture and their Aboriginal practices. In short, the old-growth forest was both a material and spiritual source supporting the First Nations' existence.

Standing against this, Rosenberg said, was MacMillan Bloedel's claim that its tree farm licence, issued by the Province, entitled it, and, indeed, instructed it—this is the alarming point, it seems to me—to clear-cut that old-growth forest. He referred to the fact that

PART II War for the Woods

when MacBlo went to log on Meares Island in November 1984, the plan was to log all the merchantable timber within the tree farm licence over the next 35 years, using clear-cut methods. That meant, as he explained, cutting down what was perhaps the oldest living cedar in the world.

Rosenberg outlined the legal history since 1984. He noted that the issues in *Meares Island* differed from those of the *Delgamuukw*, or Gitxsan, decision. In *Meares Island*, the NTC did not claim sovereignty and jurisdiction. Rather, this case was about rights, much like *Sparrow*—that is, whether or not rights had been interfered with.

There had been no surrenders to the Crown, said Rosenberg. Neither the Tla-o-qui-aht, the Ahousaht or their ancestors had ever been conquered in a war with any European nation, and they had never entered into a treaty or deed of surrender of any title to any sovereign, including the Crown. In order to establish Aboriginal rights, the First Nations had only to show that their ancestors were on Meares Island prior to the assertion of British sovereignty in 1846, by the Oregon Treaty. They had occupied Opitsat before the traders came there. St Francis Xavier parish documents of Christie Industrial School showed that the Tla-o-qui-aht were descendants of the original Clayoquots. Their chief was still Wickaninnish, and these people still lived in their village at Opitsat on Meares Island. The Kelsemaht had their connection at Cloolthpich, also on Meares Island. The Kelsemaht, he reminded the court, had been amalgamated with the Ahousaht Band by the Department of Indian Affairs, and still had a reserve at Cloolthpich. In short, the First Nations still existed, had not died away.

Rosenberg then turned to the position of the Crown. From the date of sovereignty, 1846, he reminded the court, the Crown had always been in a position of protector or fiduciary to the Indians. Any extinguishment of Aboriginal rights by the Crown would have had to be clear, plain and explicit. "Anything less would not have satisfied the Crown's obligations to the Indians," he reasoned. The extinguishment of Aboriginal rights may have been a hotly debated issue in colonial times. It continues to be hotly debated

Contested Ground

today. But the Crown did not extinguish the Aboriginal rights; that was the key issue.

As to the validity of MacBlo's tenure, Rosenberg noted it was based on a lease dated March 15, 1905. That lease lapsed for a time, and since 1926 there was no valid lease or licence for MacBlo or its predecessors to log on Meares Island. He concluded that the evidence showed that it was the Tla-o-qui-aht and Ahousaht who had the right to conserve the forests on Meares Island, and, further, that neither MacBlo nor the Province had the right to clear-cut log the trees. "The aboriginal rights continue, have never been extinguished, and a[re] constitutionally protected."[293]

The Supreme Court of British Columbia dismissed the petition for an injunction, and in a rare action the British Columbia Court of Appeal, which does not usually grant leave to hear such injunction cases, agreed to hear the application. The Court of Appeal decided that the trees of Meares Island would remain standing. In delivering his reasons, Mr. Justice Peter Seaton stated:

> Meares Island was occupied by Indians when Europeans first arrived. Indians were dependent on the forest for their shelter, their means of transportation and, to a lesser extent, their food and clothing. It has other intangible values for them. Their dependence on the forest in some aspects continues today . . . The material indicates that the natives have used this area over a long period. Many of the bark-stripped trees [that is, culturally modified trees] within the area being examined could be dated. The trees show use in the twentieth century, the nineteenth century, the eighteenth century and in the seventeenth century. A stump was found from which the tree had been felled in 1685 or earlier. Bark had been stripped from another tree in 1642.[294]

Seaton went on to say that the First Nations of Clayoquot Sound have been dependent on the forests as Europeans have never been. Clothes, containers, canoes, regalia, and buildings were fashioned from the trees. And then he concluded that the trees were essential to these uses, "The Indians wish to retain their cultures on Meares Island as well as in urban museums." Mr. Justice Macfarlane concurred, stating that Meares Island was no ordinary logging site, but

PART II War for the Woods

an island with special values rising above commercial ones: "In a sense it is like a park. It contains trees of great size and antiquity. It discloses the history and cultures of the Indian Nations. It contains evidence of use by the Indians over many years, and before the colonists arrived." In the end, it became clear that the justices of the British Columbia Court of Appeal acquiesced to the view put forward by Justice Seaton. This, wryly stated, was that if an injunction prevented MacBlo from logging until a court decided the company had the right to log, the timber would still be there. But if an injunction were not granted and MacBlo went ahead and logged Meares Island, "the subject matter of the trial will have been destroyed before the [Aboriginal] rights are decided." MacBlo was ordered by the British Columbia Court of Appeal to stop logging pending the outcome of the NTC's claim to Aboriginal title. And there the matter rests to this day, with roll-over or extended injunctions.[295]

Meares Island (and the subsequent injunction against MacBlo) is of enormous importance. The result put British Columbia on notice that resource extraction and other activity interfering with Aboriginal title would be subject to new limits. Court rulings gave full value to the management rights of the Natives, recognizing these rights from before the arrival of seafaring explorers and traders. In a way, the courts honoured NTC history, or at least did not dispute it. The historical record was inviolate. However, it was also true that the great trees still standing won the most attention. If they were to be subjected to the sharp and whirling blades of the chainsaw, history would be destroyed and heritage despoiled. Nobody, in the narrowest legal terms, could quarrel with MacBlo's right to cut those trees: all the paperwork verified that right. But "Native law," as Jack Woodward reminds us, has Indigenous roots. Therein lay the difference in the issues and in the case. If Moses Martin and his associates, and their backers near and far, had not proclaimed Meares Island a garden and a Tribal Park, some quite different result might have eventuated, and Meares Island would have joined the legion of clear-cut, bald landscapes of Vancouver Island and the British Columbia mainland.

Contested Ground

What about civil disobedience, or the activities of protesters, in regards to the Meares Island matter? By and large the Tla-o-qui-aht and Ahousaht were angered by the threat of clear-cutting Meares, but the form of protest they chose was largely legal and peaceful: declaring a Tribal Park, a Native garden. They did not back up their Declaration or demands with guns or threats. Still, an early warning was sent out by the court: the case for an injunction had been put in jeopardy by the unlawful conduct of some individual Native people and other protesters. In other words, civil disobedience as a means of protecting or promoting a claim of Aboriginal title would not pass without legal and judicial notice.[296] The Crown had issued a stern warning: authorities wanted peace in the Sound.

As to the Aboriginal title of Meares Island, the case demonstrated that an injunction could be used to prevent encroachment. Jack Woodward puts this in different words in *Native Law*. With regards to the injunction that has defined Meares Island's recent past, he says, "The *Meares Island* case established that a claim based on continuing aboriginal title in British Columbia is not so weak as to prevent an injunction from being granted."[297] In other words, the superior right of the Crown existed.

Less than a decade later, the centre of attention in the defence of uncut forests shifted out to the wider region around Meares. In 1993 came what is called the "Clayoquot Summer." The provincial government failed in the run-up to the crisis. Its scheme for allowing logging in over two-thirds of Clayoquot's remaining ancient forest did not address the protesters' fear that the forest would be devastated and biodiversity lost. The Western Canada Wilderness Committee estimated, in 1994, that the government had given the right to cut 600,000 cubic metres of wood—15,000 logging trucks worth— annually.[298] These are staggering figures, hard to comprehend.

People gathered from near and far in protest. Blockades were set up at Sulphur Passage, Bulson River and Clayoquot Arm. Protesters of all ages and backgrounds, from all walks of life and all parts of the world, guardians of the forest, stood on a logging road at dawn in the cold morning to block the way of the logging trucks and

PART II War for the Woods

protect the forest. Some of these otherwise law-abiding citizens—860, according to one source—were arrested and charged with criminal contempt of court because they failed to obey the injunction forbidding the blockade. Their actions were non-violent, but many of the protesters found themselves with police records, stiff fines and jail sentences. "I hold these people to be heroes," wrote Tofino author and naturalist David Pitt-Brooke in retrospect, "they should have collected awards and citations from a grateful nation. Instead, many received harsh sentences for civil contempt of court; their protest was contrary to court orders obtained by the forest industry. Perhaps someday they'll get their medals; these things take time."[299] In an age when historical apologies are regular fare for politicians, perhaps they might think of exonerating "the guilty" found in contempt of court for saving the forests. But the law does not work that way. Many of the voices of dissent can be found in *Clayoquot Mass Trials: Defending the Rainforest*, published in 1994.[300]

In the years since the Meares Island crisis and its legal resolution in the form of an injunction against logging there, many legal decisions have been made in Canada, and particularly British Columbia, that made clear not only the existence of Aboriginal title and rights in British Columbia but also the enlargement of those rights.

Calder (1973) did not demonstrate the non-existence of Aboriginal title and rights; rather, on a procedural technicality, the possibility of Aboriginal title was kept alive. Twenty-four years later, in *Delgamuukw*, reference to Indigenous laws and land tenure systems in proving Aboriginal title signalled the expansion within Canada of recognition for Indian legal traditions and control of lands and resources. In *Guerin*, 1984, the Supreme Court of Canada's ruling was that the Government of Canada had a fiduciary obligation—a responsibility to protect Native interests—that must be exercised. As these cases accumulated, Native oral traditions obtained sanctification and acceptance as evidence. The *Tsilhqot'ín* decision (2008), a triumph for David Rosenberg, showed that the Tsilhqot'ín Nation had proven Aboriginal title to lands it claimed in the Chilcotin; all the same, the court did not grant a declaration of Aboriginal title due to technicalities in the pleadings.[301] That case did not "change everything," as has widely been proclaimed by students of Indian law. As in *Meares Island*, Aboriginal title and rights have still to be defined fully. The files are incomplete; new cases are bound to appear.

Meares Island, as a judicial case, ranks at or near the top in all these cases being fought in and out of the courts in British Columbia and Ottawa. British Columbia became the key battleground by virtue of the fact that the Government of British Columbia had so long denied Aboriginal title (whereas Canada, following British policy, had always recognized Aboriginal title and rights). One might say this was a battle of the Crowns in regard to Indian rights and Aboriginal title. BC premiers and their cabinets remained resolved not to back down from their position, denying Aboriginal title in non-treaty areas. But signs of change existed: for instance, by fall 1990, Premier Bill Vander Zalm announced that the British Columbia government would commence negotiations with First Nations, still without acknowledging Aboriginal title. *Meares Island* remains a case in which the matter of Aboriginal title still has to be demonstrated—and that will mean in a court of law. Meanwhile, the injunction remains in place. And half a victory is better than no victory at all. Half a victory means permanent results.

The work of the expert researchers in interrelated fields had been magnificent, setting new standards under legal guidance, and probing critical questions about the persistence of Aboriginal use and Aboriginal claims to the island. Critical to the case was the undeniable fact that the Tla-o-qui-aht and Ahousaht had not been swept aside by history; rather, they were still in existence, their lineage definable and demonstrable by the facts. They had not lost their language or their places of occupation. They had not been conquered. They still retained Indigenous means of control and polity.

What can I say about my own modest contribution to this progression of Meares Island's history? To my satisfaction, I later learned from opposition lawyers, defending the government's position during the trial, that my report had been influential, even conclusive, in changing Victoria's hard position—the old policy and the old battle cry that all the lands of British Columbia belong to all the people. I had laid bare the history in my 156-page factum *The Documentary History of the Ahousaht, Clayoquot and Kelsemat Interests in Meares Island* (filed, Vancouver Court. 1991).

Here is my concluding paragraph, and I am glad to include it here, for it never was publicized at the time:

> The historical facts as presented in this report do not lend credence to the correctness of the Province's position. Rather they suggest usurpation of aboriginal rights in land and resources by the Province and the latter's complete denial of the same. The Crown's granting a lease of land for timber use and extraction without consent of aboriginal possessors of such resources or rights thereunto, by treaty or otherwise, is historically in contravention to the pronounced policies of the British government during the colonial period, to the actions and intention of Governor James Douglas during the period, and to the successive policies and principles of Canadian Indian administration, which is rooted in the policies of the British Imperial Government.

What is clear, in repetition, is that in preparation for trial in the *Meares Island* case, the legal and scholarly research done by our team had been thorough and impeccable, and the documentary presentations certain. Further, the arguments had been made articulately, with precision and without acrimony. Moreover, it had opened the way for the Native claims of other big cases, notably *Delgamuukw* and *Tsilhqot'in*. Nonetheless, courts have made clear that claims to Aboriginal title and rights still have to be defined by court action. That is the process and the way forward. Justices Seaton and Macfarlane called for treaty-making discussions in such cases as Meares Island. This, too, was a change. The judges were calling for *wawa*—the necessity to talk issues through and come to accommodations. Blockades and fire bombings had no future, and strong police action, like what had happened at the Clayoquot barricades in 1993, could be expected for the future.

Meares Island had the advantage of being island-specific—in other words, the seas were its borders—whereas other cases deal with larger territories and sometimes competing Native neighbours.

Legal interpretations and textbooks talk about the current state of affairs with regards to Aboriginal title recognition and other rights as a matter for "reconciliation," the current Canadian term. In fact, what is at work is "accommodation" to cultural differences and partnerships on account of the recognition of differences. "Reconciliation" is an old term of colonization and decolonization, but equality and accommodation demonstrate that the parties involved recognize what they have in common and what they can do to solve problems. The public expects that Aboriginal groups and governments and corporations will talk matters out—and come to a resolution on seemingly intractable matters of difference. It took a court case and an injunction to resolve what should have been settled out of court, without threat of violence and fear of incarceration.

But court cases there will be, in spite of the extraordinary expense involved. In a very definite and unique way, *Meares Island* was the great example of this, and it marked the path for future solutions in Indigenous matters. It is hazardous to exaggerate its importance, but it would be an error to omit its significance in the history of the Province of British Columbia. In its own special and unique way, *Meares Island* as a case in law has a symmetry and a dignity, a cause and effect, and a suitable resolution: that is enough to make it a complete story with a sensible and happy resolution. All that remains now, in this recounting, is to draw the loose ends together, to gather some details about what transpired next, and to examine the matter as a chapter in the history of British Columbia and of the west coast of Vancouver Island.

Struggles for the Clayoquot rainforest are intrinsically linked to the *Meares Island* case. In fact, it drew the world's attention to the struggle for Aboriginal rights and control. "Clayoquot Sound," Robert F. Kennedy Jr. wrote at the time of the 1993 roadblock and mass trial, "has become the flashpoint in one of the defining environmental battles of our time. In Clayoquot, the fight to save one thousand-year-old cedars and hemlocks intertwines with the aboriginal peoples' struggle to control traditional lands and their economic destiny." As environmentalists and Indigenous nations were

PART II War for the Woods

working to reconcile their respective visions, logging on a large-scale industrial basis continued. "Meanwhile," noted Kennedy, "a provincial government charged with protecting the public interest stands paralyzed between its idealism and its own giant stake in the promise of instant profits." It was the Nuu-chah-nulth, and particularly Moses Martin and the Tla-o-qui-aht, backed by environmentalists, who, in Kennedy's words, "won the first beachhead a decade ago on Meares Island by repelling MacMillan Bloedel's menacing flotilla of loggers, grapplers, and chainsaws. The ensuing legal battle produced a historic court injunction prohibiting logging on Meares until the rightful ownership of the island is established. This was the first combined victory against the logging industry's political and industrial juggernaut."[302]

11
History's Possession

Over the centuries and more, the Nuu-chah-nulth, inhabiting their ancient lands and using their native waters, managed and exploited their natural resources, taking what they wished, doing so for their own reasons and purposes. The "culturally modified trees" of Meares Island were one powerful demonstration of a traditional use of forest resources.[303] Living in a world of bounty, the Natives hardly had to think of "sustained yields" and "harvesting the forests." Those terms belonged to outsiders of the industrial age.

In earlier days, those covered in the first part of this book, these peoples had no cash or money, doing business by barter and exchange. Such credit lines as they had were based on the power of the chief and of the group or village. They were as acquisitive as any people on earth, conscious of wealth and station—and ambitious to maintain their station against any rivals or pretenders. They intermarried in order to strengthen their position, and the chiefs paid particular attention in this regard. Acquisitive for resources and sources of foodstuffs and supplies, too, they extended their tribal empires at others' expense—for example, getting the best places for salmon fishing or to watch out for the return of herring or the grey whales. They lived in a world of internecine tensions. They went to

PART II War for the Woods

war to enlarge their patrimonies. Many remembered the old wars that ended in 1855. Fewer societies could have been as self-conscious as these nations that in the 1980s formed the Nuu-Chah-Nulth Tribal Council, which, after all, was a political entity of necessity to test the courts and obtain favourable rulings. They had the rising tide of history on their side.

The Nuu-chah-nulth had possessed Meares Island since time out of mind. In those distant days of the sea otter chiefs, the lands and seas of Wickaninnish offered unlimited sustenance, though late winter could bring food scarcity if not enough dried and cured salmon were to hand. Shellfish was abundant. Resources of the sea and land are and have been the lifeblood of the Nuu-chah-nulth nations. First, and perhaps since time immemorial, it was the whale. Then came the era of the sea otter, which invited the world's mariners to local waters and drew the nations into a global and international network. Not to be forgotten are salmon and other fish species, including pilchard and dog salmon (for oil).

After the era of sea otter prosperity came a couple of decades of quietude and readjustment—an in-between time. Empires, governmental and bureaucratic, commercial and industrial, were advancing relentlessly, dancing to different drummers, so to speak, than those of the older and traditional Native ways. Indian agents and Indian land commissioners came to Nuu-chah-nulth territories after 1855 and returned more frequently as the century wore on. In the mid-1870s, missionaries made visits and intrusions, and their influence was mighty, some might say catastrophic. With them came the power of government, heretofore only advisory and distant. The Canadian state changed all that, and whereas British Columbia held control of the land and the resources of that land (including mines and forests), the Government of Canada had legislative jurisdiction over, and fiduciary or patriarchal authority and obligation for, "Indians, and lands reserved for the Indians." This was the greatest act of equalizing First Nations and bands in the federation. Canada's authority was exerted over provincial authority. This, we need to remind ourselves, was completely in keeping with British imperial policy, most notably in regards to matters of trusteeship (that is, the fiduciary powers and responsibilities of the Crown and its ministers in Ottawa).

The Nuu-chah-nulth had been witness to all these changes. They had survived or adapted to them all. They entertained the outsiders, did not beat them off. They seem to have made no direct complaint, no concerted political action. They accepted the international treaty requirement that they would no longer hunt the whale, something some of their distant kin, the Makah, are now contesting. By and large, the Nuu-chah-nulth peoples and nations accommodated themselves to these changing scenarios. They adapted to circumstances and, not least, they survived.

The sea otter brought them into a worldwide web of commerce, linking Meares Island with India, China (and Macau), London, Boston, the Falkland Islands, the Hawaiian Islands, Kamchatka and Japan. The armed merchant sailing ship of the late eighteenth century was the means for establishing this web. The Nuu-chah-nulth were content with navigating their inland channels and ranging along the coast in their great canoes—and the Nootka canoes, large and small, were regarded as the premier vessels on the Northwest Coast on account of the craftsmanship and, above all, the cedar forests. Global met local and vice versa. When in 1911 an international treaty declared the sea otter a mammal that could not be hunted, some of the Nuu-chah-nulth objected strongly to an infringement on their Aboriginal rights.[304]

Meares Island, and the greater Clayoquot Sound area, were drawn back into the global spotlight by the Meares Island crisis of 1984 and the subsequent Clayoquot non-violent protest of 1993.

There are many legacies of all this. Some are memories, faded somewhat by the ravages of time, of the quiet fights and struggles behind the scenes. Others are more tangible.

Meares Island reinforced in law the importance of culturally modified trees and places with archaeological potential. This

PART II War for the Woods

demonstration of antiquity formed a key factor in preserving the Island from the systematic use of the chainsaw across its forested terrain. There was export value to the concept. Removing culturally modified trees, which mark the historical presence of Indigenous peoples, is like erasing the DNA of the First Nations: this is the view of Chief Rande Cook (known as Makwala), who was speaking of a 2019 clear-cut at Schmidt Creek, above Robson Bight on the east coast Vancouver Island.[305]

Klah-keest-ke-uss, Chief Simon Lucas of the Hesquiaht Nation, put it this way: "The very survival of the Nuu-chah-nulth people depends on the survival of old-growth forests. Old-growth forests are our most important places of worship. Within forests we are completely surrounded by life; within forests we can renew our spiritual bonds with all living things."[306]

Perhaps nothing epitomizes the general public's desire to protect places such as Clayoquot Sound as much as the initiative taken by a multiplicity of cultural and political entities to recover, or at least preserve, what remains of primeval seas, shores, islands and forests. Following the 1993 anti-logging arrests, delegates to the World Conservation Congress, meeting in Montreal in 1996, called for Clayoquot Sound to be designated as a United Nations international biosphere reserve. BC's Environment Minister, Paul Ramsay, said the application to the UN aimed to have the area recognized for environmental and conservation values while creating chances for sustainable development.[307] This, then, was the new policy—save, protect, and develop on a sustained basis.

The wheels move slowly on environmental protection. In January 2000, with support of local First Nations and communities, as well as the federal and provincial governments, Clayoquot Sound was designated a UNESCO Biosphere Reserve, one of more than 700 such places around the world that "promote solutions reconciling the conservation of biodiversity with its sustainable use."[308] The designation acknowledges in broad compass Aboriginal title and treaty rights, and does not prejudice ongoing negotiations. Much educational work has been done, engaging younger voices—the same demographic that would have manned the barricades in 1993. A ten-year review, completed in August 2010, provides glowing evidence of new partnerships forged, recovery projects undertaken and solid on-the-ground efforts to save this magical place, which some think is as close to paradise on earth as exists.[309]

Of course, protected areas and old-growth forests boost tourism and help recreational businesses but a new and stark factor has entered into man's capabilities to survive in the face of global warming and climate change. Old growth can "capture carbon" better than any other item in the forest. And in the new language of carbon emissions and climate urgencies, "carbon sequestration" may be another way to possess Meares Island's great forests and damp, heavily carpeted valleys. Maybe Meares Island will be reduced, in some bureaucrat's table, to a number in "carbon capture," some fragment of benefit to humankind in the future.

Many of the forces for possession of Meares Island these days have a similar paper, administrative character. For the island remains wrapped up in the commercial legalities of various tree farm licences; the rules, definitions and regulations of its two Indian reserves (Crown land); and, similarly, its assorted water access permits and hydro power line permits. For some there is, also, the dark legacy of Kakawis and the old Indian School property. And, not to be forgotten, its trap-line permits. Yes, it appears to be First Nations land. But let's make this clear: it is nonetheless tied up in the red tape of history and regulation, both federal and provincial. It may be a Tribal Park—for which this historian will be eternally grateful—but it is also possessed by the historical tentacles of empire. Empires are based on power, and those powers are seldom relinquished, seldom lapse. Such powers may be transferred—London to Victoria, for instance, or in the case of Indian reserves, Victoria to Ottawa. Under stress in one locale, the exercise of power may move to margins that promise greater freedom of action and less management oversight. The legal system is the broker here, dividing the authority of law, preserving the power of the Crown, which has fiduciary obligations in regards to "Indians, and lands reserved for Indians."

PART II War for the Woods

As we have seen, the unique characteristics of old-growth forests make them prize targets for logging companies, for the yield from first-growth trees far exceeds that from second-growth. Sadly, current provincial governments have not placed moratoria on all old-growth areas. At the end of the twentieth century, the Government of British Columbia brought forth the Vancouver Island Land-Use Plan (2000), with the aim of ensuring that a critical mass of old growth continued to exist. Certain areas were dutifully identified as special management zones. One such, Nahmint Valley near Port Alberni, lies in traditional territories of the Hupacasath and Tseshaht First Nations. Readers will recall the discussion, in Chapter 7, when Stamp and Sproat arrived to begin logging in nearby lands—and how the Tseshaht had protested. Now both environmental activists and First Nations had played an important role in advising on the new land-use plan.

However, the plan lacked teeth, as Vicki Husband, one of the environmentalists consulted by government, has declared.[310] She was right. Two investigations, one conducted by the Ministry of Forests and another done outside the ministry, show that the government agency responsible for auctioning provincial logging permits was not complying with rules designed to ensure sufficient old-growth forest is retained to avoid loss of biodiversity.[311] Rules were ignored by those holding permits, oversight by government was error-ridden, and forest ecosystems were destroyed. Old-growth trees were topped or fallen. Scholars and environmentalists watched with alarm, and political and environmental journals or websites like *Narwhal*, *Walrus*, *Focus* and *Tyee* chronicled the forest's demise, predicting dire outcomes. A 2018 report from the University of Victoria's Environmental Law Centre reported that "in high productivity areas such as valley bottoms, less than 10 per cent of the original old growth remains. 'On Vancouver Island, only about a fifth of the original, productive old-growth rainforest remains unlogged. More than 30 per cent of what remained standing in 1993 has been destroyed in just the last 25 years.'"[312] The forest industry's advance on the ancient forests continues unabated under the questionable surveillance of BC's Ministry of Forests, Lands and Natural Resources Operations. The stock of old growth is diminishing, moving toward a vanishing point that looms closer and closer.

From time to time, though ever so rarely these days, some previously undiscovered segment of old-growth forest is chanced upon by explorers of the forests of west coast Vancouver Island. Such was the case in 2019, when Mossome Grove ("Mossy and Awesome") was found in the San Juan River Valley, near Port Renfrew. The six-hectare grove has been described as one of the most beautiful forests on Earth, with "tall, straight solid Sitka spruce" and "the ninth-widest big-leaf maple in BC," all draped with moss and ferns. Mossome Grove stands on Crown land but—and here's the rub—it is unprotected. The location remains undisclosed and unprotected. Like those who find shipwrecks, the discoverers want to keep the scavengers and unwanted intruders away. But members of the Ancient Forest Alliance are hoping that the grove will be, as one of them put it, "the new poster child for B.C.'s endangered ancient forests."[313]

In contrast, in 2021, Native demands for a share of the economic benefit from resource extraction in old-growth forests became a factor in plans to log in the Fairy Creek watershed, one of Vancouver Island's last untouched watersheds, near Port Renfrew. Here the Pacheedaht have a revenue-sharing agreement, and they will receive compensation for logging in their territory.

Apart from one patch on Lone Cone, Meares Island has never been clear-cut. This makes it different from much of the surrounding landscape, where great swaths of grey reveal the extent of clear-cutting. And, of course, there is always "romance," the beauty of a place far away, one out of mind almost, dreamlike and precious—life on the perfect edge of Canada and the continent.

There is no denying the importance of tourism in the new era possessing Meares Island. For the island stands opposite Tofino as a world apart from the customary clear-cut mountainous hillsides that can be viewed from that spot. "Out here on this wild edge, where sand, sea, and sky merge, people have always found a lot of space for thinking, dreaming, recharging," says Adrienne Mason, writer of science, nature and history.[314] I am too hard-headed to be a travel writer, but I like what some of them do in their line of work.

Tourists may visit for a day or two, sensing the majesty of that place. Hundreds of thousands are drawn there each year. They are drawn there by the reputation of untouched and wild places, where land meets the sea in this unique labyrinth of sea channels and islands. David Pitt-Brooke, a naturalist, writes on this matter from his experience as an environment education officer for Parks Canada, which administers Pacific Rim National Park: "They come with an urgency that sometimes borders on desperation, these refugees, searching for wonderment and beauty in the natural world, qualities rare in their ordinary daily lives. They come for understanding and enlightenment. They come to experience an alternative lifestyle, seeking some sense of acceptance in this place, if only in a modest capacity as observers. They come to touch the earth, looking for an antidote to their growing isolation from the natural world, the bane of modern urban existence."[315]

Brooke-Pitt mediates between the real world and the imaginary and idealized one. For, as he explains, tourists come to take away memories and mental images of what they have held for just a brief moment in their ever-so-short lives. They have come from all over the world to take in the beauty and to hold it in precious memory (for it seldom fails, as your historian knows). The town of Tofino, with its shops, eateries, bakery, galleries, co-op, and liquor store, has its own fascination. It is true that the tourists take away only a superficial knowledge of the place—for one thing, few realize that Tofino's water supply comes from Meares Island. Still, they have sensed what were once primeval forests, unmarked channels, uninterrupted vistas and clouds surrounding the tops of mountains. And here is where a fine book such as Pitt-Brooke's *Chasing Clayoquot* can allow readers in faraway places to possess the lands and seas of Wickaninnish. His writing, and that of others, are forms of possession, of a grasp that has not come away empty-handed.

At one supreme and idealistic level, Meares Island is Tla-o-qui-aht traditional territory. The Ahousaht likewise possess Meares Island, as do the remnant Kelsemaht. However, there are dark underpinnings to this long saga of who controls what. Meares Island will surely always be contested ground—though not a place for political firestorms, roadblocks, civil disobedience and legal quarrels. Quietude is Meares Island's hallmark: this is not a place for bravado and barricades; no, the Nuu-chah-nulth do not operate by force or threat. Their ways are those of peace and respect, generously given and graciously received. In the larger history of human relations across seas, islands and continents, this is a good state of affairs.

Now, perhaps, there beckons a new dawn. Tourism favours the Native users of Meares Island and provides much-needed income. Visitors are enthralled by the place, and seem to touch the eternal there. Meares has no dock, but when the captain navigates close to a rock, guide Tsimka Martin jumps ashore and helps others make a safe arrival. This is the first Tribal Park in Canada, she says, and of course it is the birthplace of the Clayoquot Sound protests and the "War of the Woods," as locals call it. Moses Martin had been a logger by trade. He had a change of heart when he saw how logging was destroying a salmon stream. His words echo down the years: "You're welcome to visit our park, but leave your saws in the boat."

Tsimka Martin reminds the visitors that the loggers were greeted by songs and drumming. Boardwalks now aid the travellers, and the large hemlock, alder, Sitka spruce and old-growth cedars are a wonder to behold. Visitors stop by an ancient tree. One traveller recounted his emotions when looking at a thousand-year-old tree: "Its reach-for-the-sky height and enormous circumference make me want to stop and just breathe. What was happening a millennium ago? First Nations here were fishing salmon, hunting whales and moving between camps. The Vikings had barely made contact with the other side of Canada—the other side of the world, really."[316]

Meares Island stands under its two mountain landmarks, its dark forests coming down to salt water and the pathways to wider seas; its valleys are largely undefiled by industrial activity. Here and there stand the giants of the forests, and somehow they have resisted what seemed almost inevitable a generation ago.

Notes

NOTES ON NAMES AND TERMS

1. See map in Eugene Arima and John Dewhirst, "Nootkans of Vancouver Island," in Wayne Suttles, ed., *Handbook of North American Indians*, vol. 7: *Northwest Coast* (Washington: Smithsonian Institution, 1990), 392. This work provides a concise study of Nootka ethnology. See also Eugene Arima and Alan Hoover, *The Whaling People of the West Coast of Vancouver Island and Cape Flattery* (Victoria: Royal BC Museum, 2011).
2. Métis are people of mixed Native and European descent, with a distinct culture.

PREFACE

3. Archaeologists and tree experts had discovered numerous Native heritage sites and culturally modified trees— immense trees, still standing, that had seen human use hundreds of years earlier: for example, bark stripped from them or canoe forms cut out of the trunk. The distinguished archaeologist John Dewhirst completed his report for the Nuu-Chah-Nulth Tribal Council (NTC) on the Native history and sites of occupation on Meares Island. His longstanding scholarship on this subject dates to his research with William Folan at Nootka Sound and Eugene Arima (and others) in other NTC locations. See Folan and Dewhirst, eds., *The Yuquot Project*, 3 vols. (Ottawa: Historic Parks and Sites Branch, Parks Canada, 1980–1981); Arima and Dewhirst, "Nootkans of Vancouver Island."

INTRODUCTION

4. Decisions and issues discussed in David M. Rosenberg and Jack Woodward, "The Tsilqot'in Case: The Recognition and Affirmation of Aboriginal Title in Canada," *UBC Law Review* 48:3 (2015): 943.
5. Here the authority is Philip Drucker, *The Northern and Central Nootkan Tribes* (Washington, DC: Smithsonian Institution, Bureau of America Ethnology, Bulletin 144, 1951).
6. William Reid, with photos by Adelaide De Menil, *Out of the Silence* (Toronto: New Press, 1971), 18, 21.

ACKNOWLEDGEMENTS

7. Although it is now on Flores Island, Ahousat, the original home of the Ahousaht people, was on Vargas Island. John Walbran notes that the name means "people living with their backs to the land and mountains," which is more appropriate to the village site on Vargas than the one on Flores. Walbran, *British Columbia Coast Names, 1592–1906* (Vancouver: J.J. Douglas, 1971), 14.

CHAPTER 1

8. John Dewhirst, "Nootka Sound: A 4,000 Year Perspective," in Barbara S. Efrat and W.J. Langlois, eds., "Nu-tka—The History and Survival of Nootkan Culture," *Sound Heritage* 7, no. 2 (1978): 1.
9. Foreword to Earl Maquinna George, *Living on the Edge: Nuu-Chah-Nulth History from an Ahousaht Chief's Perspective* (Winlaw, BC: Sono Nis, 2003), 6.
10. In the 1950s the Government of British Columbia awarded certain tree farm licences in the area to logging companies. One licence in Clayoquot Sound was awarded to BC Forest Products on condition that the company build a road around Kennedy Lake. When completed (after much drilling and blasting of the rock face), this road connected to a logging road owned by the Kennedy Lake Logging Division of MacMillan Bloedel, which in turn connected to the Tofino-Ucluelet highway. Logging roads of the Sproat Lake Division were linked to the whole, thus forming Highway 4 from Tofino/Ucluelet to Alberni, which opened in 1959. In short, the logging truck access

Notes

was a feature in ending the isolation of Tofino and thus Meares Island. See Howard McDiarmid, *Pacific Rim Park* (published by the author, 2009), 35.
11. Father A.J. Brabant's *Reminiscences* first appeared, serially, in 1900 in *Messenger of the Sacred Heart*, published in New York, under the title "Vancouver Island and its Missions." In 1925 the *Reminiscences* were included in Charles Moser, *Reminiscences of the West Coast of Vancouver Island* (Victoria, BC: Acme Press,1926). Moser succeeded Father Brabant in charge of the Hesquiat Missions in 1910. In 1977 the enterprising Charles Lillard, conscious of the need to retain the integrity of Brabant's work, edited a new version: *Mission to Nootka, 1874–1900: Reminiscences of the West Coast of Vancouver Island* (Sidney, BC: Gray's Publishing, 1977).
12. Philip Drucker, *Cultures of the North Pacific Coast* (Scranton, PA: Chandler, 1965), 25.
13. Conversation with Peter Webster, April 19, 1989. For additional details of Webster's recollections of time and place, see his *As Far as I Know: Reminiscences of an Ahousat Elder*, illustrated by Kayatsapalth (Campbell River, BC: Campbell River Museum and Archives, 1983).
14. Vincent A. Koppert, *Contributions to Clayoquot Ethnology*, Anthropology Series No. 1 (Washington, DC: Catholic University of America, 1930), 1, 4–7.
15. Hoskins' narrative, March 1792, in Frederic W. Howay, ed., *Voyages of the "Columbia" to the Northwest Coast 1787–1790 and 1790–1793* (1941; Portland, OR: Oregon Historical Society Press in cooperation with The Massachusetts Historical Society, 1990), 279–80.
16. [Admiralty], *The Vancouver Island Pilot: Containing Sailing Directions for the Coasts of Vancouver Island, and Part of British Columbia* (London: Hydrographic Office, 1864), 181.
17. B. Magee, log of the *Jefferson*, quoted in Mary Malloy, *Boston Men on the Northwest Coast: The American Maritime Fur Trade 1788–1844* (Kingston, ON: Limestone Press, 1998), 115.
18. Extract of the navigation by Pantoja, late May 1790, in Henry Raup Wagner, ed., *Spanish Explorations in the Strait of Juan de Fuca* (1933; New York: AMS Press, 1971), 170.

CHAPTER 2

19. The reader is referred to the essential work on this topic, Robert Lloyd Webb, *On the Northwest: Commercial Whaling in the Pacific Northwest 1790–1967* (Vancouver: UBC Press, 1988), ch.1.
20. For discussion, see Barry Gough, *Juan de Fuca's Strait: Voyages in the Waterway of Forgotten Dreams* (Madeira Park, BC: Harbour Publishing, 2012). On the various passages reputed to exist, see appendix to Gough's *Fortune's a River: The Collision of Empires in Northwest America* (Madeira Park, BC: Harbour Publishing, 2007).
21. An Act of 18 Geo. II, c. 17 (1744) offered a reward of 20,000 pounds sterling for a passage through Hudson Bay to the Pacific; the Act of 16 Geo. III, c. 6 (1776), amended it for the discovery of "any northern passage" for vessels by sea between the Atlantic and Pacific. This latter act came into effect on the eve of Cook's sailing. Other promises were made to Cook by those in power, but the details are matters of speculation. He sailed with every expectation of advancement, social and financial.
22. Robert Ballard Whitebrook, *Coastal Exploration of Washington* (Palo Alto, CA: Pacific Books, 1959), 45–53.
23. Richard E. Wells, *Calamity Harbour: The Voyages of the Prince of Wales and the Princess Royal on the British Columbia Coast 1787–1788* (Sooke, BC: Richard E. Wells, 2002), Appendix 2—which reprints a letter from Captain Duncan to George Dixon, 1791, from Dixon's *Further Remarks on the Voyages of John Meares* (London: Stockdale and Goulding, 1791).
24. J. Richard Nokes, *Almost a Hero: The Voyages of John Meares, R.N., to China, Hawaii, and the Northwest Coast* (Pullman: Washington State University Press, 1998).
25. F.W. Howay, "Early Relations with the Pacific Northwest," in Albert Taylor and Ralph Kuykendall, eds., *The Hawaiian Islands* (Honolulu: Captain Cook Sesquicentennial Committee and the Archives of Hawaii Commission, 1930), 36.
26. I discovered these characteristics when researching his life for a biographical entry in *The Dictionary of Canadian Biography, vol. 5 (1983)*, http://www.biographi.ca/en/bio/meares_john_5E.html.
27. On the origins of the trade in British hands, see Vincent T. Harlow, *The Founding of the Second British Empire, 1763–1793*, vol. 2: *New Continents and Changing Values* (London: Longmans, 1964), 419–31; on Meares' character, see 432.

209

28. A close reading of Meares' account always repays dividends. The full title is John Meares, *Voyages Made in the Years 1788 and 1789, from China to the North West Coast of America, to Which Are Prefixed, An Introductory Narrative of a Voyage Performed in 1786, from Bengal, in the Ship Nootka; Observations on the Probable Existence of a North West Passage; and Some Account of the Trade between the North West Coast of America and China; and the Latter Country and Great Britain* (London: Logographic Press, 1790). Henceforth cited as Meares, *Voyages*. His forty-page account of the fascinating "introductory voyage" appears as a preface.
29. Various sources may be consulted on this subject, including Horace Davis, *Record of Japanese Vessels Driven Upon the Northwest Coast of America and its Outlying Islands* (Worcester, MA: Charles Hamilton, 1872); and especially Katherine Plummer, *The Shogun's Reluctant Ambassadors*, rev. ed. (Portland: Oregon Historical Society Press, 1991).
30. Meares, *Voyages*, 143; and more generally on the approach to Clayoquot Sound and the encounter with Wickaninnish, 134-42.
31. Here I have drawn, with gratitude and appreciation, from Rick Charles' 1990 notes for his etching "Friday Evening." Mr. Charles had the advantage of matching the Meares account with his own extensive knowledge of this difficult entrance to Tofino Harbour.
32. Also spelled Muquinna, Macuina, Maquilla. On his life, see Robin Fisher's entry in *Dictionary of Canadian Biography*, vol. 4 (1979): 567–69, http://www.biographi.ca/en/bio/muquinna_1795_4E.html.
33. The Memorial is the essential document for understanding the Nootka Sound crisis, and the British position on trade and navigation. The full title is *Authentic Copy of the Memorial to the Right Honourable William Wyndham Grenville, One of His Majesty's Principal Secretaries of State, By Lieutenant John Mears, of the Royal Navy; Dated 30th April 1790, and Presented to the House of Commons, May 13, 1790. Containing Every Particular Respecting the Capture of the Vessels in Nootka Sound* (London: J. Debrett, 1790). See also Nellie B. Pipes, ed., *The Memorial of John Meares to the House of Commons Respecting the Capture of Vessels in Nootka Sound* (Portland, OR: Metropolitan Press, 1933).
34. José Mariano Moziño, *Noticias de Nutka: An Account of Nootka Sound in 1792*, ed. and trans. Iris H. Wilson Engstrand (Seattle: University of Washington Press, 1991), 88.
35. Quoted by Lynn Middleton, *Place Names of the Pacific Northwest Coast* (Victoria: Elldee, 1979), 132.
36. Meares, *Voyages*, 32, 224.
37. Barry Gough, "Forests and Sea Power: A Vancouver Island Economy, 1778–1875," *Journal of Forest History* 32, no. 3 (July 1988): 117–24.
38. BCARS CM/757, BC Archives; reproduced in Wells, *Calamity Harbour*, 190.
39. I am grateful for the observations of my colleague Jim Gibson. See James R. Gibson, "Bostonians and Muscovites on the Northwest Coast, 1788–1841," in Thomas Vaughan, ed., *The Western Shore: Oregon Country Essays Honoring the American Revolution* (Portland: Oregon Historical Society and the American Revolution Bicentennial Commission of Oregon, 1975), 81–119. The American merchant quoted at p. 83 is William Sturgis.
40. Karl W. Kenyon, *The Sea Otter in the Eastern Pacific Ocean* (Washington, DC: Department of the Interior, Bureau of Sport Fisheries and Wildlife, Number 68, 1969), 136.
41. Barry Gough, *The Northwest Coast: British Navigation, Trade and Discoveries to 1812* (Vancouver: UBC Press, 1992), chs. 4–6.
42. The observation derives from Philip Drucker. See Tom McFeat, *Indians of the North Pacific Coast* (Toronto: McClelland and Stewart, 1966), 87.
43. Robert Haswell (August 31, 1788) refers to him as the principal or superior chief of his tribe. Quoted in Derek Pethick, *First Approaches to the Northwest Coast* (Vancouver: J.J. Douglas, 1976), 130.
44. Michael Roe, ed., *The Journal and Letters of Captain Charles Bishop on the North-West Coast of America, in the Pacific and in New South Wales, 1794–1799* (Cambridge: Hakluyt Society, 1967), 106–7. Henceforth cited as Roe, *Bishop's Voyages*.
45. Valerie Sheer Mathes, "Wickaninish, a Clayoquot Chief, as Recorded by Early Travelers," *Pacific Northwest Quarterly* 7, no. 3 (July 1979): 110–20; also, by the same, "Wickannanish," *Daily Colonist* (Victoria), *Islander*, December 9, 1979, p. 15.
46. The reader's attention is drawn to the views of William Sturgis, age 17, in the employ of the Boston firm Perkins & Co. See S.W. Jackman, ed., *The Journal of William Sturgis* (Victoria: Sono Nis, 1978), 44.

Notes

47. Quoted in Robin A. Fisher, "Wikinanish," *Dictionary of Canadian Biography*, vol. 4 (1979), 768, http://www.biographi.ca/en/bio/wikinanish_4E.html.
48. W. Kaye Lamb, ed., *George Vancouver: A Voyage of Discovery to the North Pacific Ocean and Round the World 1791–1795* (London: Hakluyt Society, 1984), 2:917.
49. J.C. Beaglehole, ed., *The Journal of Captain James Cook*, vol. 3, part 1 (London: Hakluyt Society, 1967), 306.
50. George Woodcock, *Peoples of the Coast: The Indians of the Pacific Northwest* (Edmonton: Hurtig, 1977), 9.
51. Moziño, *Noticias de Nutka*, 91.

CHAPTER 3

52. For a recent statement of this, see Richard Ravalli, *Sea Otters: A History* (Lincoln: University of Nebraska Press, 2018), 37–47.
53. James Kenneth Munford, ed., *John Ledyard's Journal of Captain Cook's Last Voyage* (Corvallis: Oregon State University Press, 1963), 70.
54. In a dictionary of Chinook jargon or trade language, we find the spelling "Mah-kook-house," meaning store, or trading house. See *Dictionary of the Chinook Jargon, or Indian Trade Language of the North Pacific Coast* (Victoria: T.N. Hibben, 1899), 15. I have used the 1972 reprint. On possible pre-contact origins of Chinook jargon (and further linguistic elucidations), see Drucker, *Cultures of the North Pacific Coast*, 169–70.
55. James Cook and James King, *A Voyage to the Pacific Ocean ... in the years 1776 ... 1780* (London, 1784), 3:437ff. For discussion of this and the consequences, see Barry Gough, "James Cook and the Origins of the Maritime Fur Trade," *The American Neptune* 38, no. 3 (1978): 217–24.
56. W. Kaye Lamb and Tomas Bartroli, "James Hanna and John Henry Cox: The First Maritime Fur Trader and His Sponsor," *BC Studies*, no. 84 (Winter 1989–90): 3–36, esp. 32–36 (for the voyages of the *Mercury* aka *Gustavus III*).
57. Winee never returned to the paradise of the Pacific. We find her shipping on board with Meares in the *Felice*, but sadly she died; she was buried at sea. The first Hawaiian contact with the Northwest Coast was thus made not by a man but by a woman. See Frederic W. Howay, "Early Relations between the Hawaiian Islands and the Northwest Coast," in Albert P. Taylor and Ralph S. Kuykendall, eds., *The Hawaiian Islands: Early Relations with the Pacific Northwest* (Honolulu: Archives of Hawaii Commission, 1930), 11–12; Meares, *Voyages*, 10, 28, 36.
58. Quoted in Beth Hill, *The Remarkable World of Frances Barkley: 1769–1845* (Sidney: Gray's Publishing, 1978), 37. She gives Clayoquot Sound as 49° N. See, in regards to Barkley Sound especially, R. Bruce Scott, "Discovery of Barkley Sound," *Daily Colonist* (Victoria), *Islander*, December 24, 1969, 6–7, 15.
59. See Anne E. Bentley, "The Columbia-Washington Medal," *Proceedings of the Massachusetts Historical Society*, 3rd series, 101 (1989): 120–27. The medal was commissioned by Boston merchant Joseph Barrell and was struck in silver, copper and pewter on behalf of the investors.
60. From Haswell's first log, in F.W. Howay, ed., *Voyages of the `Columbia' ... 1787–1798* (Boston: Massachusetts Historical Society, 1941; reprint, Portland: Oregon Historical Society Press, 1990), 78; J. Richard Nokes, *Columbia's River: The Voyages of Robert Gray, 1787–1793* (Tacoma: Washington State Historical Society, 1991), 88.
61. F.W. Howay, "The Maritime Fur Trade," in F.W. Howay, W.N. Sage and H.F. Angus, *British Columbia and the United States* (New Haven, CT: Yale University Press; Toronto: Ryerson, 1942), 6.
62. Howay, "The Maritime Fur Trade," 7.
63. Details and analysis from F.W. Howay, "The Introduction of Intoxicating Liquors amongst the Indians of the Northwest Coast," *British Columbia Historical Quarterly* 6, no. 3 (July 1942): 157–69. Also, Hoskins' narrative in Howay, *Voyages of the "Columbia,"* 260.
64. E. Bell, journal, Nootka 1792, in Lamb, *Vancouver: Voyage of Discovery*, 2:612.
65. Gough, *Juan de Fuca's Strait*, 108.
66. Quimper's diary of the voyage, quoted in Wagner, *Spanish Explorations*, 84.
67. Quimper's diary, June 2, 1790, entry, in Wagner, *Spanish Explorations*, 86.
68. There were thefts of British property, but Cook chose not to make reprisals. As Captain Charles Clerke said, it was better to "put up with the loss of some trifles, than bring matters to a serious decision." On this point, and further discussion, see the astute comments by Robin Fisher in Robin Fisher and Hugh Johnson, eds., *Captain James Cook and His Times* (Vancouver: Douglas & McIntyre, 1979), 96.

69. Warren Cook, *Flood Tide of Empire: Spain and the Pacific Northwest, 1543–1819* (New Haven, CT: Yale University Press, 1973), 278–81, gives the essential details based on Quimper's diary, copies of which are in Mexican and Spanish archives. See also Wagner, *Spanish Explorations*, 85–86.
70. Quimper's diary, June 5, 1790, entry, in Wagner, *Spanish Explorations*, 87.
71. Whitebrook, *Coastal Exploration*, 54–63.
72. Elliot Snow, ed., *The Sea, the Ship and the Sailor* (Salem, MA: Marine Research Society, 1925), 295–97. This book was reprinted by Dover in 1986 as *Adventures at Sea in the Great Age of Sail: Five Firsthand Narratives*.
73. These vessels were to have examined northern waters in search of a northwest passage. However, heavy winds faced on their intended northerly course, and worries of insufficient provisions and lateness of season, obliged the commander, Francisco de Eliza, to adjust his plans and head south—and thence to Clayoquot Sound and other locales, sweeping round the southern end of Vancouver Island, examining various islands and passages, revealing ports on the northern coast of what is now Washington State (Port Discovery, Port Angeles and Neah Bay). This reconnaissance and its cartography lie beyond this current study and are not examined here. It may be speculated that had Eliza gone north in search of a passage and not south to Clayoquot, we would have been impoverished by the absence of the valuable chart of Clayoquot Sound compiled by officers and pilots under him.
74. On this, see Gough, *Juan de Fuca's Strait*.
75. This may be followed in Wagner, *Spanish Explorations*, which prints translations of Eliza and Pantoja. For further details, see Jim McDowell, *Uncharted Waters: The Explorations of Jose Narváez (1768–1840)* (Vancouver: Ronsdale, 2015), ch. 5.
76. On this see Freeman Tovell, *The Far Reaches of Empire: The Life of Juan Francisco de la Bodega y Quadra* (Vancouver: UBC Press, 2008), 159.
77. Quoted in Wagner, *Spanish Explorations*, 145.
78. McDowell, *Uncharted Waters*, 77.
79. Wagner, *Spanish Explorations*, 35.
80. Robin Fisher, "Arms and Men on the Northwest Coast, 1774–1825," *BC Studies*, no. 29 (Spring 1976): 3–18. It may be added that there is no doubt in the historical record (and some of the cases are cited by me in this work) that Europeans worried about the arms buildup in Native hands, fearing the worst. Fisher is correct, too, that other historians, F.W. Howay, Wilson Duff and Christon Archer, have exaggerated the destructive effect of the introduction of firearms. There was no "fatal impact" here caused by firearms. Disease and liquor are matters of a different order.
81. Roe, *Bishop's Voyages*, 84.
82. Ravalli, Sea Otters, 55. See also F.W. Howay, ed., *The Journal of James Colnett aboard the* Argonaut (Toronto: Champlain Society, 1940), 20–21. Henceforth cited as Colnett, *Journal*.
83. For Colnett's account of these difficult proceedings, see James Colnett, *A Voyage to the South Atlantic and Round Cape Horn into the Pacific Ocean, for the Purpose of Extending the Spermaceti Whale Fisheries, and Other Objects of Commerce, by Ascertaining the Ports, Bays, Harbours, and Anchoring Births, in Certain Islands and Coasts in Those Seas at Which the Ships of the British Merchants might be Refitted* (London: W. Bennett, 1798), 96–102.
84. Colnett, *Journal*, 201.
85. On this point, see Webb, *On the Northwest*, 8.
86. Colnett, *Journal*, 201.
87. Colnett, *Journal*, 202.
88. Meares, *Voyages*, 32, 224.
89. W. Kaye Lamb, "Early Lumbering on Vancouver Island," *British Columbia Historical Quarterly* 2 (January 1938): 31.
90. Serious students of imperialism are advised to consult this essential treatise on how empire works both ways: R.E. Robinson, "Non-European Foundations of European Imperialism: Sketch for a Theory of Collaboration," [1972] in Wm. Roger Louis, *Imperialism: The Robinson and Gallagher Controversy* (New York: New Viewpoints; London: Franklin Watts, 1976), 128–51.
91. Meares to Colnett, April 17, 1789, Macau, for Messrs. Etches, Cox and Co., in *Mr. Mears's Memorial, dated 30th April 1790 (Ordered to be Printed 13 May 1790)*, no. 1, pp. 6; copy in FO 72/16, p. 62v, National Archives, Kew, England.
92. Meares to Colnett, April 17, 1789, in *Mr. Mears's Memorial*.

CHAPTER 4

93. Pethick, *First Approaches*, 129–30.
94. The essentials are given in Wilson Duff, "Koyah," *Dictionary of Canadian Biography*, 4 (1979): 419–20, http://www.biographi.ca/en/bio/koyah_4E.html. Also Duff and Michael Kew, "Anthony Island, a Home of the Haidas," *British Columbia Provincial Museum Report* (Victoria, 1957), 37–64 (also published separately 1958). In the historical record, see Joseph Ingraham's account: Mark D. Kaplanoff, ed., *Joseph Ingraham's Journal of the Brigantine HOPE on a Voyage to the Northwest Coast of North America, 1790–92* (Barre, MA: Imprint Society, 1971), 179–81.
95. E. Bell, journal, Nootka 1792, in Lamb, *Vancouver: Voyage of Discovery*, 2:612.
96. For discussion of this matter, see Lamb, *Vancouver: Voyage of Discovery*, 2:612, n. 1.
97. John Walbran, *British Columbia Coast Names, 1592–1906* (Vancouver: J.J. Douglas, 1971), 321. Captain George Vancouver, RN, said that American traders held Marvinas Bay in great repute.
98. This document and similar ones (such as at Clayoquot with Wickaninnish) were likely drawn up by Stoddart, the clerk. For wider examination, see Gough, *Fortune's a River*, 139–52.
99. Kendrick-Maquinna deed, July 21, 1791, printed in Scott Ridley, *Morning of Fire: John Kendrick's Daring American Odyssey in the Pacific* (New York: William Morrow, 2010), 234. Ridley provides observations on the Nootka transactions and prints a map of the four land purchases there (p. 236).
100. This segment is printed in F.W. Howay, "An Early Colonization Scheme in British Columbia," *British Columbia Historical Quarterly* 3, no. 1 (January 1939): 56.
101. An explanation here is necessary and helpful to those who wish to know about boundaries and claims to sovereignty. To the north, Russian claims were limited at 54° 40′ N by separate treaties with the United States (1824) and Britain (1825). To the south, the United States inherited Spain's claims to empire in the Pacific Northwest through the 1819 treaty with Spain. That, therefore, left the British and American claims as sole rivals. The Hudson's Bay Company dominated the trade of this region and called this trading district the Columbia Department (later the Western Department).
102. For all its expansionist bluster, a competent history of Gray, Kendrick and the "Kendrick deeds" is to be found in Hall J. Kelley, Discoveries, *Purchases of Land etc. on the North West Coast Being Part of an Investigation of the American Title to Oregon* (Boston, 1838). Copy in BC Archives, Victoria.
103. I have underlined the significant words for emphasis.
104. J. Kendrick to T. Jefferson, March 1, 1793, in Kelley, *Discoveries, Purchases*, 7–8.
105. Kendrick to Jefferson, in Kelley, *Discoveries, Purchases*, 7–8.
106. Kelley, *Discoveries, Purchases*, 7.
107. Quoted in Kelley, *Discoveries, Purchases*, 10.
108. Robert Greenhow, *The History of Oregon and California, and the Other Territories of the North-West Coast of North America*, 3rd ed. rev. (New York: D. Appleton and Co., 1845), 228–30.
109. Francis Paul Prucha, *American Indian Policy in the Formative Years: The Indian Trade and Intercourse Acts 1790–1834* (Cambridge, MA: Harvard University Press, 1962), 144.
110. [Edward Bell], *A New Vancouver Journal*, 39, published with Edmond S. Meany, ed., *Vancouver's Discovery of Puget Sound: Portraits and Biographies of the Men Honored in the Naming of Geographic Features of Northwestern America* (Portland, OR: Binfords & Mort, 1957).

CHAPTER 5

111. Quoted in Samuel Eliot Morison, *Maritime History of Massachusetts 1783–1860* (Boston and New York: Houghton Mifflin, 1921), 55.
112. Haswell, in F.W. Howay, ed., *Voyages of the "Columbia" to the Northwest Coast 1787–1790 and 1790–1793* (Boston: Massachusetts Historical Society, 1941; reprint, Portland: Oregon Historical Society Press, 1990), 303.
113. Boit's log, September 18, 1790, in Howay, *Voyages of the "Columbia*," 381.
114. Haswell's second log, in Howay, *Voyages of the "Columbia*," 305.
115. Boit's log, undated entry, in Howay, *Voyages of the "Columbia*," 382.
116. Haswell's second log, October 3, 1791, in Howay, *Voyages of the "Columbia*," 306.

117. Haswell's second log, October 3, 1791, in Howay, *Voyages of the "Columbia,"* 304.
118. Haswell's second log, September 21, 1791, in Howay, *Voyages of the "Columbia,"* 304.
119. Boit's log, quoted in Jack Fry, "Fort Defiance," *The Beaver*, 298 (Summer 1967): 18. This article provides a valued synopsis of the search for and finding of this important historical site.
120. Haswell's second log, October 12, 1791, in Howay, *Voyages of the "Columbia,"* 305.
121. Boit log, in Howay, *Voyages of the "Columbia,"* 390–91.
122. C.F. Newcombe, ed., *Menzies' Journal of Vancouver's Voyage* (Victoria: Provincial Archives, 1913), 17.
123. See text and notes in Lamb, *Vancouver: Voyage of Discovery*, 2:502–3; Meares, *Voyages*, p. lvi.
124. Speculation existed that beyond the Rocky Mountains lay a river flowing to the Pacific Ocean. Jonathan Carver, a British colonial military officer under the direction of Major Robert Rogers (himself a believer in these prospects), set out on an expedition from the Great Lakes to explore western lands and waters in 1766; he journeyed for two years. From his travels a growing appreciation developed for the idea of going up a branch of the Missouri River and discovering the source of the Oregon River, also known as the River of the West, on the other side of the Continental Divide. The 1778 map that accompanied the publication of Carver's narrative showed alluring possibilities of that river linking up with the Strait of Anian and Juan de Fuca Strait. These were bold claims that kept alive the mysteries of a still un-mapped far west beyond the Continental Divide. See Gough, *Fortune's a River*, 346–47.
125. Edmund Hayes, ed., *Log of the Union: John Boit's Remarkable Voyage to the Northwest Coast and Around the World, 1794–1796* (Portland: Oregon Historical Society, 1981), xxiii–xxiv.
126. Journal of Bodega y Quadra, October 21 and December 23, 1792, Huntington Library, Pasadena, CA; F.W. Howay, *A List of Trading Vessels in the Maritime Fur Trade, 1785–1825*, consolidated ed., compiled, edited and corrected, with additional materials, by Richard A. Pierce (Kingston, ON: Limestone Press, 1973), 167. Separate lists of trading vessels were originally published between 1930 and 1934 in vols. 24 to 28 of the Royal Society of Canada, *Proceedings and Transactions*.
127. George Vancouver, *A Voyage of Discovery to the North Pacific Ocean* (London, 1798), 2:226. See, on this episode, F.W. Howay and T.C. Elliott, "Voyages of the *Jenny* to Oregon, 1792–94," *Oregon Historical Quarterly* 30 (1929): 197–206. Also Roe, *Bishop's Voyages*, xxv. A most unsubstantiated affair, lacking collaborative evidence.
128. Wisconsin-born Hayes (1895–1986), a Princeton graduate and officer in the US Army in the First World War, went to Oregon to head up certain timber operations, becoming prominent in Weyerhaeuser Co. See Philip S. Hayes, *Boxing the Compass* (privately printed, 1998)—a copy is held by the Oregon Historical Society. Many of Hayes' manuscripts, including his collection on the *Tonquin*, are held by that society, as are many paintings he commissioned from Hewitt Jackson and some similarly commissioned ship models.
129. Edmund Hayes, "Gray's Adventure Cove," *Oregon Historical Quarterly* 68, no. 2 (June 1967): 101.
130. Davidson completed four illustrations relating to this voyage. Three, specifically related to Vancouver Island, are in G. Davidson, Sanborn Collection, Oregon Historical Society Museum. Reproduced in Thomas Vaughan and Bill Holm, *Soft Gold: The Fur Trade and Cultural Exchange on the Northwest Coast of America*, rev. ed. (Portland: Oregon Historical Society Press, 1990), 213, 216, 217.
131. Samuel Eliot Morison, "The *Columbia*'s Winter Quarters of 1791–1792 Located," *Oregon Historical Quarterly* 39 (March–December 1938): 7.
132. E. W. Giesecke, "Search for the Settlement Ship *Tonquin*: Astor's Lost Vessel of 1811," unpublished Ms., 1998, p. 60. In 1947 one of Davidson's illustrations became publicly known; the second in 1966 (see *Vancouver Province*, August 16, 1966).
133. I have not been able to locate the Vancouver publication. See, however, also by George Nicholson, "Schooner *Adventure* Built at Clayoquot," *Daily Colonist* (Victoria, BC), June 5, 1966, 3, 14.
134. Donald H. Mitchell, "The Investigation of Fort Defiance: Verifications of the Site," *BC Studies*, no. 4 (Spring 1970): 3–20; Donald H. Mitchell and J. Robert Knox, "The Investigation of Fort Defiance: A Report on Preliminary Excavations," *BC Studies*, no. 16 (Winter 1972–1973): 32–56.
135. Hayes, "Gray's Adventure Cove," 110.
136. Haswell's narrative, in Howay, *Voyages of the "Columbia,"* 36–40, gives many details of the event.

137. John Boit, "New Log of the Columbia," Edmond S. Meany, ed., *Washington Historical Quarterly* 12, no. 1 (January 1921): 24–26. See, for further details, Cook, *Flood Tide of Empire*, 342–43.
138. Haswell's narrative, in Howay, *Voyages of the "Columbia,"* 312–13.
139. Menzies journal, entry for April 29, 1792, in C.F. Newcombe, ed., *Menzies's Journal of Vancouver's Voyage, April to October 1792* (Victoria: Archives of British Columbia, Memoir 5, 1923), 14.
140. See, on this extraordinary exchange dated October 2, 1795, Roe, ed., *Bishop's Voyages*, 106–7. It is Professor Roe's view that "Wickanninish's desire to obtain a vessel no doubt prompted him to plan attacks on European visitors."(p. 107, n. 1).
141. Malloy, *"Boston Men" on the Northwest Coast*, 179.

CHAPTER 6

142. Robert Levine, " Introduction: Native Language and Culture," in *Sound Heritage* 4, nos. 3 and 4 (1976): 1.
143. In my day, only one in every ten PhD theses, when modified to make a potential book, achieved publication. One in a hundred historians had a second book published.
144. Edmund Hayes to B.M. Gough, July 30, 1968, Gough fonds, Wilfrid Laurier University Archives.
145. My contribution: "The Northwest Coast in Late 18th Century British Expansion," in Thomas Vaughan, ed., *The Western Shore: Oregon Country Essays Honoring the American Revolution* (Portland: Oregon Historical Society and the American Revolution Bicentennial Commission of Oregon, 1975), 47–80. The cover page displays Hewitt Jackson's illustration of Robert Gray's *Columbia Rediviva* at the mouth of the Columbia River, 1792.
146. A catalogue was produced: Thomas Vaughan and Bill Holm, *Soft Gold: The Fur Trade and Cultural Exchange on the Northwest Coast of America* (Portland: Oregon Historical Society Press, 1982). A second edition, revised and enlarged, was published in 1990.
147. Thomas Vaughan and Bruce T. Hamilton, "Artist Hewitt Jackson Re-creates the Pageant of Northwest Maritime Exploration," *The American West: The Magazine of Western History* 17, 1 (January/February 1980): 37.
148. The key document Mr. Hayes needed was the report from Rear Admiral Joseph Denman to Secretary of the Admiralty, Adm. 1 /5878, Y107, National Archives, Kew, Surrey, England. Any serious student of this incident should consult related reports from Denman in Adm.1/5878. The story has often been mis-told. Anthropologists, oddly, neglect reading the pertinent naval reports, but rely on Sproat (*Scenes and Studies of Savage Life*), who was not even there.
149. Alexander Mackenzie, *Voyages from Montreal* (London, 1801), 410. Mackenzie followed this up with several communications to leading ministry statesmen of the time.
150. When compared to the 1804 map of the west Lewis and Clark had in their possession at the commencement of their journey, the geographical additions are prodigious. All the same, the Columbia River is not shown with accuracy and the Fraser River not at all.
151. Bernard De Voto, *The Course of Empire* (Boston: Houghton Mifflin, 1953), 539.
152. "Journal of David Thompson," T.C. Elliott, ed., *Oregon Historical Quarterly*, March 1914, 57.
153. On the various accounts of Thompson's arrival at Astoria, see Jack Nisbet, *The Mapmaker's Eye: David Thompson on the Columbia Plateau* (Pullman: Washington State University Press, 2005), 114–18. Thompson's intricate travels may best be followed in Barbara Belyea, ed., *Columbia Journals: David Thompson* (Montreal: McGill-Queen's University Press, 1994).
154. Quoted in H.H. Bancroft, *History of the Northwest Coast* (New York: Bancroft, 1886), 2:163.
155. Mark D. Kaplanoff, ed., *Joseph Ingraham's Journal of the Brigantine Hope on a Voyage to the Northwest Coast of North America, 1790–92* (Barre, MA; Imprint Society, 1971), 224–27.
156. Roe, ed., *Bishop's Voyages*, 108.
157. Quoted in George W. Fuller, *A History of the Pacific Northwest, with Special Emphasis on the Inland Empire*, 2nd ed. rev. (New York: Alfred A. Knopf, 1966), 98.
158. Of all the narratives and histories of this event, Seton's is the most accurate and complete. See Robert F. Jones, ed., *Astoria Adventure: The Journal of Alfred Seton, 1811–1815* (New York: Fordham University Press, 1993), esp. 72, 91–92.

159. Roe, ed., *Bishop's Voyages*, 107.
160. Walbran, *British Columbia Coast Names*, 93.
161. Quoted in Robert H. Ruby and John A. Brown, *The Chinook Indians: Traders of the Lower Columbia River* (Norman: University of Oklahoma Press, 1988), 139.
162. Details from Joe Martin, Father Brabant and Eli Enns come from Claudia Cornwall, "The Suicide Bomber of Clayoquot Sound, Revived," *The Tyee*, March 14, 2008.
163. Robert F. Jones, *Annals of Astoria: the Headquarters Log of the Pacific Fur Company on the Columbia River 1811–1813* (New York: Fordham University Press, 1999), 194–95.
164. In Jones, *Annals of Astoria*, 41.
165. B.A. McKelvie, *Tales of Conflict* (Vancouver: Vancouver Province, 1949), 5.
166. Walbran, *British Columbia Coast Names*, 93.
167. A.J. Brabant to John Devereux, May 15, 1896, in Walbran misc. papers, BC Archives; quoted in Ruby and Brown, *The Chinook Indians*, 139.
168. See the map, prepared from information given to Hosie, in Gough, *Fortune's a River*, 286.
169. For an introduction see David W. Griffiths, *Tonquin: The Ghost Ship of Clayoquot Sound* (Tofino: Tonquin Foundation, 2007), http://www.tofinotime.com/articles/A-T709-10frm.htm.
170. Jackman, ed., *Journal of William Sturgis*, 113–20.
171. Camille de Roquefeuil, *A Voyage Round the World between the Years 1816–1819* (London: 1823), 27.
172. On the Barkley Sound visit, see R. Bruce Scott, *Barkley Sound: A History of the Pacific Rim National Park* (Victoria: published by the author, 1972), ch. 5.
173. James Gibson, *"Opposition on the Coast": The Hudson's Bay Company, American Coasters, the Russian-American Company, and Native Traders on the Northwest Coast, 1825–1846* (Toronto: Champlain Society, 2019), 55.
174. In turn by Commander Belcher and Captain Richards.
175. Roy L. Taylor and Barry Gough, "New Sighting of Sea Otter Reported for Queen Charlotte Islands," *Syesis* 10 (1977): 177.
176. John Vaillant, *The Golden Spruce: A True Story of Myth, Madness, and Greed* (Toronto: Alfred P. Knopf Canada, 2005), 72; quoted in N.A. Sloan and Lyle Dick, *Sea Otters of Haida Gwaii: Icons in Human-Ocean Relations* (Queen Charlotte: Archipelago Management and Skidegate: Haida Gwaii Museum, 2012), 108–9.
177. Woodcock, *Peoples of the Coast*, 101.

CHAPTER 7

178. See the remarkable volume that contains excerpts from writings by E. Belcher and Midshipman Francis Guillemard Simpkinson, published as Richard A. Pierce and John H. Winslow, eds., *H.M.S. Sulphur on the Northwest and California Coasts, 1837 and 1839: The Accounts of Captain Edward Belcher and Midshipman Francis Guillemard Simpkinson* (Kingston, ON: Limestone Press, 1979), 29–34, 107–114.
179. Here I use Woodcock's estimates, *Peoples of the Coast*, 115.
180. The reader's attention is drawn to the outstanding treatise on this: John S. Galbraith, *The Hudson's Bay Company as an Imperial Factor, 1821–1869* (Berkeley and Los Angeles: University of California Press, 1957), esp. ch. 14 on Company control of Vancouver Island.
181. Captain G.H. Richards, RN, noted that sea otter were rare in the 1860s. He acquired a small pelt, but larger ones, if and when available, were terribly expensive to purchase (one pelt = 40 blankets). For details, see Linda Dorricott and Deidre Cullon, eds., *The Private Journal of Captain G.H. Richards: The Vancouver Island Survey (1860–1862)* (Vancouver: Ronsdale, 2012), 120 n.99, 204. See also Richard Mackie, *Trading Beyond the Mountains: The British Fur Trade on the Pacific, 1793–1843* (Vancouver: UBC Press, 1997), 286.
182. It is generally believed that the Chinook jargon or trade language was not in use on the west coast of Vancouver Island, but the sources on this are elusive and inconclusive.
183. Charles Edward Barrett-Lennard, *Travels in British Columbia, with the Narrative of a Yacht Voyage Round Vancouver Island* (London: Hurst & Blackett, 1862), 131–32.
184. Jim Hamilton, "Sproat Met the Indians . . . and Nearly Came Out Second Best," *Daily Colonist, Islander*, June 29, 1969, pp. 4, 5. For the end of the story and more details, see Gilbert Malcolm Sproat, *The Nootka: Scenes and*

Studies of Savage Life, ed., and annotated by Charles Lillard (Victoria: Sono Nis, 1987). Sproat's original book was published in London in 1868 and is regarded as a competent early example of ethnography as well as a classic account along Homeric lines.

185. Sproat, *The Nootka*, 187.
186. John Edwin Mills, "The Ethnohistory of Nootka Sound, Vancouver Island" (PhD dissertation, University of Washington, 1955), 14, copy in Simon Fraser University Library. Also M. Swadesh, "Motivations in Nootka Warfare," *Southwestern Journal of Anthropology* 4, no. 1 (Spring 1948): 76–93.
187. Harold Driver, *Indians of North America*, 2nd ed. rev. (Chicago: University of Chicago Press, 1969), 313–15, esp. 315.
188. Arima and Hoover, *The Whaling People*, 141–48.
189. Koppert, *Contributions to Clayoquot Ethnology*, 104–5.
190. Margaret Mead, quoted in Keith F. Otterbein, "The Anthropology of War," in John Honigmann, ed., *Handbook of Social and Cultural Anthropology* (Chicago: Rand McNally College Publishing Company, 1973), 923.
191. Edward Sapir and Morris Swadesh, comps., *Native Accounts of Nootka Ethnography*, Publication 1 (Bloomington: Indiana University Research Centre in Anthropology, Folklore, and Linguistics, October 1955).
192. Sapir and Swadesh, *Native Accounts of Nootka Ethnography*, 346–49.
193. Arima and Hoover, *The Whaling People*, 148–59.
194. Webster, *As Far as I Know*, 64. His account of the war, and stories related to it, are printed at 59–64.
195. The war texts, collected by Edward Sapir, are minutely examined in Morris Swadesh, "Motivations in Nootka Warfare," *Southwestern Journal of Anthropology*, 4 (1948): 76–93.
196. I refer specifically to Barrett-Lennard and to Sproat, whose works are referenced elsewhere. Both had first-hand knowledge of the war chief, and he features in the story of the murder of the Maltese trader Barney in 1855. Sitakanim is the spelling of his name according to Father Moser (who says Sitakanim died at Clayoquot village in 1897). There is an undated photo of Sitakanim and his son Curley in Moser, *Reminiscences of the West Coast*, 174.
197. Gilbert Malcolm Sproat, *Scenes and Studies of Savage Life* (London: 1868), 63. Here I cite the original edition.
198. Barrett-Lennard, *Travels in British Columbia*, 130–31.
199. See Galbraith, *Hudson's Bay Company as an Imperial Factor*.
200. The Colonial Office guided the process, favoured the Company over other aspirants and "made the deal." The process was complicated but the Colonial Office held the ground. See Barry M. Gough, "Crown, Company, and Charter: Founding Vancouver Island Colony—A Chapter in Victorian Empire Making," *BC Studies*, no. 176 (Winter 2012/13): 9–54.
201. Walter N. Sage, *Sir James Douglas and British Columbia* (Toronto: University of Toronto Press, 1930), 185–86.
202. Douglas could not keep out foreigners, only foreign traders or others unconnected with the HBC. See Derek Pethick, *James Douglas: Servant of Two Empires* (Vancouver: Mitchell Press, 1969), 156–67.
203. For the history of liquor legislation in the colonies of Vancouver Island and British Columbia, 1850–1876, see Barry M. Gough, *Gunboat Frontier: British Maritime Authority and Northwest Coast Indians, 1846–1890* (Vancouver: UBC Press, 1984), App. 2, 219–23.
204. Kenton Storey, *Settler Anxiety at the Outposts of Empire: Colonial Relations, Humanitarian Discourses, and the Imperial Press* (Vancouver: UBC Press, 2016), chs. 2, 4 and 7. This contains vital examination of the local press of Victoria, BC.
205. This subject is complex. Evidence, though extensive in the historical record, is fragmentary and often incidental; censuses were inaccurate, and the results possibly underestimated, overrated or exaggerated, etc. One conclusion may be drawn: smallpox appeared and reappeared in irregular fashion in many Northwest Coast locations and had profound effects. See Cole Harris, *The Resettlement of British Columbia: Essays on Colonialism and Geographic Change* (Vancouver: UBC Press, 1997), 3–30, 276–81. Important to keep in mind is the fact that in Clayoquot Sound there was not a pervasive displacement of Indigenous peoples by newcomers or colonists. In a way, then, Clayoquot Sound is an anomaly in BC history. What smallpox epidemics were experienced here, as in 1855, did not eradicate the local population, though they may have weakened or destroyed some groups, forcing amalgamation with other nations. Once again, the lack of homogeneity of the villages and individual nations is a striking feature.
206. [Admiralty], *Vancouver Island Pilot*, 1864 ed., 182.
207. R.E. Gosnell, *Year Book of British Columbia, 1911/1914* (Victoria: Legislative Assembly, 1914), 158.

208. Dominion Bureau of Statistics, *Canada Year Book, 1952–53* (Ottawa: Queen's Printer, 1953), pp. xxvi-xxvii. The figure for 1871 is exaggerated: it had been boosted for per capita income benefits from Canada. The same source gives 178,657 for 1901; 694,263 for 1931; and 1,165,210 for 1951.
209. Koppert, *Contributions to Clayoquot Ethnology*, 4.
210. Even before the proclamation of Governor Blanshard's commission as governor for the Colony of Vancouver Island on March 11, 1850, imperial law had enacted a measure for the trial and punishment of persons guilty of crimes and offences committed in Indian territories—that is those north and west of Hudson's Bay Company chartered territory. This informal version of "the law marches west" meant that the jurisdiction of the courts of justice in the Provinces of Lower and Upper Canada were to be considered in such cases as if the offences had been committed within the jurisdictions of the Canadian courts (Act of 14 Geo. 3, c. 138). In 1818 the 49th parallel west to the Rocky Mountains (then known as the Stony Mountains) defined the southern boundary of Indian territories; the 1825 boundary with Russia defined the British territories claimed as far as Russian-held Alaska. See J.H. Pelly to Earl Grey, September 13, 1849, enclosing the Company's memorandum on the subject, in "Hudson's Bay Company," *Parliamentary Paper*, Cmd. 542, UK House of Commons, printed July 12, 1850. Vancouver Island law superseded this that same year.
211. See Gough, *Gunboat Frontier*, 108–28, for discussion of the affairs of the Hesquiaht (1864), which marked the major episode of gunboat diplomacy on the west coast of Vancouver Island. It must be observed that the authorities did not intervene in internecine and inter-tribal matters—only when British persons (or whites) and their property were preyed upon by Indigenous peoples.
212. George Nicholson, *Vancouver Island's West Coast* (Victoria: George Nicholson, 1965), 73–74. Here I follow Admiralty documents on piracy and punishment detailed in my *Gunboat Frontier*, ch. 8.
213. Captain J.C. Prevost to Captain M. deCourcy, March 11, 1859, encl. in M. deCourcy to Governor Douglas, March 12, F 1218, BC Archives; see also R. Bruce Scott, *Barkley Sound: A History of the Pacific Rim National Park* (Victoria: n.p., 1972), 43–47.
214. Margaret Horsfield and Ian Kennedy, *Tofino and Clayoquot Sound: A History* (Madeira Park: Harbour Publishing, 2014), 89–92.
215. In 1855, Banfield (or Bamfield) was trading at Clayoquot with partner Peter Francis. Their small schooner *Jibo* kept up a lucrative trade in dogfish oil, trading blankets, calico, beads and other articles. The 1855 murder of the Kyuquot trader Barney, a Maltese, is recounted in Moser, *Reminiscences of the West Coast*, 171–75.
216. Documents for this incident are referenced in Gough, *Gunboat Frontier*, notes 26–56, on pp. 247–50.
217. Gough, *Gunboat Frontier*, 125–28.
218. A handsome vessel on old-fashioned lines, built in 1839, she was an 810-ton paddlewheel steamer of 240 horsepower, with a nominal complement of 125 officers and men, and a comfortable main room with fireplace, where twelve officers could dine at table. *Hecate* had a full sail rig. Although imagined to be powerful enough to contend with local tide rips and currents, she was not; she nearly came to grief when she hit rocks on the south shore of Juan de Fuca Strait; damage had to be repaired at Mare Island, San Francisco, there being no suitable dock yet available in Esquimalt Harbour, the usual rendezvous of British warships in Vancouver Island and British Columbia waters. Esquimalt became station headquarters in 1862, though for a time that designation reverted to Valparaiso, before being reinstituted, remaining so until the Pacific Station was closed down in 1905. Lack of a dockyard of suitable capacities became a political complication, only resolved in 1887.
219. On Richards in BC waters and elsewhere, see Barry Gough, *Britannia's Navy on the West Coast of North America 1812–1914* (Barnsley, UK: Seaforth; Victoria: Heritage House, 2016), 183–87. See also next note.
220. Richards' progress may be followed in Dorricott and Cullon, *Private Journal of Captain G.H. Richards*, 122–26; quotation at 122.
221. Gowlland journal, July 23, 1861, in Dorricott and Cullon, *Private Journal of Captain G.H. Richards*, 123.
222. Richards journal, August 4, 1861, in Dorricott and Cullon, *Private Journal of Captain G.H. Richards*, 125.
223. Entries from John T.E. Gowlland's ms. journal, June 27, 1861, Mitchell Library, Sidney, New South Wales; copy, microfilm 447-A, BC Archives.
224. Charles Forbes, *Vancouver Island: Its Resources and Capabilities as a Colony* (Victoria: Colonial Government, 1861), 20.

Notes

225. Walbran, *British Columbia Place Names*, 303–304, contains particulars. Information from R. Blagborne.
226. Rear Admiral R.L. Baynes, the Commander-in-Chief, knew all about this and apparently authorized it.
227. Barrett-Leonard, *Travels in British Columbia*, 116.
228. Information from R. Blagborne.
229. Stubbs was later stipendiary magistrate and gold commissioner for West Kootenay. Walbran, *British Columbia Coast Names*, 475.
230. Barrett-Lennard, *Travels in British Columbia*, 128–29.
231. Blanshard's testimony of June 15, 1857, in "Report from the Select Committee on the Hudson's Bay Company; together with the Proceedings of the Committee, Minutes of Evidence," *Parliamentary Papers*, 224.260—Sess.2 (1857), 291–92.
232. Drucker, *Cultures of the North Pacific Coast*, 196. See pages 196–97 for details and elaboration of this theme.
233. Herman Merivale, *Lectures on Colonization and Colonies* ([1861 ed.; reprint New York: Augustus M. Kelley, 1967), 116.
234. Bob Bossin, ed., "Forming Tender Ties: Fur Trader Frederick Thornberg," in Saeko Usukawa et al., *Sound Heritage: Voices from British Columbia* (Vancouver: Douglas & McIntyre, 184), 20–22. Quotation at 21. Thornberg gives important details about Native language, Chinook jargon or trade language, and Lucy Ha-a-pes, who he married, in 1885, in "Indian fashion."
235. Again, I cite Bossin's work. See *Sound Heritage*, 120–29.
236. Margaret Horsfield, *Voices from the Sound: Chronicles of Clayoquot Sound and Tofino 1899–1929* (Nanaimo: Salal Books, 2008), 8.
237. The original is in the Alberni Valley Museum. John Sendey, *The Nootkan Indian: A Pictorial* (Port Alberni: Alberni Valley Museum, 1977), 63.
238. In 1905 the Canadian Pacific Railway had purchased the Esquimalt & Nanaimo Railway.
239. See Norman R. Hacking and W. Kaye Lamb, *The Princess Story: A Century and a Half of West Coast Shipping* (Vancouver: Mitchell Press, 1974) for details on these ships. Details on the *Tees* are found at pp. 150–59. See also Gordon Newell, ed., *The H.W. McCurdy Marine History of the Pacific Northwest* (Seattle: Superior Publishing, 1966), 16, 65; and Robert D. Turner, *Those Beautiful Coastal Liners* (Victoria: Sono Nis, 2001), 35–36.
240. R. Atleo, remembrance, in Turner, *Those Beautiful Coastal Liners*, 122.
241. Hacking and Lamb, *The Princess Story*, 300.
242. Interview by Nancy Turner, May 1996, in Turner, *Those Beautiful Coastal Liners*.
243. Quotations (and discussion of this subject) from Clayton Evans, *Rescue at Sea: An International History of Lifesaving, Coastal Rescue Craft and Organizations* (Annapolis: Naval Institute Press, 2003), 208.
244. The lifeboat, No. 580, named *Bamfield Creek*, was initially 28 HP (gas fuelled), increased to 35–40 HP, and capable of 10 statute MPH, full throttle. She sported a sail rig of two masts, with jib, plus fore-and-aft lug sails; also five thwarts for ten oars. I am grateful for detailed information on this particular vessel to Timothy R. Dring, *Canadian and U.S. Coast Guard Rescue Craft: A History of Collaboration and Development* (for Bamfield Lifeboat Centenary & Historical Symposium, Bamfield, June 2008). Copy in author's possession.
245. See Adrienne Mason, *Long Beach Wild: A Celebration of People and Place on Canada's Rugged Western Shore* (Vancouver: Greystone, 2012), ch. 7.

CHAPTER 8

246. Barbara S. Efrat, "The Hesquiat Project: Research in Native Indian Aural History," in W.J. Langlois et al., eds, *Sound Heritage* 4, nos. 3 & 4 (1976): 6–11. Quotation at p. 8.
247. Details on the Meares Island Easter Festival 1984 and what transpired on Meares Island and elsewhere that year are from Horsfield and Kennedy, *Tofino and Clayoquot Sound*, 502–503.
248. According to Horsfield and Kennedy, "Neither FOCS or the First Nations condoned tree spiking" (in *Tofino and Clayoquot Sound*, 503).
249. Jack Woodward, *Native Law* (Toronto: Carswell, 1989), 206.

250. Woodward, *Native Law*, 216–19. For further discussion, see Brian Slattery, "Understanding Aboriginal Rights," *Canadian Bar Review*, 66 (1987).
251. Norman H. Clark, introduction to James G. Swan, *The Northwest Coast, or, Three Years' Residence in Washington Territory* (Seattle: University of Washington Press, 1972), xiii–xiv.
252. Discussion of these matters is documented in my contribution to comparative frontiers, Barry Gough, "Indian Policies of Great Britain and the United States in the Pacific Northwest in the mid-Nineteenth Century," *The Canadian Journal of Native Studies* 2, no. 2 (1983): 321–37. My emphasis there was on the nature and causes of violence and the maintenance of order among both Native and non-Native residents. Violence on the British Columbia frontier has been greatly exaggerated by present practitioners, particularly when compared to the adjacent United States frontiers, including Alaska (see sources in next note).
253. George W. Fuller, *A History of the Pacific Northwest, with Special Emphasis on the Inland Empire*, 2nd ed. (New York: Alfred A. Knopf, 1966); Dorothy O. Johansen, *Empire of the Columbia: A History of the Pacific Northwest*, 2nd. ed. (New York: Harper & Row, 1967). Richard Kluger, *The Bitter Waters of Medicine Creek: A Tragic Clash Between White and Native Americans* (New York: Alfred A. Knopf, 2011) examines the Puget Sound wars and treaty-making of the 1850s. More generally, see Roxanne Dunbar-Ortiz, *An Indigenous Peoples' History of the United States* (Boston: Beacon Press, 2014), chs. 7–11.
254. Quoted in George A. Walkem, Attorney General, Province of British Columbia, August 17, 1875 (from *British Columbia Sessional Papers*, 1864), in "Report of the Government of British Columbia on the Subject of Indian Reserves," in *British Columbia, Papers Connected with the Indian Land Question, 1850–1875* (Victoria: Government Printing Office, 1875), 7. This was approved by the Executive Council.
255. Gosnell, *Year Book of British Columbia 1911/1914*, 242.
256. P. O'Reilly to Chief Commissioner of Lands and Works, February 21, 1889, Indian Reserve Commission Papers, Box 4, No. 395/89, and same to same, January 11, 1889, ibid., No. 98/89, BC Archives.
257. Margaret Horsfield and Ian Kennedy, *Tofino and Clayoquot Sound: A History* (Madeira Park: Harbour Publishing, 2014), 242–43.
258. O'Reilly to Chief Commissioner of Lands and Works, April 26, 1890, Indian Reserve Commission Papers, No. 1152/90, and same to same, April 26, 1894, ibid., Box 5, No. 1376/94, BC Archives.
259. Documents for this paragraph: Certificate of Pre-Emption, No. 1711, in Ministry of Lands, Parks and Housing (LPH) Schedule—Crown Grants of Land and Minerals, Meares Island—Lot 642, Clayoquot District. Certificate of Purchase No. 4294, February 7, 1905, and Water Record No. 95, January 30, 1905, all in LPH Schedule—History of Water Licenses, Meares Island—Final Water License No. 4377.
260. Brabant's reminiscences, first published 1900, have been republished, most recently as *Mission to Nootka, 1874–1900*, ed. Charles Lillard (Sidney: Gray's Publishing, 1977). The 1926 edition (Acme Press, Victoria) by Rev. Charles Moser, is the classic but hard to find. A new, critical edition would be a welcome addition to the literature. For biographical treatment, see Jim McDowell, *Father August Brabant, Saviour or Scourge?* (Vancouver: Ronsdale, 2013); cf., Joseph Van Der Heyden, *Life and Letters of Father Brabant* (Louvain: J. Wouters-Ickx, 1920). As a chapter in missions and ethnohistory, see Barry M. Gough, "Father Brabant and the Hesquiat of Vancouver Island," *Study Sessions, Canadian Catholic Historical Association* 2, pt. 2 (1983): 553–68.
261. Governor Douglas to Earl Grey (Colonial Secretary), May 28, 1852, C.O. 305/3, p. 113, National Archives, Kew, England.
262. Patricia Meyer, ed., *Honore-Timothee Lempfrit, OMI: His Oregon Trail Journal and Letters from the Pacific Northwest, 1848–1853* (Fairfield, WA: Ye Galleon Press, 1985), 34–37.
263. On September 7, 1874, Brabant was at Opitsat, with Bishop Seghers, on reconnaissance. Brabant wrote, "We found the Indians very much excited over the news that a man-of-war [the gun vessel *Boxer*] was anchored to the leeward of Vargas Island with the Superintendent of Indian Affairs [Dr. I.W. Powell] on board." Further details in Moser, *Reminiscences of the West Coast*, 25–27.
264. Horsfield and Kennedy, *Tofino and Clayoquot Sound*, 93–114 (on missionaries) and, correlative to them, 258–63 (on schools).
265. Earl Maquinna George testifies powerfully to how the ending of this international economy, in which Nuu-chah-nulth sailors and hunters had critically important roles, foreclosed Indigenous well-being and futures. See his *Living on the Edge*, 35, and esp. 61–67.

Notes

266. Deed and plan of L. 642 (Crown Grant No. 740 162) and allied documents from the Land Title and Survey Authority of British Columbia, copies in author's possession. Brabant's Land Act document bears the date February 25, 1905.
267. Moser, *Reminiscences of the West Coast*, 154–55.
268. Lenard Monkman, "Genocide against Indigenous Peoples Recognized by Canadian Museum for Human Rights," CBC News, May 17, 2019, https://www.cbc.ca/news/indigenous/cmhr-colonialism-genocide-indigenous-peoples-1.5141078
269. "Christie (Tofino)" on the National Centre for Truth and Reconciliation, University of Manitoba website, https://collections.irshdc.ubc.ca/index.php/Detail/entities/43.
270. Moser, *Reminiscences of the West Coast*, 154.
271. "Christie (BC)" on the Indian Residential School History & Dialogue Centre website, https://collections.irshdc.ubc.ca/index.php/Detail/entities/43.
272. The full apology is accessible at https://www.cccb.ca/wp-content/uploads/2017/10/oblate_apology_english.pdf.
273. "Matsquiaht" on Maaqutusiis Hahoulthee Stewardship Society website, https://www.mhssahousaht.ca/matsquiaht.

CHAPTER 9

274. See Guppy, *Clayoquot Soundings*, following p. 32. See also next note.
275. Timber Lease, Sutton Lumber & Trading Company Limited, March 1, 1912. This document was backdated to March 15, 1909, for unspecified reasons thereon.
276. I owe this observation to Michael Edgell.
277. J.D. Chapman and D.B. Turner, eds., *British Columbia Atlas of Resources* (British Columbia Natural Resources Conference, 1956), 53.
278. Chapman and Turner, *British Columbia Atlas of Resources*, 53.
279. Michael C.R. Edgell, "Forest Industry," in Charles N. Forward, ed., *Vancouver Island: Land of Contrasts*, Western Geographical Series, vol. 17 (Victoria: University of Victoria, 1979), 105.
280. John Steinbeck, *Sea of Cortez*, excerpt in *The Portable Steinbeck*, rev. and enlarged ed. (New York: Viking, 1971), 512.
281. Edgell, "Forest Industry," 129. The full document is accessible at https://www.cccb.ca/wp-content/uploads/2017/10/oblate_apology_english.pdf.
282. Quoted in Horsfield and Kennedy, *Tofino and Clayoquot Sound*, 498.
283. Edgell, "Forest Industry," 115.
284. See the table on the summary of tree farm licences in Edgell, "Forest Industry," 120. The Tofino (No. 20) had a productive area of 133,166 hectares, and this constituted 9.6 percent of Vancouver Island's total percentage. These are 1977 figures.
285. Edgell, "Forest Industry," 107.
286. Ian S. Mahood, *The Land of Maquinna* (privately printed, 1971), 2.
287. Andrew Struthers, *The Green Shadow* (Vancouver: New Star Books, 1995).
288. Horsfield and Kennedy, *Tofino and Clayoquot Sound*, 501.
289. Horsfield and Kennedy, *Tofino and Clayoquot Sound*, 497–506.
290. Horsfield and Kennedy, *Tofino and Clayoquot Sound*, 501.

CHAPTER 10

291. Stephen Hume, "Park Plan Threat to 1,000 Jobs," *Victoria Times Colonist*, December 8, 1984. In 2009 a protocol was signed between the Province of British Columbia and the Haida Nation. Forestry continued on Haida Gwaii but the protocol and other statements and declarations demonstrated that Haida Gwaii was drawing tourists from around the world who came to see old-growth forests, wildlife and Haida culture.

292. Council of the Haida Nation, *Athlii Gwaii: Upholding Haida Law at Lyell Island [1985]* (Locarno, 2019). See also, Islands Protection Society, ed., *Islands at the Edge: Preserving the Queen Charlotte Islands Wilderness* (Vancouver: Douglas & McIntyre, 1984).
293. Opening statement by D. Rosenberg, September 30, 1991, Supreme Court of British Columbia; copy in Gough files.
294. *MacMillan Bloedel Ltd. v. Mullin; Martin v. R. in Right of B.C.* (1985) 61 B.C.L.R. 145, 1985 CanLII 154 (BC CA), [1985] 3 W.W.R. 577 (B.C.C.A.). Available at the Canadian Legal Information Institute website at https://canlii.ca/t/1p6pb.
295. For a resume of these cases, with specific recognition of the importance of *Meares Island*, see Douglas C. Harris, "A Court Between: Aboriginal and Treaty Rights in the British Columbia Court of Appeal," *BC Studies*, no. 162 (Summer 2009): 137–64, esp. 149–50. See also items in next note.
296. Woodward, *Native Law, 219; MacMillan Bloedel Ltd. v. Mullin* (1984), 61 B.C.L.R. 145 at 154 (C.A.).
297. Woodward, *Native Law*, 219.
298. *Western Canada Wilderness Committee Educational Report 1994*, quoted in Ron MacIsaac and Anne Champagne, eds., *Clayoquot Mass Trials: Defending the Rainforest* (Philadelphia, PA/Gabriola Island, BC: New Society Publishers, 1994), 40.
299. David Pitt-Brooke, *Chasing Clayoquot: A Wilderness Almanac* (Vancouver: Raincoast Books, 2004), 280.
300. MacIsaac and Champagne, *Clayoquot Mass Trials*.
301. Among the many publications on the evolution of the British Columbia Aboriginal title and rights issues, cases and decisions, see Woodward, *Native Law*, most recent edition. See also, for articulate commentary, Maria Morellato, ed., *Aboriginal Law Since Delgamuukw* (Aurora, ON: Canada Law Book, 2009).
302. Robert F. Kennedy Jr., Foreword, in MacIsaac and Champagne, *Clayoquot Mass Trials*, vii.

CHAPTER 11

303. In consequence of *Meares Island* and the subject expert examinations, findings and reports, "culturally modified trees" became an accepted concept in archaeological/anthropological studies.
304. On this point, see generally Todd McLeish, *Return of the Sea Otter: The Story of the Animal that Evaded Extinction on the Pacific Coast* (Seattle: Sasquatch, 2018).
305. Judith Lavoie, "Old Growth in the Crosshairs," *Focus Magazine*, July 5, 2019, https://www.focusonvictoria.ca/focus-magazine-july-august-2019/old-growth-in-the-crosshairs-r10/.
306. Quoted in Adrian Dorst and Cameron Young, *Clayoquot, On the Wild Side* (Vancouver: Western Canada Wilderness Committee, 1990), 141.
307. Canadian Press Report in *Globe and Mail* (Toronto), October 24, 1996.
308. "Biosphere Reserves," on the UNESCO website, https://en.unesco.org/biosphere.
309. George Francis, Sharmalene Mendis-Millard, and Maureen Reed, with help from Colleen George, *Clayoquot Sound Biosphere Reserve: Periodic Review, August 2010*, on the Clayoquot Biosphere Trust website, https://clayoquotbiosphere.org/our-biosphere-reserve/periodic-review.
310. Judith Lavoie, "Why is a B.C. Government Agency Violating Old-growth Logging Rules?" *Times Colonist (Victoria)*, October 20, 2019, pp. D1 and D4, https://www.timescolonist.com/islander/why-is-a-b-c-government-agency-violating-old-growth-logging-rules-1.23981779. Originally published by the *Narwhal*: thenarwhal.ca.

Notes

311. The results of the investigations were obtained by the Ancient Forest Alliance through a Freedom of Information request, and reviewed by the *Narwhal*. Quoted in Lavoie, "Why Is a B.C. Government Agency Violating Old-growth Logging Rules?"
312. Quoted in Lavoie, "Why Is a B.C. Government Agency Violating Old-growth Logging Rules?"
313. Jeff Bell, with photos by T.J. Watt, "A Beautiful Forest," *Times Colonist* (Victoria, BC) January 13, 2019, D1 and D2.
314. Mason, *Long Beach Wild*, 192.
315. Pitt-Brooke, *Chasing Clayoquot*, 4.
316. From "Natural Wonder," in *CAA Magazine*, Fall 2015, 26–27, quotation at 27.

Index

Ships mentioned in the text are indexed under "ships." Images in the photo insert are indicated with a *p* and are set in italics. For example, *p1* is an image on the first page of the insert.

Aborigines Protection Society, 172
Abraham, Dorothy and Ted, 154
Admiralty, 25, 37, 105, 108, 129–30, 145, 148–49. *See also* Richards, George Henry; Royal Navy
Adventure Cove, 87, 92–93, 94, 95, 97
Ahous Business Corporation, 178
Ahousaht Nation
   fight to protect Meares Island, 163–64, 191, 193
   Indian reserves, 173
   and *Kingfisher*, 107–8, 144
   on Meares Island, 22–23, 136, 178, 190, 195–96, 207
   at Nootka Sound cannery, 157
   relations with Europeans, 55, 67, 146, 157 (*see also* sea otter trade)
   social structure, 2
   war with Otsosat, 135–36
   See also Clayoquot Sound; Meares Island case; Nuu-chah-nulth nations
Ahousat, *p2*, 20, 37, 108, 154, 155, 176
air travel, 19, 157, 159
Alaska, 27–28, 32, 40, 50, 114–15, 124, 131
Aleut people, 39, 113
Alta California. *See* California
Ancient Forest Alliance, 205
Apānas (Maquinna's daughter), 44
Arima, Eugene, 135
Arnet Island, 153
Astor, John Jacob, *p1*, 111, 113, 114, 115. *See also* Pacific Fur Company; ships: *Tonquin*
Astoria, 105, 112, 113–14, 115, 118
Atleo, Richard, 157

Baker, James, 91
Baker Lake v. Minister of Indian Affairs and Northern Development, 166

Bamfield, 158
Banfield, William, 143
Baranov, Alexander, 117
Barkley, Charles, 33, 51
Barkley, Frances, 35, 51
Barkley Sound, 62, 124, 132–34, 136, 141–42
Barnet, Thomas, 61
Barrett-Lennard, Charles Edward, 24, 136–37, 149–50
Bartlett, John, 61–64
BC Forest Products, 182
Beale, Daniel, 50
Belcher, Edward, 128
Bell, Edward, 56, 76, 82–83
Berger, Thomas, xxi
Bering, Vitus, 27, 39
Bishop, Charles, 99, 116, 119
Blanshard, Richard, 137–38, 139, 151
Bodega y Quadra, Jan Francisco de la, 29, 35, 80
Boit, John, Jr., 85, 86, 87, 88, 90, 95–96, 97, 98–99
Bossin, Bob, 154
Boston traders, 40, 49, 52–55, 56–57, 67, 92–93, 115, 116, 126. *See also* Gray, Robert; Kendrick, John
Brabant, Augustin Joseph, 20–21, 120, 122, 173–77
British Columbia
   colonial history, 137–40, 151–52, 167
   Indian reserves, 173
   and Indigenous Peoples, 169–72
   Indigenous population, 140–41
   Indigenous rights, xxiv, 189, 190, 192, 194–95
   Indigenous treaties, 151, 169, 189, 195, 196
   Land Act, 172–73
   logging industry, 163, 179, 180–81, 182–83, 184, 185, 204–5
   public school acts, 176

   See also Meares Island case
Broughton, William Robert, 89, 91
Browning, George, 146, 148

Calder (legal case), 166, 194
California, 39–40, 49, 181
Callicum, 59
Canada
   Indian reserves, 173
   and Indigenous Peoples, 139, 163–64, 168, 171–72, 190, 194, 200–1
   Indigenous title and rights, xxiii, xxiv, 195
   Japanese internment, 159
   lifesaving stations, 158
   residential schools, 177–78
   See also Meares Island case
Canton (China), 31, 36, 39, 49
Carrasco, Juan, 58, 66
Carver, Jonathan, 90
Chegchiepe, 175
China, 39, 41, 104. *See also* Canton (China)
Chirikov, Aleksei, 27
Christie, Alexander, 177
Christie Indian Industrial School, 7, 20, 174, 176–78, 203
civil disobedience, 193–94
Clark, Norman H., 167–68
Clark, William, 110. *See also* Lewis and Clark expedition
Clayoquot (Stubbs Island), 23, 150, 158
Clayoquot (Tla-o-qui-aht) Nation
   Indian reserves, 173
   on Meares Island, 23
   population, 141
   relations with Europeans, 67, 76–77, 91–92, 96, 97–98, 116 (*see also* sea otter trade)
   smallpox, 140
   social structure, 2
   trade, 55, 75, 116

224

Index

war with other First Nations, 23, 120, 134, 136–37
See also Clayoquot Sound; Martin, Moses; Meares Island; Nuu-chah-nulth nations; Opitsat; ships: Tonquin; Tla-o-qui-aht Nation; Wickaninnish
Clayoquot Sound
  approaches by sea, 20, 24, 33–34, 44–45, 145–46, 147–48
  attacks on shipping, 142–44
  colonization, 7, 129, 131, 151–59
  description, 19, 20–21, 23–25
  European accounts of, 2–3, 25, 51, 65–66, 147, 150
  historical photography, 154–55
  historical records, 5
  Indian reserves, xi, 164, 173
  international biosphere reserve, 202–3
  "Kendrick deeds," 3, 77–82
  logging, 7, 12, 162, 179–80, 187, 193–94
  map, xv
  missionaries, 20–21 (see also Brabant, Augustin Joseph)
  modern histories, 8–9
  population, 66, 140, 141, 154
  Royal Navy survey, 129–30, 145–49, 155
  shared federal and provincial jurisdiction, 171–72
  smallpox, 7, 140
  Spanish visits, 58–60, 64, 65–66
  tourism, 20, 149–50, 156, 181, 185, 186, 203
  trade in 1700s, 47, 48–49, 55, 56–57, 72, 116–17, 123–24 (see also Colnett, James; Gray, Robert; Meares, John; sea otter trade)
  trade in 1800s, 7, 11, 124–25, 130–31, 138, 141, 149, 150, 152
  See also Meares Island; Nuu-chah-nulth people; ships: Tonquin; Wickaninnish; specific nations
"Clayoquot Summer," p6, 193–94, 197–98, 201
Cleaskinah, 62
climate change, 203
Cloolthpich, 23, 190
Clo-oose, 158

Colnett, James, 30, 35, 51, 57, 68–69, 70–71
Columbia River, 28, 53, 88, 90, 95, 109, 111, 115
Cook, James, 25–28, 31, 37, 40, 43, 45, 50, 72, 73
Cook, Rande, 202
"Cougar Annie," 154
Cox, John Henry, 34, 50, 61
Crown land, 171, 179. See also Indian reserves
culturally modified trees, 191, 199, 201–2
Curtis, Edward, 155

Dally, Frederick, 154
Davidson, George, p1, 93, 94
Dawley, Walter, 154
de Fuca, Juan, 27, 28
De Voto, Bernard, 111
Delgamuukw (legal case), 190, 194, 196
Denman, Joseph, 143, 144
Dewhirst, John, 18, 165
Dixon, George, 32, 35, 51
Dixson, Winnie, 153
doctrine of discovery, 29, 64
Dominion Lifesaving Trail, 158
Douglas, James, 138, 139, 142, 151, 169, 170–71, 174
Douglas, William, 32
Drake, Francis, 26, 27
Driver, Harold E., 134
Drucker, Philip, 21–22, 68, 151
Duffin, Robert, 35
Duffus, Dave, 19
Duncan, Charles, 30, 37, 51

East India Company, 31, 38, 49, 50
E-cha-chist, 23, 33, 118, 123, 147
Edgell, Michael, 181, 183
Efrat, Barbara, 161–62
Eliza, Francisco de, 59, 64–66
Enns, Eli, 120
environmentalists, 185, 186, 197–98, 204. See also Friends of Clayoquot Sound
Esquimalt & Nanaimo Railway, 156, 183
Evans, Clayton, 157–58
Fairy Creek watershed, 205
Fisher, Robin, 67

Flores Island, 136
Folan, William, 95
Forbes, Charles, 148
Fort Defiance, 87, 92–95
France, 55, 124
Frank, Alex, Sr., 162
Frank, George, 162
Frank, Leonard, 155
Fraser River gold rush, 7, 139, 145
Friendly Cove, 26, 35, 128. See also Nootka Sound; Yuquot
Friends of Clayoquot Sound, xx, 162, 163, 164, 186
Fuller, George, 169
Funter, Robert, 57

Galbraith, John S., 38
Galiano, Dionisio Alcalá, 29
Gentile, Charles, 154
George, Earl Maquinna, 157
Gibson, Kenneth, 94
Gitxsan Nation, 190
Gosnell, R.E., 141
Gough, Barry, 102–8, 125, 186–87, 195–96
Gowlland, John, 146, 147, 148
Gray, Robert
  circumnavigates the globe, 54, 90, 92
  destruction of Opitsat, 88, 90, 95–99
  first voyage to Northwest Coast, 52–54
  and John Meares, 35
  relations with Nuu-chah-nulth, 84, 90, 91
  second voyage to Northwest Coast, p1, 54, 85–90, 95
Great Britain
  claims on Pacific Northwest, 79, 81, 110–11
  Colony of Vancouver Island, 137–39, 168
  relationships with Indigenous Peoples, 108, 129, 172
  trade, 31–33, 37, 39, 50–52, 61–62, 73–74, 89 (see also Colnett, James; East India Company; Meares, John; South Sea Company)
  war in Europe, 29, 52, 69

225

Possessing Meares Island

war with United States, 34, 105, 113, 172
  See also Cook, James; Drake, Francis; Hudson's Bay Company; Nootka Sound crisis
Greenhow, Robert, 81
Greenpeace, 186
Griffiths, David W., 123
Guerin (legal case), 194
Guillod, Harry, 176
Guppy, Walter, 179

Hacking, Norman R., 157
Haida Gwaii, 47, 51, 55, 76, 125, 131, 170, 188
Haida Nation, 76, 140, 188
haiqua, 125
Hamilton, Bruce T., 106
Hancock's Harbour. *See* Clayoquot Sound
Hanna, James, 42, 50, 62
Haro, Gonzalo López de, 58
Haswell, Robert, 53, 54, 75, 85, 86–87, 88, 95, 97
Hayes, Edmund, 93–95, 102–3, 104, 107–8, 123
Heelboom Bay, *p7*, 163, 164
Hesquiaht Nation, 144, 161, 202
Hesquiat, 20, 21, 108, 154, 175
Hezeta, Bruno de, 29
Highway 4, 19
Hilhooglis, 22, 34. *See also* Meares Island
historiography, 6–7, 101–2, 105–6, 108
Hodgins, Jack, 152
Hoover, Alan, 135
Horsfield, Margaret, 8, 176, 185, 186
Hosie, John, 122–23
Hoskins, John, 24, 55, 87, 95
Howay, F.W., 30, 55, 92
Hudson, Thomas, 70
Hudson's Bay Company
  and Indigenous Peoples, 138–39, 142, 151, 167–68, 169, 170, 172
  origins, 109, 167
  in Pacific Northwest, 167
  on Vancouver Island, 11, 126, 130, 137–39, 151, 168–69
Hupacasath Nation, 204
Husband, Vicki, 204
Huu-ay-aht Nation, 142–43. *See also* Nuu-chah-nulth nations

hydroelectric development, 181

India, 31, 42, 49, 52
Indian Act, xi, xxiii, 137
Indian agents, 143, 176, 200
Indian reserves, 138, 164, 170–73, 203
Indian School Act, 177
Indigenous Peoples
  British Columbia policy, 169–72
  Canadian policy, 139, 163–64, 168, 171–72, 190, 194, 200–1
  colonial policy, 151, 168–69, 170–71, 172
  genocide, 177
  industrial economy, 140, 156–57, 169–70, 184
  logging, 183, 184, 204, 205
  oral traditions, 3, 6–7, 46, 194
  population decline, 139–41, 171
  reserves, 138, 164, 170–73, 203
  See also Indigenous rights; Nuu-chah-nulth people; *specific nations*
Indigenous rights
  in British Columbia, xxiv, 192, 194–95, 195
  in Canada, xx, xxiv, 195
  and civil disobedience, 193
  court cases, xxiii–xxv, 197
  existence of title, 165–67, 188, 189, 193, 194–95, 196–97
  extinguishment, 3, 165–66, 168–69, 189, 190
  and logging industry, 179–80, 188
  to Meares Island, xxiv, 2–3, 164
  See also Meares Island case; *specific legal cases*
Ingraham, Joseph, 35
International Woodworkers of America, 183
Ireland, Willard, 94
Irving, Washington, *p1*, 113

Jackson, Hewitt, 104–7
Japan, voyages to Northwest Coast, 33
Japanese internment, 159
Jefferson, Thomas, 79, 80, 110–11
Jewitt, John, 116
Johansen, Dorothy, 169
Joseachal, 118, 120

Kakawis, 176, 178, 203. *See also* Christie Indian Industrial School
Kelley, Hall J., 78–79
Kelsemaht Nation
  on Meares Island, 23, 136, 190, 196, 207
  population, 141
  relations with Europeans, 55, 67 (*see also* sea otter trade)
  social structure, 2
  war with Clayoquot Nation, 23
  See also Ahousaht Nation; Clayoquot Sound; *Meares Island* case; Nuu-chah-nulth nations
Kelsemat, 154
Kendrick, John
  arms trade, 76
  in Clayoquot Sound, 75–77, 78–79
  first voyage to Northwest Coast, 52–54
  and Koyah, 76
  land purchases, 77–82
  meeting with Robert Gray, 86
  in Nootka Sound, 77–78
  relations with Nuu-chah-nulth, 84
"Kendrick deeds," 3, 77–82
Kennedy, Arthur, 144
Kennedy, Ian, 8, 176, 185, 186
Kennedy, Robert F., Jr., 197–98
Kennedy Lake, 23
Kenyon, Karl, 39
King, James, 50
King George's Sound Company, 51
Klah-keest-ke-uss, 202
Klatsmick, 143
Knott Brothers Logging, 182
Koppert, Vincent, 135, 141
Koyah, 76
Kwakwaka'wakw, 140
Kyuquot, 175

La Pérouse, Comte de, 55
Lamb, W. Kaye, 157
Lamesee, 120
Lane, Barbara, 96, 99, 165
Lane, Robert, 165
Lewis, Meriwether, 110. *See also* Lewis and Clark expedition
Lewis and Clark expedition, 90–91, 110, 112
lifesaving stations, 157–58

Index

logging industry
  in 1700s, 72
  in 1800s, 141–42
  British Columbia, 180–81, 184
  Clayoquot Sound, 7, 12, 162, 179–80, 187, 193–94
  Haida Gwaii, 188
  John Meares, 36–37, 72
  on Meares Island, 179–80
  old-growth forests, 182, 204–5
  Royal Commission, 182
  stewardship, 182–84
  on Vancouver Island, 132, 204–5
  See also MacMillan Bloedel (MacBlo)
Lone Cone (*wanacks*), 22, 34, 42, 182
Lone Cone Hostel and Campground, 178
Long Beach, 19, 186. *See also* Pacific Rim National Park
Lucas, Simon, 202
Lyell Island, 188
Maaqutusiis Hahoulthee Stewardship Society, 178
Macau, 39, 49
Macfarlane, A.B., 191–92, 196
Mackenzie, Alexander, 80, 109–10, 111, 113, 114
MacMillan Bloedel (MacBlo)
  in Clayoquot Sound, 180
  on Meares Island, p7, xx, 162, 163, 164, 180, 185–86, 189–90, 191–92
  on Vancouver Island, 182, 183
  See also *Meares Island* case
Magee, Bernard, 25
Mahood, Ian S., 183–84
Makah people, 201
makúk, 7, 41
Makwala, 202
Malaspina, Alejandro, 29
Malloy, Mary, 100
Maquinna
  image, p4
  and John Meares, 35, 41
  land sales, 77–80
  relations with Spanish, 58–60
  and trade, 43–44, 56, 74, 76
  and trading ship *Boston*, 116
  and Wickaninnish, 2, 43–44, 56, 83
  See also Nootka Sound

Maquinna (descendant), 129
Marder, Arthur, 6
Martin, Carl, 163
Martin, Joe, 120, 163
Martin, Moses, p7, xix, xx, xxiv, 162, 198, 207
Martin, Tsimka, 207
Martínez, Esteban José, 29, 35, 57–59, 68, 69
Marvinas Bay, 77
Mason, Adrienne, 205–6
Massachusetts Historical Society, 92
Maynard, Hannah and Richard, 154
McDougall, Duncan, 115, 121
McDowell, Jim, 66
McKay, Alexander, 114–15, 117, 121
McKelvie, B.A., 122
Mead, Margaret, 135
Meares, John
  background, p4, 29–31, 34–35
  charts, xvi-xvii
  first voyage to Northwest Coast, 32, 42, 49–50
  and James Colnett, 68, 69
  plans for trading enterprise, 30–34, 35, 36–38, 40–41, 71–72
  relations with First Nations, 73–74
  second voyage to Northwest Coast, 32–34, 36, 42–43, 44–45, 46
  seizure of ships at Nootka, 30, 57
  Voyages, 34, 42, 89
  and Wickaninnish, 42–43, 44–46
Meares Island
  claimed by Spain, 64
  declared Tribal Park, p6, xx, 162–63, 192, 193, 207
  description, p8, 18–19, 22–24
  Indian reserves, xi, 164, 173, 190, 203
  Indigenous occupancy, 2–3, 18, 136, 141, 190–91, 200, 206–7
  land title, 173–74, 177, 178, 179
  logging, 182, 205
  map, xv
  microcosm of global trade, 49
  naming, 148
  residential schools, 7, 20, 203
  and sea otter trade, 47
  sold to John Kendrick, 81
  threatened by logging, 162–64, 181–83, 185–86, 189–90

timber lease, xx, 179–80, 185, 191, 196, 203 (*see also* MacMillan Bloedel (MacBlo); *Meares Island* case)
tourism, 205–7
See also Ahousaht Nation; Christie Indian Industrial School; Clayoquot (Tla-o-qui-aht) Nation; Clayoquot Sound; Fort Defiance; Gray, Robert; Kelsemaht Nation; Meares, John; Opitsat; Tla-o-qui-aht (Clayoquot) Nation; Wicaninish (village); Wickaninnish
Meares Island case
  continuity of occupancy, 141, 190
  in court, 189–91, 196
  destruction of Opitsat, 95–97, 99
  environmental concerns, 186
  judgment, xxiii–xxiv, 191–92, 196
  legacy, xxiv–xxv, 192, 193, 194–98
  preparation for case, xix–xxiii, 165–67, 189, 196
Meares Island Planning Committee, 186
Menzies, Archibald, 89–90, 97–98
Merivale, Herman, 152
Methodist Church, 176
Métis, 172
Missionary Oblates of Mary Immaculate, 178
Mitchell, Donald H., 95
Morison, Samuel Eliot, 92–93
Morpheus Island, 93, 154
Moser, Charles, 177
Mossome Grove, 205
Mount Colnett, 22, 68
Mowachaht/Muchalaht people, 41, 92, 135. *See also* Maquinna; Nootka Sound; Nuu-chah-nulth nations
Mullin, Michael, 164. *See also* Friends of Clayoquot Sound
Mumford, John, 117
Murderers' Harbor, 53, 96–97
Musqueam Indian Band, 189

Nahmint Valley, 204
Narváez, José María, 57, 64, 65–66
navigational aids, 25, 37, 65–67, 129–30, 145, 148–49
New Caledonia, 138, 168
Newcombe, C.F., 141, 155

227

Nicholson, George, 94, 107
Nokes, J. Richard, 30
Nomukos, 175
Nookamis, 119, 120, 129
Nootka Convention (1790), 3, 69
Nootka Sound
  attack on *Tonquin*, 121–22
  cannery, 157
  and James Cook, 26–27, 40, 43, 46, 72
  and John Meares, 29–30, 33, 35–36, 41, 71–72
  land sales, 3, 35, 77–82
  Mowachaht/Muchalaht people, 41, 92, 135
  sea otter trade, 36, 41, 46–47, 50, 51–52, 109, 126
  See also Maquinna; Spain: in Nootka Sound; Yuquot
Nootka Sound crisis, 36, 41, 57–58, 68–69, 89
North West Company, 109, 111–13, 114
Northwest Passage, 27, 28, 64–65
Nova Albion, 26, 40
Nuučaańuł. *See* Nuu-chah-nulth nations
Nuu-chah-nulth Economic Development Corporation, 178
Nuu-chah-nulth nations
  and Canada, 200–1
  cash economy, 133, 140, 157, 169–70, 176, 185
  culture, 3–4, 161, 184, 191–92, 199–200
  historical photographs, 155
  importance of property, 2, 27, 43, 45–46, 135, 161, 199–200
  Indian reserves, 173
  "Kendrick deeds," 3, 77–82
  and missionaries, 21, 174–76, 200 (*see also* Brabant, Augustin Joseph)
  and old-growth forests, 3, 21–22, 147, 191, 199, 202
  population, 129, 140–41, 154
  relations with Europeans and Americans, 58–59, 67, 70–74, 91, 116, 119, 142–44, 152–53
  social structure, 2, 161
  and trade, 41, 43–47, 50, 55–56, 60, 72, 125–27, 130–31, 200, 201

villages, 20, 23 (*see also* Ahousat; Hesquiat; Nootka Sound; Opitsat)
warfare, 67, 134–37
whaling, 23, 26, 53–54
  See also Ahousaht Nation; Christie Indian Industrial School; Clayoquot (Tla-o-qui-aht) Nation; Clayoquot Sound; Hesquiaht Nation; Huu-ay-aht Nation; Kelsemaht Nation; Meares Island; Mowachaht/Muchalaht people; Tla-o-qui-aht (Clayoquot) Nation; Tse-shaht Nation
Nuu-chah-nulth Tribal Council, 8, 163, 164–65, 184, 189, 190, 200. *See also* Meares Island case

O'Brian, Patrick, 71
old-growth forests, p8, 182, 189–90, 193, 202, 203–5, 208. *See also* Meares Island
Oo-tsus-aht Nation, 135–36
Opitsat
  approaches by sea, 62
  destroyed by Americans, 88, 90, 95–99
  historical photographs, p2, p3, 155
  Indian reserve, 173
  missionaries, 174, 176
  Nuu-chah-nulth occupation of, 3, 23, 44, 147, 154, 190
  refuge for Maquinna, 58–60
  Royal Navy survey, 147
  sold to John Kendrick, 78, 81
Oregon, 26, 40, 78–79, 81, 93, 136
Oregon Historical Society, 103–4, 123
Oregon Treaty (1846), 138, 190
O'Reilly, Peter, 173

Pacheedaht Nation, 205
Pacific Fur Company, 109, 111, 112–13. *See also* Astor, John Jacob; Astoria; ship *Tonquin*
Pacific Rim National Park, 19, 158, 186, 206
Palm, Rod, 123
Pantoja, Juan, 25, 66
Parks Canada, 186, 206
Philippines, 31, 38
photography, in Clayoquot Sound, 154–55
Pitt-Brooke, David, 194, 206

Port Alberni, p4, 132, 141–42, 151, 156, 183, 204
Port Cox, xvii, 24, 34, 42, 50, 65, 70, 146–47
Port Renfrew, 205
Portlock, Nathaniel, 32, 51
Portugal, flags of convenience, 38, 39, 50
Presbyterian Church, 176
Prevost, J.C., 142–43
Protestant churches, 176
Puget, Peter, 44, 89

Queen Charlotte Islands, 47, 51, 55, 76, 125, 131, 170, 188
Quimper, Manuel, 58–61

Rae-Arthur, Ada Annie, 154
railway, 156
Ramsay, Jack, 120
Ramsay, Paul, 202
Rayonier Canada, 188
"reconciliation," 197
Reid, Bill, 4
residential schools, 7, 20, 177–78, 203. *See also* Christie Indian Industrial School
Richards, George Henry, 34, 130, 145–49
Roberts, Henry, 41
Roman Catholic Church, on Vancouver Island, 20, 21, 174–77. *See also* Brabant, Augustin Joseph; Christie Indian Industrial School
Roquefeuil, Camille de, 124
Rosenberg, David, xxi, xxii, 165, 189–91, 194
Rosenberg, Paul, xxi, xxii, 165
Rosenberg, Rosenberg and Woodward, xxi, 165, 189. *See also* Woodward, Jack
Royal Canadian Air Force, 159
Royal Commission on Forest Resources, 182
Royal Navy, 108, 128, 129–30, 138, 142–44, 145–49, 155, 168. *See also* Admiralty; Richards, George Henry
Russia, 27–28, 32, 39, 48, 111, 113, 128, 167

San Blas (Mexico), 29
San Juan River Valley, 205

Index

Sapir, Edward, 135
sea otter trade
    arms trade, 45, 56
    in Clayoquot Sound, 19–20, 47, 57, 200
    contributions to navigational charts, 37–38
    cultural misunderstandings, 101 (see also ships: Tonquin)
    decline, 100, 123–26, 201
    description, 38–39
    dominated by Americans, 54–55
    global reach, 35, 38–39
    and liquor, 55
    logistics, 41, 46–47, 51–52
    in Nootka Sound, 36, 41, 46–47, 50, 51–52, 109, 126
    origins, 50–51
    protocols, 45, 59–60, 67–68, 99, 115–16, 119
    and Spanish, 38, 39, 64–65
    See also Astor, John Jacob; Colnett, James; Gray, Robert; Kendrick, John; Meares, John
sea otters, 35, 38, 124, 125
Seaton, Peter, 191, 192, 196
Second World War, 159
Seghers, Charles John, 175
Sendey, John, 155
Seton, Alfred, 118
ships
    Adventure, 88, 91
    Argonaut, 58, 69–70
    Boston, 116
    Chatham, 89, 91
    Columbia Rediviva, p1, 52–53, 54, 56–57, 85–92, 99
    Discovery, 28, 82, 89, 106, 107
    Felice Adventurer, 32–34
    Gustavus III, 61–62
    Hecate, 145–50
    Imperial Eagle, 33, 51
    Iphigenia Nubiana, 32–33, 36
    John Bright, 144
    Kingfisher, 107–8, 143–44
    Lady Washington, 52–53, 54, 77
    Maude, 156
    Nootka, 32, 42
    North West America, 33, 57, 57–58
    Plumper, 145
    Prince of Wales, 32, 68–69
    Princess Maquinna, p5, 156, 157, 159
    Princess Norah, 156
    Princess of Alberni, 157
    Princess Royal, 58, 69
    Resolution, 28
    Ruby, 99, 116
    San Carlos, 64–66
    Santa Saturnina, 64–66
    Satellite, 142
    Sea Otter, 32, 42, 50
    Sparrowhawk, 144
    Swiss Boy, 142
    Tees, p4, 156
    Templar, 149–50
    Tonquin, p1, 94, 102–3, 104, 108–9, 111, 113–15, 117–23
    Valencia, 158
Sierra Club of BC, xx, 186
Sitakanim, 136–37, 175
smallpox, 7, 139–40
South Sea Company, 49, 50
Spain
    in Clayoquot Sound, 58–60, 64, 65–66
    contributions to navigation, 65–67
    "Kendrick deeds," 80
    in Nootka Sound, 29, 30, 36, 40, 52, 61, 64, 69, 77
    in North America, 27, 29, 39–40, 49, 60–61, 66–67, 111
    sea otter trade, 38, 39, 64–65
    seizes British ships, 57–58
    voyage accounts, 2–3
    war with Britain, 29, 52
    See also Martínez, Esteban José; Nootka Sound crisis; Quimper, Manuel
Sparrow (legal case), 188–89, 190
Sproat, Gilbert Malcolm, 132–34, 136
Stamp, Edward, 132
steamships, 156–57
Steinback, John, 181
Stevens, Godfrey, 162
Stockham, Thomas, 154
Stockham Island, 154
"Strait of Anian," 27
Strait of Juan de Fuca, 26, 28, 51, 89, 145
Strawberry Isle Marine Research Society, 123
Struthers, Andrew, 185
Stryd, Arnoud, 165
Stubbs, Napoleon Fitz, 150
Stubbs Island. See Clayoquot (Stubbs Island)
Sturgis, William, 124
Sutton Lumber & Trading Company, 179
Swadesh, Morris, 135
Swanston, Robert, 138

Tahsis, 44
Taylor, Roy L., 125
telegraph, 158
Templar Channel, 24, 119, 122, 150
Tent-a-coose, 122
Thompson, David, 91, 111
Thorn, Jonathan, 114–15, 116, 117–18, 119, 121
Thornberg, Frederick Christian, 152–53, 154
Tibbs, Frederick Gerald, 153
Tla a qua, 23
Tla-o-qui-aht (Clayoquot) Nation
    fight to protect Meares Island, 162–64, 193, 198
    and logging, 182
    and Meares Island, 190–91, 195–96, 206–7
    See also Clayoquot (Tla-o-qui-aht) Nation; *Meares Island* case; Nuu-chah-nulth nations
Tofino, 18–19, 24, 158–59, 176, 181, 182, 184–86, 206
Tofiño, Vicente, 19
Tootiscosettle, 54, 78
trade, global, 38, 48–49, 57–58, 72, 124, 126, 200, 201. See also Canton (China); East India Company; sea otter trade
tree farm licences, 182–83
Tseshaht Nation, 132–33, 142, 204. See also Nuu-chah-nulth nations
Tsilhqot'ín (legal case), xxii, 194–95, 196
Tsilhqot'ín Nation, xxii, 194–95
Tsimshian, 140
Turner, Nancy, 19

Ucluelet, 158–59, 186
UNESCO biosphere reserve, 202

229

United States
  claims in Pacific Northwest, 79–82, 90–91, 93, 110–11, 167
  and Indigenous Peoples, 82, 151, 168–69, 170
  traders, 39, 50, 52, 111 (*see also* Astor, John Jacob; Boston traders; Gray, Robert; Kendrick, John)
  voyage accounts, 2–3
  war with Great Britain, 105, 113, 172

Vaillant, John, 125–26
Valdéz, Cayetano, 29
Vancouver, George, 29, 56, 89–90, 98, 146–47
Vancouver Island
  colonial history, 137–40
  development, 180
  logging, 180, 181, 182, 183, 187, 204–5
  map, xiv
  population, 141
  Royal Navy survey, 25, 145
  shipwrecks, 157–58
  treaties with Indigenous peoples, 151, 169, 189

Vancouver Island Land-Use Plan, 204
Vancouver Island Pilot, 25, 148–49
Vander Zalm, Bill, 195
Vaughan, Thomas, 103, 106
Victoria
  colonial administration, 11, 137, 138
  commerce, 130, 140, 141
  Hudson's Bay Company, 11, 138, 151, 168
  Indigenous population, 7, 139, 142, 151
  Royal Navy base, 143, 168
  "Save Meares" protests, *p6*, 163

Wagner, Henry R., 66
Walbran, John, 119–20, 122
War of 1812, 105, 113, 172
Washington state, 29, 93, 136, 169
Webster, Peter S., 22–23, 136
Weeping Woman Cedar (Stevens), 162
West Coast Trail (lifesaving trail), 158.
  See also Pacific Rim National Park
Western Canada Wilderness Committee, xx, 163, 193
whaling, 23, 26, 53–54, 71, 201
White and Bob (legal case), 171
Wicaninish (village), 44, 46

Wickaninnish
  about, 1–2, 43–44, 62
  attempts to take *Columbia*, 90, 99
  land sales, 78, 79, 81, 82
  leading chief, 129
  and Maquinna, 2, 43–44, 56, 83
  relations with Europeans, 33–34, 42–43, 44–46, 59, 83, 87–88
  as trader, 44, 46, 56, 76, 116–17
  whale hunt, 53–54
  See also Clayoquot (Tla-o-qui-aht) Nation; Clayoquot Sound
Wickaninnish (1861), 147
Wickaninnish (1980s), 190
Winee (Frances Barkley's maid), 51
Wood, Charles, 146
Wood, James, 145
Woodcock, George, 46, 126–27
Woodward, Jack, xix, xxi–xxii, xxv, 96, 165–66, 192, 193

Yendell, Samuel, 81
Young, John, 81
Yuquot, 2, 18, 26, 33, 44

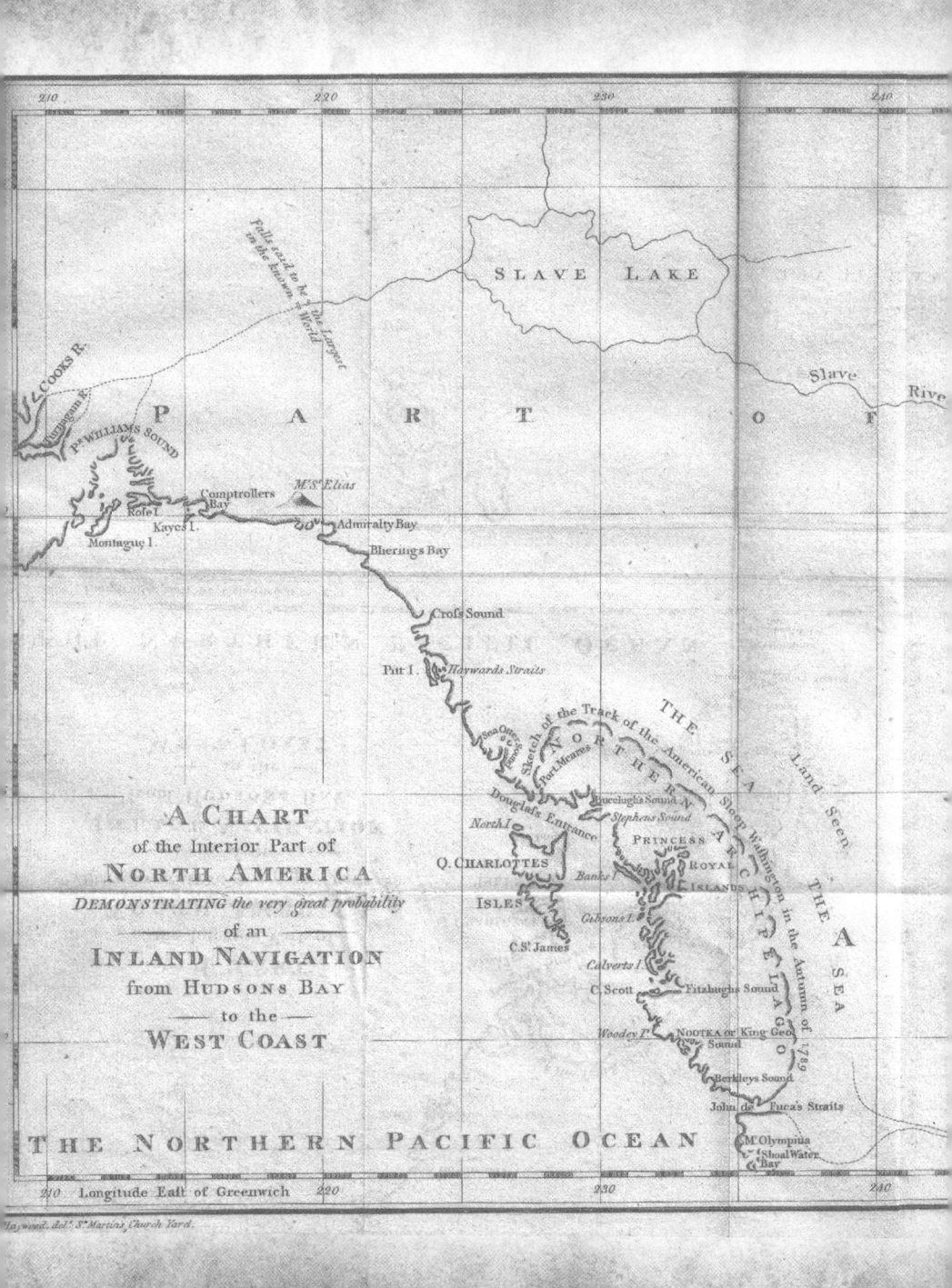

A CHART
of the Interior Part of
NORTH AMERICA
DEMONSTRATING the very great probability
— of an —
INLAND NAVIGATION
from HUDSONS BAY
— to the —
WEST COAST